PEN
&
PALATE

PEN & PALATE

MASTERING *the* ART *of* ADULTHOOD, *with* RECIPES

Lucy Madison
and
Tram Nguyen

Illustrations by Tram Nguyen

GRAND CENTRAL
Life & Style
NEW YORK · BOSTON

Grand Central Life & Style
Hachette Book Group
1290 Avenue of the Americas
New York, NY 10104
grandcentrallifeandstyle.com
twitter.com/grandcentralpub

First Edition: May 2016

Grand Central Life & Style is an imprint of Grand Central Publishing.
The Grand Central Life & Style name and logo are trademarks of Hachette Book Group, Inc.

The publisher is not responsible for websites (or their content) that are not owned by the publisher.

The Hachette Speakers Bureau provides a wide range of authors for speaking events. To find out more, go to www.hachettespeakersbureau.com or call (866) 376-6591.

Library of Congress Cataloging-in-Publication Data has been applied for.

ISBNs: 978-1-4555-3505-7 (hardcover), 978-1-4555-9168-8 (ebook)

Printed in the United States of America

RRD-C

10 9 8 7 6 5 4 3 2 1

For Rob and Romeo

Contents

Prologue

Lucy

I looked for Tram, but the only person I could see standing outside the baggage claim was a lanky figure with short hair, black skinny jeans, and dramatic red lipstick. *Definitely not Tram*, I thought, squinting into the distance. Last time I saw her, she had glossy black hair all the way down her back, and, like me, she wore cardigans and boot-cut jeans, no makeup to speak of. I checked my phone to make sure I hadn't missed a message. But then the creature with the hair and the jeans and, as it turned out, some towering high-heeled sandals, looked up and called my name. "Lucy!" She rushed toward me from across the street and gave me a big hug. "I barely recognized you!"

It had been two years since we'd lived in the same city, and suddenly I felt shy. Tram and I had spent most of our waking hours together in high school, but after graduation I left the Maryland suburbs for college in the Midwest and she went off to live with relatives in France. On her own she'd had European adventures, eaten all sorts of exotic foods whose names I couldn't pronounce, and possibly dated dozens of sleazily sexy Eurotrash guys. She had chopped off all her hair into a sophisticated pixie cut. I, on the other hand, had eaten a lot of bad cafeteria food and entered a mild depression. What if she had outgrown me? What if things were different between us now?

"I almost didn't see you!" I said.

"Is it because I look like a boy now?"

"Don't be ridiculous, you look amazing. I love your hair."

"My hairdresser only charged me for a man's haircut," Tram said. "What should we do?"

"What we always do," I said. "Let's eat."

I

The Chicken
That Walks

Tram

There were seven of us piled into a rented Honda Odyssey, edging slowly toward the front of the line where blue-uniformed agents awaited us. Not us, specifically, but people like us, hardened criminals with questionable morals and no regard for the law, people who smuggled illegal goods into the United States of America. As our minivan inched toward the border checkpoint from Canada into the United States, we passed official signage that warned of the penalties we would incur if we committed the exact crime we were trying to commit. The signs started off politely enough (they were Canadian, after all), with a casual, "Hey there, don't bring drugs, guns, or other illegal contraband across the border, yeah?" It escalated quickly with every passing kilometer, until the final one read: "WE KNOW WHAT YOU'RE TRYING TO DO. CONFESS OR WE'LL DEPORT YOUR ASS TO VIETNAM." I am paraphrasing, but that was the gist of it.

I was fifteen years old and had a permanent scowl etched across my face—an expression enhanced by my overplucked, perpetually angry, '90s Kate Moss–inspired eyebrows. I should have been spending the summer with my best friend, Lucy, baking cakes and reading trashy magazines, not wasting two weeks traipsing across all of the China-towns in Canada with my eternally embarrassing family. And now we were about to get arrested at the border for smuggling in hundreds of dollars' worth of illegal contraband.

I was horrified by my family's blatant disregard for the law. I was a rule follower, an indoor kid. My life until that point was about main-taining the appearance of being the perfect, obedient, grade-grubbing, piano-playing Asian daughter. I discovered early on, that if you are a small Asian girl with a serious demeanor and can pull off *Moonlight Sonata* passably well, most people just *assume* you are a musical prodigy and there's no need to learn another song ever again. But not practicing piano was as far as my disobedience went. At fifteen, I'd suppressed any inkling of a rebellious nature, neatly stashing it away for a later date in the not-so-distant future.

My sanctuary from the pressures of home was Lucy's house. Well, more specifically, Lucy's room. I'd have to make it past her parents first. Through no fault of their own, I was absolutely terrified of her par-ents. Jane and Chris were exceedingly polite to me, always graciously offering me a place with the family at dinnertime. On the table, there would be pasta with pesto, homemade from the sweet basil that her father grew in the back garden, or a beautiful margherita pizza that her mother had just pulled out of the oven. The food looked and smelled amazing, but the mere thought of sitting through a Madison family din-ner was enough to make me break out in hives. I was certain that there were rules to living of which I was woefully ignorant. I would say the wrong thing or accidentally spill food on myself. It was much better to avoid any situation that might reveal to outsiders just how uncouth and clueless I was. Instead, I would stammer, "No thanks...I've already eaten," and run upstairs to hide out in Lucy's room.

I was a graceless misfit in the real world, but somehow when I was alone with Lucy, I shed that awkward teenage skin. She laughed at my jokes, praised the little watercolors I painted, proudly displaying them on her bedroom wall. My best friend's approval meant the world to me. I'd never met anyone like Lucy. She looked like a heroine from one of those old Victorian novels I'd loved so much growing up: perfect porcelain skin, a smattering of freckles, big blue eyes, and thick, wavy, chestnut-colored locks that she was always trying to tame, but that I thought were beautiful. She was the only fifteen-year-old I knew who kept a stack of *New Yorkers* at her bedside and actually read the articles, and not just the cartoons. Sometimes I felt like my brain had to work overtime just to keep up with her quick wit, but whatever minor insecurities I'd had about myself were assuaged by the fact that she laughed just as hard at my jokes.

With a partner in crime, high school wasn't so bad. Still, Lucy and I fantasized about getting the hell out of the suburbs of Washington, DC, and moving to New York City. We would live together in an enormous, miraculously rent-controlled, pastel apartment just like the Golden Girls. We'd break hearts left and right, have a shared closet full of vintage Courrèges, and glorious shampoo-commercial locks attached to our heads. (Somehow, in this scenario, I always pictured us both as blondes.) Lucy would be an intrepid, pavement-pounding, power-suit-wearing, ball-busting lady writer, getting the inside scoop for the *New York Times*, or maybe *Us Weekly*—we couldn't decide which would be more fun. I'd always wanted to be an artist, like my crazy uncle in Brussels, but it didn't seem like the most realistic career choice, so I settled on the much more practical profession of fashion designer instead. With my friend as my muse, *Women's Wear Daily* would shower me with hosannas, hailing me as the second coming of Alexander McQueen. Lucy would often indulge my artistic aspirations, gamely modeling some chiffon monstrosity that I'd tacked together with my remedial sewing skills, nodding in enthusiastic agreement when I suggested in all seriousness that yes, it could *totally* pass for Miu Miu.

My real life, the one where I could be the feckless dreamer with vaguely artistic aspirations, was back in Maryland with my best friend. But right now I was trapped in a teal Honda Odyssey at the Canadian border creeping toward impending doom. There were a few vehicles pulled over on the side of the road. We noticed that of all the drivers that had been stopped, the ones the federal agents were taking extra time with seemed to fit a certain...profile. They were all Asians. Families that looked just like mine, the contents of their cars being methodically rifled through and confiscated. I knew it was inevitable that we would be next. I could just see it: me, my mom, my little brother, my aunt and my uncle in one of his many fishing-themed polo shirts (he wore only fishing-themed shirts that whole trip), and my cousins Tiffany and Kimberly, ages eight and seven, all facedown on the grass, with our hands cuffed behind our backs. The children would be sent to live with my grandpa Harold in the suburbs of Northern California, which was its own uniquely cruel form of punishment, and the adults (myself included) would be doomed to a life of hard labor in a rice paddy back in Nam. Probably.

I had grown up on the stories of my mother and her sisters—how, as teenagers, they'd stolen away onto a rickety old fishing boat under the cover of darkness to escape Saigon after the war. My mom, along with dozens of strangers, was trapped inside a tiny wooden vessel. They spent many long days and nights in constantly roiling waves, the boat a mere speck floating in the middle of the South China Sea. All the while, she knew there was no guarantee that this was even her ticket out. If she and her sisters had been found by the wrong people and returned to Vietnam, they'd have most certainly suffered a years-long prison sentence. And not in a cushy Martha Stewart–style American prison, but a hot jungle "reeducation camp" where several of her family members were already serving time for fighting on the losing side. They were lucky; a few days into their journey, my mom and her sisters were rescued by a ship from Hong Kong and sent to a refugee camp in Singapore.

My mom speaks fondly of that time: she remembers the kindness of the Malaysian people, and, without fail, she always remarks on how clean the city was. It was also the place where she met and fell in love with my father, a fellow refugee, about a decade her senior. He was still skinny back then (this was before he'd discovered American cable television—more specifically, that perennial dad favorite: World War II documentaries on the Discovery Channel), with deeply golden caramel skin and killer cheekbones, a bit of the Bruce Lee about him. He had an open, easy demeanor, a smirk or a Marlboro cigarette dangling from his lips, always ready with a joke. He proved irresistible to my quiet, reserved mother. They made their way to America, got married, learned English, worked multiple jobs, and sacrificed for years until they had built a comfortable life in the suburbs of DC, which included yearly trips to visit my relatives in California and a fat, state-of-the-art laser disc karaoke system.

I remember helping my parents study for their citizenship test when I was in the fifth grade, the final hurdle to this almost two-decade-long journey. The exam was full of obscure questions to which no natural-born American citizen would ever have a reason to know the answer. We crammed for weeks, me quizzing them until they had committed those useless facts to memory. My parents both passed, and a few weeks later in a stadium with hundreds of people from every corner of the earth, with hands over their hearts, they recited the Pledge of Allegiance and became citizens. With that hard-won piece of paper, they also received new, easily pronounceable names, emerging from that stadium as Nancy and Timothy. A few years later, they did the most American thing of all: they got a divorce.

It was our turn in line at the Canadian border. My mom turned to the four of us kids lined up in the back and communicated to us wordlessly with her best silent Asian tiger mom look: *Don't be a snitch.* With mounting dread, I watched my uncle roll down the window to greet the border patrol officer, a wide, not-at-all-suspicious smile on his face. I was appalled. My mother had risked her life, scrimped, and saved—and yet she was willing to throw away all those years of sacrifice. I was an innocent bystander, and she was going to drag me down with her. I saw all of the things I would never do flashing before my eyes. I'd never graduate, or attend an overpriced art school and get a BFA in something practical like fiber arts or glassblowing. I'd never bleach my hair blond, or fall in love, and I'd never get to move to New York City with Lucy to do... something creative. I could say adios to all of my teenage aspirations. Hello, Hanoi Hilton!

The officer peered down at us, his eyes masked by the reflective glare of his aviator sunglasses. "What brings you to Canada?"

My uncle told him the truth: that we were on a mini road trip through the Great White North, hitting up five cities in two weeks. He presented our documents, passports for us and birth certificates for the little kids. Nothing unusual here, no sir. The officer examined the papers, and seeing that they were legit, returned them. One hurdle jumped; now, if he would just let us on our way. We were still a few hundred feet away from freedom.

"You folks wouldn't have any food in here? Tropical fruit, for instance?"

"No sir!" My uncle shook his head dramatically, just like an innocent person with nothing to hide. My mom and aunt also were shaking their heads in unison. "We ate it all at the hotel," they said. The border agent walked around our van, crammed to the gills with suitcases, stuffed animals, and brightly colored bedding splattered with images of princesses and purple dinosaurs, his suspicious eyes resting on the tiny Vietnamese children with shit-eating grins plastered across their faces.

"All right, then. We hope you folks had a nice visit in Canada. Please come back again."

Once we were back on good old freedom-loving American soil, we let out exuberant cries of relief, cackling at how we had just pulled the wool over on those racial-profiling Canucks. Victory! When we were a safe distance from the checkpoint, my mom motioned for the kids to move. My cousins scuttled their little butts over and she pulled away the blanket that they had been sitting on, revealing the boxes stuffed full with pounds and pounds of forbidden fruit that we had just successfully smuggled back into the United States of America. My mom handed out bunches of plump, sweet, lychee nuts and we happily snacked on them on the long drive home.

I couldn't understand it at the time—why would my family go to this much trouble for tropical fruit? For some reason, probably due to a healthy Chinese-immigrant population, Canada was rife with it. My mom, who was not prone to emphatic displays of any kind of emotion, was uncharacteristically exuberant. Niagara Falls, one of the seven natural wonders of the world—just okay. But a cardboard box of bruised mangosteen from the dumpy little corner grocery store in Chinatown? She was in ecstasy. That whole trip, my mom and aunt had been on a mission, seeking out the local Asian neighborhoods, sniffing out the food of their youth. They would come back to the hotel room laden with plastic bags heavy with fruits that looked alien and exotic to my uncultured eyes. I saw real lychee nuts for the first time, something that prior to this trip I had eaten only from a can, drowning in sugary syrup. They were fresh and still on the tree branch, with the most delicate, subtle flavor, clean like sweet water. These gems bore no resemblance to the overprocessed, cloyingly sweet, candied impostors I'd known. My favorite fruit was the rambutan, oddly cute and anthropomorphic, like a Miyazaki character, colored a brilliant raspberry red with spiny cilia emerging from it like a sea anemone. I had never seen my mom, who was normally cool and unflappable, giggle like this. She and her sister were giddy, practically drunk with joy over these tastes from Vietnam, from their childhood, which had up until that moment been just a distant memory. So they gorged themselves in Canada, and then, back home, they divided up the lucre to disperse to our vast network of Vietnamese expats, delivering these gifts like skinny, tan, Southeast Asian Santa Clauses.

My family wasn't alone in its underground efforts to transport goods. Most Vietnamese people treat relatives, friends, and acquaintances traveling to Vietnam like their very own personal Federal Express. If someone goes back to the homeland, he or she polls the neighborhood and everyone puts in an order. You could get a beautifully embroidered, hand-beaded, custom-made silk wedding *ao dai* for a song; genius model airplanes crafted from old Heineken cans; DVDs from the future, of the latest Hollywood movies that hadn't even premiered yet on American big screens; and some of the more esoteric food items that were impossible to find in the States. One year, Mom asked for dried bamboo. I couldn't believe that this, of all the good things to eat in Vietnam, was what she'd asked her friend to carry back over thousands of miles of ocean. Reconstituted in water, it was disturbingly bronze and sinewy, just like Iggy Pop. We put it in soup with poached duck and a ginger dipping sauce, and after all the elements of that dish were put together, I had to admit, it was pretty good.

Every summer, we flew to California to visit my mother's side of the family. My mom is one of ten children: seven daughters and three sons. Most of them married and had multiple children, so I always looked forward to these family reunions because there were so many cousins my own age to hang out with. Each year when we'd arrive, I was surprised by how tiny everyone was. I reached my full adult height by age fifteen, topping out at barely five foot three, but next to my bird-boned aunts I felt as large and ungainly as André the Giant. At these reunions, the whole family would congregate at my grandfather's house in Northern California. He actually moved a few times during my childhood, but I could never tell the difference between the houses because they always felt exactly the same. Grandpa Harold (né Ha, but he decided that the name Harold was easier for Americans to pronounce so he changed it legally) was a hoarder. Why buy just one pair of blue-jean overalls when you could buy ten pairs of blue-jean overalls? He applied this principle to nearly everything in his life, from antique swords and vintage naked lady oil paintings to purebred Chihuahuas and his own offspring.

Upon arrival, my aunts would inspect me and coo over how tall I'd grown, how enormous my size seven-and-a-half feet were, and point at a zit and inquire if I was washing my face with soap. And then they'd ask if I'd eaten. My mom's sisters fussed around the kitchen, moving in this complex, synchronized dance to which only they knew the steps. Any outsider would know better than to try to intrude, and I was content to hover around the perimeter and watch as each sister performed her part of the meal with an effortless ease that I was too ignorant to appreciate at the time. They always ate well, but for these family reunions my aunts would cook something extra special. One of my favorite dishes was *cha ca thang long*. It started with small nuggets of catfish that were left to soak overnight in a marinade tinted a brilliant electric yellow by the freshly grated turmeric. No matter how careful you were, you always managed to find a way to splatter it onto your clothing, a small, unforgettable souvenir of that meal. One of my aunts would tend to the grill on the patio with a fan and a pair of wooden chopsticks, cooking the morsels of fish until they were just done, tender and flaky, with the tiniest hint of smoke from the charcoal. We would eat these with slender vermicelli noodles, pulled from the boiling water at just the right moment to retain that perfect amount of bounce, heaps of cooling dill, fish mint, Thai basil from my grandma's garden, and crushed roasted peanuts, all drowned in a piquant fish sauce, bright with lime juice and red chiles. Sometimes we'd wrap the whole thing in gossamer-thin rice paper wrappers. Other years, there would be a crispy rice cracker with black sesame seeds, toasted over the flame of a gas burner until the edges were tinged golden brown. We'd sit on one of Harold's many sectional sofas, with a plate piled high with food, and my aunts would make fun of me for holding my chopsticks like a white person. But I didn't care—the food was so good.

In the mornings, I would wake to the crowing of Harold's rooster. I'd spend the day exploring the grounds, digging through the garage for hidden treasures, picking persimmons from one of dozens of fruit trees, collecting fresh eggs, and feeding the chickens, ducks, and fighting roosters that he kept for fun. "But Grandpa, isn't that illegal?" I'd ask, always the rule follower. He'd just shrug and say, "Not if the police don't know about it." The highlights of our days were mealtimes, punctuated by the occasional trip to various Asian grocery stores where my mom would stock up on specialties that she couldn't get back home in Silver Spring.

On our way back to Maryland, at the airport I would help my mom unload the luggage from my uncle's car. There would be the regular hodgepodge of mismatched suitcases that we'd arrived with, alongside the falling-apart paper shopping bags filled with a lunch that my aunt had packed for us so that we wouldn't have to eat the dreaded plane food. Underneath the suitcases was always a new addition for our journey east: some years it would be an enormous cardboard box, wrapped up in layers of duct tape, with our names and home address written on all sides in giant block letters. This year, I noted with mounting concern, it was a big orange plastic cooler, the kind that people bring to a tailgate party. It was obvious that whatever was in there wasn't going to be cans of Budweiser and bratwurst.

And then, not for the first time or last, I asked myself: Why couldn't we travel like normal people? I envied those cool American families I'd see at the airport, seasoned travelers with sassy, matching rolling suitcases. I wouldn't even mind joining the ranks of those idiots who brought along full-size bed pillows and stuffed animals, as that was a common enough sight to be almost acceptable behavior. At least they didn't look like they were emigrating from the homeland every time they boarded a plane.

Cautiously, I asked my mom, "What's in the box?"

"Ga di bo."

"Huh?"

"Ga di bo."

I know the word for *ga*; it means "chicken." But *di bo*? That translates to...

"The chicken that walks?"

"Yes. The chicken that walks."

While I was busy taking my grandpa's electric wheelchair for joyrides to Round Table Pizza with my cousins, my mom and my aunts were at the farm store where Harold bought all his livestock. They had come home with twenty-four live young chickens. These were slender, free-range, organic birds, hence the "di bo" part. They weren't super-sized and pumped up on steroids like their American brethren, and they tasted almost exactly the same as the chickens my mom grew up eating in Vietnam. I never heard a peep from these birds, because my mom and her sisters spent the afternoon in the garage chopping off their heads, plucking their feathers, and packing them in this crazy box for her to take home to Maryland.

Parents will embarrass you. I knew that. I'd read most of the Judy Blume oeuvre, after all. But I felt like my family had that extra edge that went above and beyond the usual teenage humiliation. Most people did not live like this. Lucy's family certainly didn't. I was pretty certain that the Madisons bought their chickens in grocery stores. In Maryland. Their luggage was filled with clothing, books, and toiletries— not frozen poultry. I had reached new depths of embarrassment, ones previously unknown to me. Either I could sit here and quietly die of humiliation, or I could let go and accept my fate. These chickens, and all the dishes that my mom would make with them, were a reminder of the place where she had grown up. She knew it was a little weird, but my mom didn't care what other people thought. And, as it turned out, I didn't really care either. The only person whose opinion mattered to

me was Lucy. She would probably laugh at the situation, but she'd be laughing right alongside me, not at me. Besides, you couldn't go to jail for transporting poultry across state lines. Temporary teenage mortification aside, if the payoff was a few weeks' worth of delicious meals, it was totally worth it. I couldn't wait to see how this played out.

We hauled that cooler onto the scale and I propped my arms on the counter and watched as the travel agent took down our flight information.

When the woman asked, "What's in the box?" I leaned in. "Twenty-four frozen chickens."

And then, my mom caught my eye, and I think I detected the barest hint of a smile.

GINGER CHICKEN AND RICE SOUP WITH SLAW

For me, this is the ultimate comfort food, the Vietnamese version of chicken soup. It's what my mother would make for me whenever I was ill. I could expect a cool hand on my forehead, a warm bowl of this rice porridge, and a not-too-gentle scolding for getting sick in the first place. But this dish should not be limited to invalids. After trudging through the snow in subzero weather, the kind of cold that turns your skin red and raw and instantly transforms your mascara into crunchy little icicles, there is nothing better than coming home to this for dinner.

This soup is also a great way to really show off the charms of a quality free-range, organic chicken and it uses all the parts of the whole bird in a really satisfying manner. The chicken is poached gently in a broth with aromatic ginger and onions for sweetness, and then the meat is removed from the bones and added to a tangy cabbage slaw that is served alongside the porridge, resulting in a simple dish that is truly greater than the sum of its parts. The addition of the slaw may seem unusual, but it adds a lovely crunch and brightness and a welcome verdant green from a generous handful of herbs.

Serves 6
Prep time: 30 minutes; Cook time: 2 hours

For the soup:

2 quarts low-sodium chicken broth

1½ quarts water

2 pounds bone-in chicken parts, preferably organic and free-range

1 large whole onion, peeled

1 (4-inch) piece fresh ginger, peeled

2 tablespoons kosher salt, plus more for seasoning

1½ cups jasmine rice, uncooked

4 scallions, green parts only, chopped

For the slaw:

½ medium head green cabbage, finely shredded (about 4 cups)

¼ teaspoon kosher salt

½ small red onion, thinly sliced

½ cup loosely packed cilantro, chopped

½ cup loosely packed Vietnamese mint*, chopped

For the dressing:

¼ cup lime juice (about 3–4 medium limes)

2 teaspoons sugar

1 tablespoon fish sauce, plus more as desired (I prefer the Three
    Crabs brand)

1 Thai bird's-eye chili, minced

1 large clove garlic, minced

*Vietnamese mint, also called *rau ram*, has a distinctive earthy, herbaceous flavor. It is available in many Southeast Asian grocery stores, but feel free to substitute mint or Thai basil if you can't track it down.

For serving:
   ¼ cup neutral oil, such as canola or grape-seed
   2 medium shallots, thinly sliced
   Fresh cracked black pepper
   Lime wedges

In a large stockpot, bring the chicken broth, water, chicken, onion, ginger, and 2 tablespoons salt to a boil. Reduce heat to low and simmer, partially covered, for 50 to 60 minutes, or until the chicken is cooked through and reaches an internal temperature of 160°F when pierced with a meat thermometer. Remove the chicken from the pot and plunge into an ice bath to stop the cooking. After it has cooled enough to handle, shred the chicken and reserve the meat for the slaw. Return the bones to the pot and simmer for an additional 30 minutes.

While the stock is bubbling away on the stove, prepare the slaw. In a colander placed over a large bowl, toss the shredded cabbage with ¼ teaspoon salt and let sit for at least 20 minutes to draw the excess water from the cabbage. In a small bowl, soak the sliced onion in cold water to take the edge off. Let sit for at least 10 minutes and then drain thoroughly.

In a small bowl, assemble the dressing by whisking together the lime juice, sugar, fish sauce, chili, and garlic. In another large bowl, toss the reserved poached chicken, cabbage, onion, cilantro, Vietnamese mint, and dressing together. Let the slaw rest about 30 minutes prior to serving to allow the flavors time to meld. Add fish sauce to taste.

In a separate skillet, lightly toast the rice on medium-low heat, stirring frequently to keep from burning, for about 5 minutes, or until the rice is a lovely pale blond. Add the toasted rice to the stock. Here it will make the most satisfying sizzling sound. Simmer on low, partially covered, for an additional 40 minutes, or until the rice is tender and falling apart. Fish out the bones, onion, and ginger. Add the chopped scallions. Season to taste with salt.

In a small saucepan, heat ¼ cup oil over medium-low heat. Add the shallots and fry, taking care to stir frequently so they do not burn, for about 10 minutes, or until golden brown. Remove from the oil with a slotted spoon and place on paper towels to drain.

Ladle the rice soup into six deep bowls, topping with a generous portion of slaw. Garnish with fried shallots and fresh cracked black pepper. Serve immediately with lime wedges.

TURMERIC FISH WITH DILL (*CHA CA THANG LONG*)

Serves 2
Prep time: 45 minutes active prep; 30 minutes to 24 hours marinating time; Cook time: 15 minutes

For the marinated fish:

5 tablespoons vegetable oil, divided

3 tablespoons minced shallots

2 large cloves garlic, minced

1 tablespoon minced galangal (about a 1-inch piece; ginger may be substituted)

2 teaspoons fish sauce

1 teaspoon sugar

¼ teaspoon ground turmeric

1 pound skinless catfish fillets, cut into 2-inch pieces (another oily fish, such as salmon, may be substituted)

Freshly ground black pepper

1 bunch dill, chopped into 4-inch pieces

1 bunch scallions, green parts only, chopped into 4-inch pieces

Continued

For the nuoc cham:

   2 tablespoons fish sauce

   2 tablespoons lime juice (about 1 medium lime)

   3 ounces water

   ½ teaspoon sugar

   1 small clove garlic, minced

   1 Thai bird's-eye chili, minced (optional)

For serving:

   ¼ cup peanuts

   8 ounces rice vermicelli, cooked according to package instructions

   1 medium head lettuce, leaves torn into large pieces

   Few sprigs Thai basil and mint

To assemble the marinade, in a large bowl, mix together 3 tablespoons of the oil, the shallots, garlic, galangal, fish sauce, sugar, and turmeric. Add the catfish, coating each piece with the marinade. Cover with plastic wrap and refrigerate for at least 30 minutes or up to 24 hours.

Preheat the broiler on high for 5 minutes. Place a wire rack atop a baking sheet and oil lightly. Arrange the catfish pieces on the wire rack and season with pepper. Discard the remaining marinade. Broil on high for 6 to 10 minutes, until the fish is beginning to turn golden brown. Flip the pieces over and broil the other side an additional 6 to 10 minutes, until golden brown in places and the fish flakes easily with a fork.

While the fish is broiling, heat the remaining 2 tablespoons oil in a skillet over medium-high heat. Add the dill and scallions and cook for about 3 minutes, until wilted.

For the nuoc cham, in a small bowl, mix together the fish sauce, lime juice, water, sugar, garlic, and chili. Stir until the sugar is completely dissolved.

In a small pan, dry roast the peanuts over medium-high heat for 1 to 2 minutes, until they are lightly toasted and fragrant. Give them a little toss every once in a while, and monitor closely to prevent burning. Transfer to a mortar and pestle and crush lightly. If you do not have a mortar and pestle, a plastic bag and something heavy to pound the peanuts with works just as well.

To serve, arrange a bed of wilted dill and scallions on a platter, and then place the broiled fish atop the greens. Garnish with crushed roasted peanuts and serve with rice vermicelli, lettuce, herbs, and nuoc cham to taste.

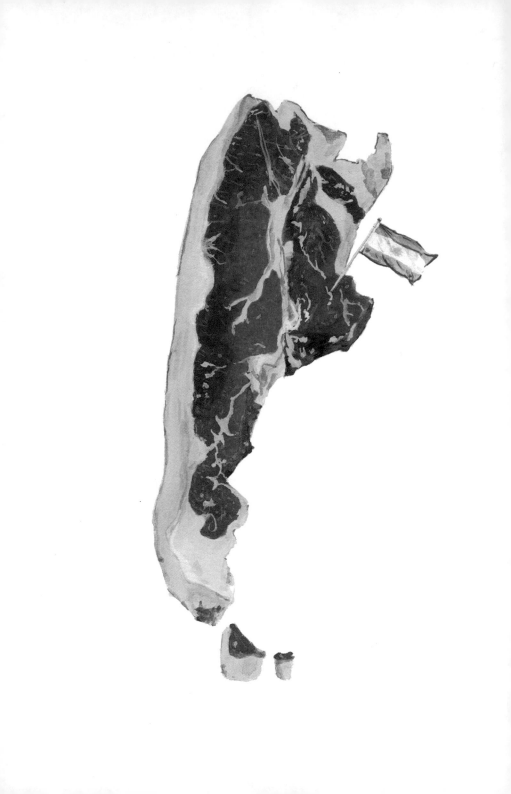

2

Cheap Steaks

Lucy

When I look into your future, I see...hard work. Studies." The psychic opened her eyes and looked at me.

Well, yeah, I thought. *Duh.* I was a college student. "But can you see anything else? Like what I'm supposed to do with my life?"

"I sense uncertainty," she said. "You are searching, but your path is still undetermined. If you come back, perhaps I can tell you more."

She paused.

"My rates go up for repeat visits."

"Even the psychic thinks I'm boring!" I said to my friend Ann, who I'd dragged along on my visit to Madame Tallulah's. I was 19, adrift, desperate for any sign of how things would turn out for me. I couldn't picture it, but maybe a clairvoyant could. "She looked into my future and she saw nothing."

"Lucy, I'm pretty sure you took the wrong lesson from that experience," Ann said. "She's a fraud. While you were getting your reading done, her kids were trolling for tips in the living room."

If anyone was a fraud, I thought, it was me. So far college hadn't turned out at all like I'd imagined. I had left high school feeling strong and ready. "I'm gonna nail this college girl thing," I whispered as I loaded my suitcase with enormous turtleneck sweaters and eight-hundred-page Victorian novels. But as soon as I arrived on campus in the Chicago suburbs, my confidence disappeared. My roommate thought my Dickens novels were lame. My Gap corduroys turned out to be less fashionable than I had imagined. My classmates not only seemed smarter than me, they also appeared to know exactly what they wanted to do with their lives. I tried to find a sense of purpose in writing, but that backfired, too. I submitted an article to the school magazine and went into a tailspin when my editor rewrote the whole thing.

"I dropped out of the newspaper. I don't want to be a journalist anymore," I told Tram on a phone call during my freshman year at Northwestern.

"What are you gonna do instead?" she asked.

"I'm working on a play about emotionally unhinged college students."

By my sophomore year, I had fallen into a depressive pattern. A regular day might involve lying on my dorm room bed, listening to Lucinda Williams on repeat, and eating sugary cereal until my tongue turned green. Occasionally I'd throw some Russian poetry into the mix, which didn't help. I filled journals with page after angst-ridden page describing how alone I felt, all the while turning down invitations to go socialize.

It wasn't that I had no friends—I had made some great ones in those first two years of college. But even into my sophomore year I still felt like an outsider. The high school I attended was huge and incredibly diverse, too big to support a strict social hierarchy. People drifted from group to group, trying on identities like they were thrift-store sweaters. College was different. Sororities and fraternities dominated campus life, setting rigid guidelines for how students perceived one another.

There was the slutty sorority; the nice sorority; the blonde sorority; the best sorority. If you chose not to be in any sorority, like me, you were more or less not worth categorizing.

I was also shocked by how much money my classmates seemed to have. People had gone to tony boarding schools. They owned fancy cars, wore $200 jeans. I had gone to public school my entire life, and my dad had lost his job shortly before I went away to school. We had never been rolling in it to begin with, and now money was an issue. I was worried about being able to afford the next semester; meanwhile, the kids around me had credit cards that their parents paid off. One girl from my Spanish class traveled back and forth from Baltimore to Chicago in a private jet.

I became anxious and dyspeptic, the grumpy black storm cloud hunched in the corner of every party. Even worse than my unhappiness was the idea that it might be permanent.

Then one day, at the end of sophomore year, I got a call.

"Lucy! Guess what!" said Tram. "I'm moving to Chicago!"

Tram and I had been best friends since sophomore year of high school. I had spotted her down the hallway wearing a vintage houndstooth coat and carrying a fat, serious-looking novel.

"Who's that?" I asked my good friend Naomi.

"Oh, you don't know Tram?" she asked. "You're going to love her."

At first I thought I was going to have to work overtime to convince Tram to hang out with me. She was smart, stylish, and self-assured—even at fifteen, she seemed to have a sense of who she was and what she was good at. She knew the best bands to like (sad, skinny, and British) and what jeans to wear (flares, before they were popular). I, on the other hand, didn't know myself at all. I felt ungainly and awkward in my lumpy adolescent body, like I was walking around in someone else's hand-me-downs. I had no sense of where I fell in the spectrum of human existence: Was I smart, stupid, or just smart enough to know exactly how stupid I was? Was I hideously ugly, or passably attractive? How did I appear to the outside world? I genuinely had no idea, but I feared it wasn't good. Tram, cool and quietly confident, sophisticated but unpretentious, seemed out of my reach.

But Naomi introduced us, and within a few months Tram and I became inseparable. She came to my house after school and we'd hang out until dinnertime, usually in the kitchen. Both of my parents baked regularly—cakes for birthdays, whole wheat bread for sandwiches, piping-hot scones for weekend breakfasts—and I loved the rituals of it. I was an anxious child, but the sifting, the kneading, the rhythmic ticking of the timer calmed me down. On a dreary day, you could pop a tray of cookies in the oven and fill the house with the sweet aroma of caramelized sugar and butter. Baking was cozy and intimate, and around the time that Tram and I became friends I decided I wanted to become good at it—so after school, while she sat on the counter stool, I made cakes.

Tram didn't eat the cakes—"Too sweet, yuck!" she said—but she did enjoy making them beautiful. She bought books on cake decorating, and a tool kit, and soon she was piping intricate roses and making elaborate basketweave patterns. After a while she started using real flowers, too, edible varieties like pansies and nasturtiums, which she brushed with simple syrup and coated with sugar. We spent hours in my kitchen, covered in white dust, procrastinating on our chemistry homework until my mom kicked us out to make dinner.

Tram was always invited to our family meals, but she rarely stayed. I didn't think much of it. We had grown up eating different food. When I went to Tram's house there was often some sort of wildly unfamiliar broth bubbling on the stove, which I would always politely refuse. She would offer me golden crepes filled with shrimp and bean sprouts, fresh off the frying pan, and I'd opt instead for a bowl of jasmine rice doused in soy sauce—a much less intimidating option. Tram's mom would avert her eyes politely as I scarfed it down, the rice spilling out of my inexpertly wielded chopsticks.

*   *   *

Not all of my friends cared about food like I did, but Tram understood. Her mother was a serious cook. Even if I was too nervous to try the mung bean cakes her mom had bought for the autumn harvest festival, I was still deeply impressed by how pretty they were, with their intricate designs and ornate red and gold packaging. Tram was equally baffled by my family's affection for hummus, but she admired that we ate it on slices of my dad's homemade bread. We had a mutual sense of respect for how the other ate.

Food became central to our friendship. We lived in the DC suburbs, and cheap, amazing restaurants were all around us. When we first became friends, Tram took me to her favorite Vietnamese spot in Silver Spring and introduced me to pho. Together, we tried chicken souvlaki at a Greek restaurant in Dupont Circle, and we devoured the spongy injera at an Ethiopian place in the Eastern Market. The two of us became experts at eating well on a dime.

And while we ate, we talked. We talked about our families, our favorite bands and books and movies, our innermost secrets and hidden ambitions. Where would we go to college, and then where would we go after that? Would we ever have boyfriends? Who was more of a babe, Ewan McGregor in *Trainspotting* or Joseph Fiennes in *Shakespeare in Love*? By the end of high school, Tram knew me almost as well as I knew myself. It was possible she knew me *better* than I knew myself. As I headed off to college, and as Tram left for France, our friendship felt like the one thing that would never change.

So when Tram called before my junior year to tell me she was attending art school in Chicago, I was thrilled but also a little scared. She was my best friend. I needed her to like me, but at the time I didn't especially like myself. I was sure that as soon as she arrived she would discover my new sad-sack state and ditch me. And that would be unbearable.

The night before she landed in Chicago, I didn't sleep at all. I was wracked with anxiety. I imagined an interminable, awkwardly silent trip from the airport back to Evanston, where Tram would realize how little we still had in common. As I tossed and turned in my bed I pre-emptively lamented the end of our friendship. By the next morning, I had accepted its demise as a sad reality.

But when I actually saw Tram, I knew everything would be fine. We both looked different after a few years apart, but the internal machinery of our friendship was the same. We went to dinner at the Thai restaurant in my neighborhood, and as I slurped at my bowl of panang curry I told her about my friends, my job at a bakery, my bare-bones apartment with its stark white walls.

"Oooh, let's paint it!"

I was skeptical. Back home in Maryland, I had been up for any project, at any time. These days, however, my extracurricular creative activities were minimal, unless you counted the thousands of unsent text messages I'd drafted to the faux-communist senior on whom I had an unrequited crush.

"Come on! It'll be fun," Tram said. "We'll bring home our leftovers and blast David Bowie. I am an expert painter."

Twenty minutes later, we were at the Ace Hardware store, picking out a bright shade of blue.

"Lucy, do you have a stepladder? How high are your ceilings?"

"I don't know but I'm out of money, so we'll have to wing it," I said.

I did not have a stepladder, and the ceilings were exactly a foot higher than either of us could jump. I know, because for the rest of that year I had a white twelve-inch border circling the top of my bedroom wall. It never bothered me.

Within weeks of her arrival in Chicago, Tram and I were back to all our old habits. We party-hopped with her art school roommates. We played drinking games with my friends in Evanston, who loved Tram's sense of humor and adventurous attitude. We made our own Halloween costumes, and even though not everyone understood why Tram was wearing an expertly crafted replica of Björk's famous swan dress, she and I were on the same page. Once, at the concert of a doe-eyed Norwegian singer, Tram and I unintentionally showed up in the exact same outfit—down to the scarf that she had split in half and divided between us.

Above all, we ate. On a visit to Evanston, Tram brought a salmon fillet and taught me how to broil it. When we were low on funds, I'd take the El to her shoebox-sized apartment and we'd eat ramen and pizza rolls. But whenever we could scrounge together some cash, we went out. I loved going out to dinner with Tram, because it wasn't just about the food—we were exploring Chicago, trying to understand the city and where we fit into it. We scavenged the Indian restaurants on Devon Avenue, piling our plates with pakora and dal on mountains of fluffy saffron rice. We scarfed down heaping bowls of bucatini at a cozy Italian spot in Southport. We went to Pilsen to eat Salvadoran pupusas bursting with cheese and chicken and topped with a peppery slaw. When my senior year rolled around, we made our ritual official: on the first Saturday of every month we'd eat at a restaurant one of us had picked out, and in the process we'd get to know a new part of the city. It was a way to escape from our daily responsibilities, to force ourselves out of our apartments and carve out time for each other even when we were overwhelmed with schoolwork, jobs, and drama.

Maybe it was the Chicago winter. Maybe it was the dull panic that resulted from having our whole undecided lives before us. But eating our way around the city seemed like a good distraction from all the uncertainty we faced. Tram was trying to figure out if the art school she had chosen was the right fit. I was a few months away from graduating, and while I had some murky visions of being a writer in New York City, I had no concept of what that actually meant, or if I was talented enough to pull it off. Ultimately what we both wanted was for someone to tell us what to do and who to be.

"Why can't anyone just spell it out for us?" Tram asked one day over pork tamales in Wicker Park.

"Actually, there might be someone who can," I said. My Evanston psychic had been a bust, but I hadn't given up hope.

Tram and I adjusted our routine slightly. Now, in addition to restaurants, we were also looking for psychics. We quickly found one who happened to be located right across the street from an Argentine restaurant. And when we stepped into her waiting room and saw it was full of personal finance magazines, we thought it was the mark of a true professional. *Here come the answers*, I thought while flipping through a copy of *Forbes*, waiting for my turn with the crystal ball.

Tram went first. After a few minutes she came out of the other room, upset.

"What's wrong?" I asked. "What did she see?"

"I don't want to talk about it," she said. "But she said there is something seriously wrong with me."

At dinner, I attempted to distract Tram from her troubles by babbling about the menu. I had studied abroad in Buenos Aires, and the steak in South America was like nothing I'd ever had. Argentine meat was grass-fed and organic by definition, full of flavor, and usually grilled to perfection. I got mine with chimichurri sauce and yucca fries—a classic *porteño* dish, which I presented to Tram as proudly as if I had invented it myself. The steak was juicy and tender, and it had a potent garlicky kick thanks to the bright-green sauce I poured all over it. The fries were crispy and salty, just the way I liked them. We downed glass after glass of malbec—another Argentine favorite I had proudly adopted, even though I didn't actually like it much—and I rattled on and on about

Argentine street meat, hoping to cheer Tram up with vivid descriptions of blood sausage.

When that didn't work, I took a more straightforward tack.

"Tram, there is nothing wrong with you," I told her. "Psychics aren't real. This is probably just a front for her hooker business."

I reminded Tram that she had so many friends who loved her, who relied on her. Take me, for example: Before Tram came to Chicago, I had been miserable and insecure. I had forgotten who I was and what I liked about myself. I had assumed my college friends wanted me to be a certain type of person—wealthy, preppy, frat-party-loving—but Tram showed me that they didn't actually care. With her around, I remembered how to be myself, and why that might not be the most terrible thing in the world.

We were young and delicate; our self-confidence was tenuous; we were grasping so hard at our identities that our knuckles were white and our hair was practically standing on end. The future felt scary and uncertain, equal parts thrilling and deeply, deeply depressing. But at the very least, even if we weren't quite sure of who we were, we had a sense of who we wanted to become. We wanted to be worldly, adventurous, fashionable, creative, and slightly mystical. We wanted to be the type of women who genuinely enjoyed malbec, who smoked cigarettes, and who knew the most authentic psychic in town. We wanted to be a little slutty but not, like, actual prostitutes. We wanted to eat good steak on the cheap.

I wasn't very strong. I was not even remotely resilient. But Tram was both of those things, and even if she didn't know it, I knew it about her. I found that comforting. With her around, I'd always be okay.

CHARCOAL-GRILLED FLAT IRON STEAK WITH CHIMICHURRI SAUCE

I had been out of the country only once before when I went to study in Argentina for a few months during college, and as soon as I got there I realized I wanted to become the kind of person who traveled—even if I had to save up every cent for the rest of my life to do it. The day I arrived in the city, my host mom took me on a walk around town. It was February, the height of summer down there, and as we meandered through the cobblestone streets of this vibrant, fascinating place, I noticed that a lot of people were grilling on the streets and sidewalks. They were not cooking hamburgers and hot dogs: they were firing up steaks, sweetbreads, and blood sausages, every part of the cow you could imagine, plus a little chicken. I swiftly learned that this custom—cooking a boatload of beef on a simple iron grill, called a *parilla*—was a huge part of Argentine life. When my American friends and I befriended the locals, they invited us to their *asados* (barbecues). When we went out to dinner, we ordered a variety of meat on a *parilla*, which was set right on our table. I loved it all, but my favorite was the flat iron steak. Tender and juicy with deep, rich flavors, it's great for grilling and goes perfectly with chimichurri salsa—a delicious, garlicky sauce that's ubiquitous in that part of the world.

Serves 4
Prep time: 15 minutes; Cook time: 10 minutes

For the chimichurri sauce:
  3 tablespoons red wine vinegar
  1½ cups roughly chopped flat-leaf parsley
  ¼ cup chopped cilantro
  4 cloves garlic, peeled and smashed
  ¼ teaspoon lemon zest

1 teaspoon kosher salt, plus more as desired

½ teaspoon freshly ground black pepper, plus more as desired

½ teaspoon crushed red pepper flakes

½ cup extra-virgin olive oil

For the steak:

4 (10- to 12-ounce) flat iron steaks, 1 inch thick, at room temperature

Salt and pepper

To make the sauce, combine the red wine vinegar, parsley, cilantro, garlic, lemon zest, salt, pepper, and crushed red pepper flakes in a food processor; pulse until combined and about the consistency of pesto. Stir in the olive oil and add additional salt and pepper to taste. Refrigerate for at least 30 minutes before serving.

Season each steak generously with salt and pepper.

Grilling instructions: Fire up a charcoal grill to high heat. To get the best flavor out of your steak, use natural, organic charcoal bricks and no lighter fluid.

Once the grill is hot, put the steaks directly over the flame and cook for 4 to 5 minutes per side for medium-rare doneness. Remove the steak from the grill and let it rest for 5 minutes. Slice it against the grain and top generously with chimichurri sauce. Serve immediately.

Stovetop instructions: To cook the steak on the stovetop instead of the grill, heat a cast-iron pan (not oiled) over high heat for 15 minutes. Open up all the windows and get your vents going because this method is *very smoky*, and your apartment will smell like steak for days. Add 2 tablespoons of a neutral oil, such as canola or grape-seed, and the steak, and cook each side until it has developed a nice crust, about 5 to 6 minutes for medium rare.

BAKED YUCCA FRIES

Serves 4
Prep time: 20 minutes; Cook time: 30 minutes

1 (3½-pound) yucca, peeled
½ cup extra-virgin olive oil
1 teaspoon salt
1 teaspoon freshly ground black pepper
1 teaspoon smoked paprika, plus more for sprinkling

Preheat the oven to 450°F. Slice the yucca into ½-inch-thick pieces about 3 inches long. Place the yucca in a large pot and cover completely with room-temperature water. Cover and bring to a boil. When the water is boiling, reduce the heat to medium low and cook the yucca for another 10 minutes, pot partially covered. Drain and cool under cold running water. Dry thoroughly.

In a large bowl, toss the yucca with the olive oil, salt, pepper, and smoked paprika. Spread the fries out on a baking sheet and bake for 10 minutes. Flip the fries and bake for another 10 minutes, or until lightly browned and crispy. Sprinkle with paprika to serve.

3

Friends

Tram

The ticketing agent at the check-in desk raised one skeptical eyebrow at the giant cardboard box, lines of duct tape crisscrossing its surface. My name and new address in Chicago was scrawled on the side of it. I struggled to lift it onto the scale and then held my breath. It came in at sixty-eight pounds, just two pounds shy of Southwest's luggage weight limit. She rolled her eyes and pointed at the box: "*This* is how our guys end up hurting their backs."

I felt a tiny twinge of guilt for the baggage handlers, but what was I going to do? My crazy cardboard box was filled—not with dozens of frozen chickens—but with books, CDs, clothes, my old Singer sewing machine, and a rice cooker. My entire life, basically. I couldn't imagine moving to a new city without every single item in it, including that paperback copy of *The Unbearable Lightness of Being* (which I was certain would help me make friends in art school). I looked forward to meeting new people in Chicago, but what I was most excited about was finally being reunited with Lucy.

After I'd graduated high school, I wasn't sure what I wanted to study in college, so I took some time off and lived with relatives in Toulouse, France. My European family was an enterprising bunch. One of them was a fashion designer, another owned her own hair salon, and my great-aunt and great-uncle ran a popular Vietnamese restaurant. I tried on various professions, helping out at their businesses during the week. I peeled carrots and onions, stitched perfect blind hems, swept floors, and by the end of my stay had learned how to expertly perform "le shampooing."

I got fat on a daily *croque monsieur* habit; gobbled up buttery *pain au chocolat* every morning with my *chocolat chaud*; sampled oozy French cheeses brought by my uncle in Lyon; and developed a deep fondness for the Toulousain dish, the absurdly rich *cassoulet*. I loved Toulouse; the food, the foreignness, and the beautiful terra-cotta walls of the town that glowed pink at dusk. It was as far from the mundane suburbs of Maryland as I could get at the time. It would have been perfect, save for the fact that I was desperately lonely. Despite four years of high school French, my grasp on the language was still pretty dismal. I had no friends, my relatives were odd and overprotective, and I missed home.

My lifeline at the time was a thick stack of envelopes from Lucy that grew weekly. She wrote to me about her new life at school, the cool friends she'd met, the horrors of dorm food ("Mashed potatoes from a box!"), and her new crush. I returned her letters, all the unspoken feelings and new experiences pouring forth from me onto the pages. I told her of day trips to medieval castles, the excruciatingly awkward conversations that I'd have with the cute boy who worked at the salon, and how for my eighteenth birthday, my great-uncle accidentally took me to a cabaret that ended up being more of a strip club. Alone in my little bedroom, I'd devour those letters again and again, her bubbly, looping script written in blue ink on loose-leaf notebook paper comforting and familiar. Reading Lucy's words, and writing to her, was almost as good as having her with me.

Finally, after a few years apart, Lucy and I would be together again.

After an ecstatic, tearful reunion at the airport, she drove me in a borrowed minivan back to her place in Evanston to hang out before school started. We ate at a BYOB Thai place for dinner and downed a bottle of something called "Nest Ale" that we'd bought because it had a cute little owl on the label. If the rest of my time in Chicago was anything like that first day, I was golden.

The next morning, Lucy drove me to my new apartment. The halls were teeming with parents and their embarrassed offspring, exchanging teary good-byes. My mom had asked if I wanted her to come to Chicago to help me move, but I had waved her off. It seemed silly to pay for an extra plane ticket. I was an adult; I could handle moving to a new city all by myself. But standing in front of all these strangers, it finally hit me that this was my life now. I was suddenly grateful for Lucy's reassuring presence beside me.

I shared a crowded two-bedroom apartment in Boystown with three other girls. Monica and Lisa were from Indiana and Cincinnati, respectively. They'd arrived a few days earlier and hit it off immediately, so they called dibs on the larger room with the en suite bath. My roommate Donna was a tall, statuesque brunette from Lima, Ohio. Donna loved *Friends*, the TV show, so much that she couldn't fall asleep unless she watched at least three episodes every night. She was not my first choice for a roommate, but I didn't know anyone else in Chicago and I was desperate for friends. Lucy was almost an hour's ride away on the train in Evanston and she had her own life; I didn't want to be the clingy, hometown loser dragging her down with my lameness. Donna seemed nice enough; at any rate, she was very clean and polite. Along with the *Friends* DVD box set, she had brought an enormous crate of premium toilet paper with her from Lima, and she generously offered to let us use it gratis—so I could deal with that dumb Rembrandts song on a loop.

Donna was a morning person. She set the alarm for 6 a.m., even on the weekends, to get a jump start on the day and to provide her ample time to complete her toilette. The hour or two she spent setting her long brown hair in hot rollers, followed by the precise application of enough makeup to outfit an entire flotilla of midwestern beauty queens, allowed her to squeeze a few more episodes of *Friends* into her daily routine. Donna loved the color pink and she chose to dress exclusively in those rosy hues, from her puffy coat down to her platform sneakers. A few hours after her alarm buzzed, I would stumble out of bed and smear on some black eyeliner and we'd walk to class together, Donna's corkscrew curls bouncing merrily like Jimmy Dean sausage links in the wind.

When I'd started packing for my move from Maryland to Chicago, my mom placed a little bag of white powder and two brand-new bottles of soy sauce and fish sauce, carefully wrapped in Vietnamese newspapers, among the small pile of cookware and the books I had planned to bring with me. I scoffed at the baggie of MSG and pushed the bottle of fish sauce back at her. Was she crazy? "Why not throw some dried squid and durian in with my stash while you're at it?" I snapped.

My mom just looked at me for a moment, and then she unwrapped the fish sauce and placed it back in the pantry. It would have been easier if she had yelled at me, or even given me a cold, withering stare, but she said nothing. I felt a pang of shame at my behavior, but I pushed it aside. I wasn't budging on this. The foreign, funky, fermented anchovy sauce seemed too far a step in the wrong direction, broadcasting loudly to these new people that yes, indeed, I was doomed to life as a social pariah.

I had been burned early on in elementary school, labeled the weird kid with the strange food. I'd open my plastic lunch box and remove a small Tupperware container, simultaneously anticipating and dreading what was to come. Inside that container, lovingly packed by my mother, was last night's dinner: slow-cooked pork shoulder braised in a caramel sauce and coconut juice, atop her homemade sweet pickled mustard greens and rice. She always kept a giant glass jar by the window in the kitchen, layering mustard greens and scallions in a sweet brine to ferment. I'd ask my mom every day if they were ready, watching as the leaves faded from bright green to muted olive in the sun. I loved these sweet, crunchy pickles.

I tried to keep a low profile during lunchtime, but, inevitably, Jessica or Stephanie or some other third-grade mean girl would peer over my shoulder and squeal, "Ewwww! What is that?!" in disgust, mouths full with white bread and bologna sandwiches. Once, they even called the lunchroom monitor over to our table to complain about my meal (a delicious stir-fry of calamari, tomatoes, and Chinese celery). I endured it for a while, but my eight-year-old self couldn't take this much scrutiny every day, and I soon found myself demanding Lunchables and Capri Sun for school lunch until my mom relented. They couldn't possibly find anything to critique in those perfectly uniform die-cut squares of processed meat and cheese, which I happily brought to school even though, if I was honest with myself, I thought they kind of sucked.

In Chicago, I decided I'd stick with cooking "American" dishes in my new apartment, foods that were recognizable and unchallenging to midwestern palates. Also, simplicity was key, as I'd never really cooked much beyond fried eggs and rice. *But how hard could it possibly be?* I figured there would be some kind of learning curve, sure, but I'd had years of experience. I made dozens of cakes with Lucy. I did prep work in my family's restaurant in France, and I had spent my whole life helping my mom out in the kitchen.

My mother used to sell homemade Vietnamese delicacies to the local businesses when I was growing up. Every week, the house would be filled with the scent of warm coconut milk simmering on the stove. She'd make glutinous rice sweets in an enormous triple-stack aluminum steamer, alternating stripes of translucent jade, delicately scented with pandan leaf, and yellow mung bean paste. She'd set me to work prepping the ingredients for dessert soups, studded with the unlikely combination of chickpeas and thin strips of seaweed, dried longan, and crunchy tapioca jewels, dyed a garish red with McCormick food coloring until they glistened like pomegranate seeds. You would never find these desserts in *The Joy of Baking*; they looked more like some Lucite confection designed by Ettore Sottsass than anything resembling a food.

We made *pâté chaud*, one of the few good things that came of the French occupation in Vietnam. We'd take puff pastry squares and fill them with ground pork flavored with scallions and fish sauce, black pepper, and always a bit of sugar. I'd help her assemble them, crimping the edges closed with the tines of a fork and brushing them with an egg wash. I would watch in satisfaction as they rose miraculously in the oven, turning a deeply appealing golden brown. After an interminable wait, I'd burn my fingers peeling the layers of flaky pastry back one by one, the hot steam escaping as I savored each bite. These Vietnamese treats were great and all, but my little brother Jimmy and I would really go nuts when my mom would dabble in more exotic "American food." One day we made cherry turnovers, which involved opening a can of Libby's cherry pie filling. It was syrupy sweet, tasted exactly like cold medicine, and bore no resemblance to any cherry found in nature. As you bit into it, the filling would seep out shiny and lurid, like a bottle of Revlon nail lacquer. I loved it.

I had never really flown solo in the kitchen, nor had I ever cooked American food, but naturally I assumed that I knew my way around a stove. For my first dinner in Chicago, I decided on a whole roast chicken. It was a budget-friendly option, and I could make a single bird last for a few days of meals. I attempted to prepare it the way my mom always had: marinated overnight in a simple brine of white wine and salt, and then rubbed with butter and roasted in the oven. I left it in the oven for too long, the concept of a meat thermometer foreign to me. The bird was reduced to tender mush, but the skin was golden and beautifully crisp. I ate it with rice and a salad with a really simple but delicious homemade vinaigrette made with fried shallots.

As we sat down to dinner in front of the TV to watch an episode of *Friends*, my roommates peered curiously at my plate. A short while later, the comments began. They found eating meat on the bone gross, which was baffling to me. Why would you waste your time and money buying boneless, skinless chicken breasts? They taste like nothing, cost more, and everyone knows that dark meat is superior. They questioned my little jar of homemade dressing, and asked me things like: Why is your lettuce brown? Is it rotten? It was not rotten; it was red leaf lettuce, which I'd bought because it was the kind my mom always got; she said the leaves were tenderer. The living room had become my third-grade cafeteria all over again. I finished off my chicken that week alone, away from prying eyes.

My new roommates ate mostly things out of boxes and cans: Nissin Cup Noodles, Zatarain's Jambalaya Mix, Starkist tuna salad, Ragú Old World Style spaghetti sauce, and every single pasta dish Chef Boyardee had on offer. Donna didn't actually cook anything ever. She preferred to eat her SpaghettiOs cold, straight from the tin. Monica fried a lot of ground beef and occasionally had a salad of preshredded iceberg lettuce and neon orange Hidden Valley French dressing. My third roommate, Lisa, ate only one dish the entire time we lived together: Hillshire Farm sausage and green bell peppers, on Uncle Ben's white rice, which she'd cook in a little bag in the microwave. Every time, without fail, she'd sit down to her meal, do a little shimmy of pleasure, and announce to the room, "Mmm...sausage and peppers." They washed everything down with liters and liters of Coca-Cola.

The next week, I made spaghetti with jarred sauce, topped with grated Parmesan for dinner. There couldn't possibly be anything to object to here. My dinner was a not-too-distant relative of Donna's can of cold SpaghettiOs, but even then, Monica shook her head and said, "I've just never heard of anyone eating spaghetti without meat," while draining the grease from her seemingly endless supply of ground beef.

In between classes we'd roam the Chicago neighborhoods in large packs, an odd assortment of new friends who had nothing in common save for the proximity of our living quarters. We'd take the Red Line train down to Chinatown, where they screeched at the sight of ducks hanging in the window of a restaurant, glistening red with crispy skin. They looked delicious to me, not so different from a rotisserie chicken, but I kept that to myself. Donna bought a lucky bamboo plant. I was intimately familiar with this world; it was as normal as the Jewel-Osco and Dominick's grocery stores were to people out here, but of course I said nothing because I was still trying to maintain a low profile. Not that it was really working, I'd discovered. The first question a lot of strangers asked me was: "Where are you from?" I knew what they were asking, but I always answered, "DC." And then the inevitable follow-up question: "But where are you *really* from?" Or they would just guess, shouting out "Ni hao ma!" or "Konichiwa!"

This didn't bother me much at first, but it got old quickly. It was odd having my ethnicity be my singular identifying characteristic. Some of my new acquaintances had never even heard of Vietnam, which was baffling to me because this country did fight a long-ass war over there. There are entire Tom Cruise movies on the subject.

I had never been particularly invested in my identity as a Vietnamese American. As far as I was concerned, religion and my ethnic identity were neutral markers, like being a brunette or having green eyes. When I was a little girl, my mom tried to teach me about my culture by taking me to an autumn harvest festival celebration held at the local middle school. There was a market set up, with ladies selling steamed banana-leaf-wrapped goodies and moon cakes filled with sweet beans. I watched pretty young girls my age in flowing *ao dai* perform a quaint fan dance on the stage.

On the drive home, I listened with half an ear open as my mom told me how much she used to look forward to the autumn festival back in Vietnam. With a family that large there was never enough of anything to go around, so Harold could spring for only one lantern for all the children to share. She'd watch with envy all of the other little boys and girls playing with lanterns of their own; she'd admire their bright candy colors, intricately patterned and hand-painted to look like dragons or carp.

I looked at the small paper lantern in my lap that my mother had bought for me that day. I thought about how lucky I was, so privileged to be able to avoid spending my weekends stuck in fan dance rehearsal or, worse, at Vietnamese Sunday school, learning to speak the language properly.

I'd spent most of my young life ignoring or actively suppressing my cultural background because it seemed to cause me nothing but embarrassment with the outside world. So it was a surprise to me that in Chicago I felt genuine excitement when I discovered that there was a Vietnamese neighborhood just a few stops away on the El. I'd make secret solo trips to Little Saigon so I could enjoy the flavors from home, free from my roommates' scrutiny. As soon as I stepped out of the station at the Argyle stop my heart leapt. There were actual rickshaws parked in front of one of the restaurants. Like Donna's lucky bamboo, they were obviously pandering to tourists, but to me it was a sign of home. Not that I'd actually been a passenger in one or had even seen a rickshaw before in my entire life, but I knew people who had. I was rickshaw-adjacent. Little Saigon comprised only a few blocks, and half of the vendors were Thai or Chinese, but it was familiar. I would sneak off after classes to consume enormous bowls of *bun bo hue*, my face hovering over the steam, inhaling the scent of star anise and cinnamon, long-simmered beef stock, and bright, herbaceous Thai basil. I worried that I would come home smelling foreign, the evidence of my Asian food habit emanating from my pores. After several weeks of denying myself a home-cooked meal, I couldn't take it anymore. I gave in and went grocery shopping, finally seeing the heaps of ong choy and bitter melon, the shelves lined floor to ceiling with pickled vegetables, in an entirely new light. These foods were home. I picked up a bottle of fish sauce and a bag of MSG.

I invited Lucy over to my new place to make spring rolls. I wasn't sure if she had actually eaten them before, but she was game. I prepped all of the ingredients: poached shrimp, sliced along the grain so that they'd roll more easily; vermicelli noodles that I'd accidentally overcooked; and piles of (brown) lettuce, basil, and mint. I made a simple hoisin-based sauce and topped it with crushed peanuts that I'd lightly toasted on the stove. I explained how to construct a spring roll so that the contents would not spill out, rolling it tightly the way you'd do with a burrito. Just as we sat down around the coffee table to eat, I felt that old fear rise in me. Would Lucy squeal in disgust just like Donna? I had nothing to worry about. This was my best friend, and she knew me better than pretty much anyone in the world. Even if something was unfamiliar to her, Lucy would never treat me or what my family ate as strange. It was a relief to know that I had at least one good ally in this new place. I could be my true self, cracking jokes to a receptive audience. I'd felt so stifled those first few weeks on my own, so cautious to iron out anything that could be perceived as a flaw, I had nearly become someone I no longer recognized.

It's easy to have a strong sense of who you are when you are surrounded by your natural environment and the people you trust. There isn't a lot of risk involved. Back home, I had my room; my vintage clothes; my lists of top five bands, books, movies—material things I had mistaken for an actual identity. I'd brought these with me to Chicago, but it wasn't enough to stave away that feeling of being unmoored and uncertain. I'd become a bland, watered-down version of myself. The foods I ate, and the strong flavors, the textures, and the memories that came with them, were a part of who I was. All it took was an afternoon with my best friend to see my real self reflected back at me, a reminder that I shouldn't be ashamed of who I was, for liking what I liked. After all, Lucy liked me, and she was pretty much the best person I knew.

I gave up trying to hide my "weird" food. My roommates might have been more vocal in their distaste, but I was no different in judging the meals they ate. I'd forgotten that those girls were a long way from home as well, and my hoisin sauce was as foreign to them as cold SpaghettiOs were to me. Also, I had spent all of that money at the Asian market, and I wasn't about to let those groceries go to waste.

Monica used to refer to me as the "gourmet chef," which I'm sure was meant in an entirely sarcastic way at first. But after a few weeks of living together, she and Lisa started to come around, casually remarking that hey, if I ever wanted in on these sausage and peppers or to help make a dent in Monica's ground beef supply, I was welcome to join them. And maybe they could try one of those Asian burritos, too?

CARAMEL AND COCONUT–BRAISED PORK

This is the kind of lazy comfort food I love, because it requires very little active time in the kitchen but pays off handsomely. Pork shoulder is braised in a coconut broth and left to cook for hours on the stove, until the meat is fork-tender and has absorbed all of that rich caramel sauce. You should avoid using pasteurized coconut water or juice, which I personally find has a strange, off-putting flavor. My favorite brand of coconut water is Harmless Harvest's 100% Raw Coconut Water (you can find it at Whole Foods). Another great alternative is frozen young coconut juice, which is available in most Asian grocery stores. I often serve this with a slaw made of bright, crunchy chives and bean sprouts, which lends a satisfying crunch and helps cut through the richness.

Serves 6
Prep time: 15 minutes; Cook time: 2 hours 15 minutes

4 tablespoons neutral oil, such as canola or avocado
6 tablespoons sugar
1 medium shallot, chopped
6 whole dried arbol chiles
1 (3-pound) boneless pork shoulder, trimmed of excess fat and cut into 1½-inch pieces

3 cups coconut juice

2 tablespoons soy sauce

2 tablespoons fish sauce

In a 4½-quart Dutch oven or heavy-bottomed pot, heat the oil over medium-low heat. Add the sugar and cook, stirring frequently with a wooden spoon to keep the mixture from sticking, for 3 to 5 minutes, until the sugar has dissolved and the mixture has turned a light tan color. Raise the heat to medium and add the shallot and chiles. Cook for 3 to 4 minutes, until the shallots are lightly golden. Add the pork, coconut juice, soy sauce, and fish sauce. Partially cover, reduce heat to low, and cook for about 2 hours, or until the pork is tender and almost falling apart.

CRUNCHY SPROUT AND CHIVE SLAW

Serves 6

Active prep time: 5 minutes; 30 minutes to marinate

¼ cup Champagne vinegar

2 teaspoons sugar

1 teaspoon kosher salt, plus more as desired

12 ounces bean sprouts

4 ounces chives, cut into 2-inch lengths

Fresh ground black pepper for seasoning

In a large bowl, mix together the vinegar, sugar, and salt. Stir to dissolve. Add the bean sprouts and chives, tossing gently to combine. Cover and refrigerate for at least 30 minutes before serving. Season with salt and pepper to taste.

4

The Cheese Puff Gypsy of Avenue C

Lucy

I arrived in New York City with $300 in my wallet and fifty pounds of canned beans in the back of my dad's minivan. I had made good on my goal to move to the city right after college, and while I had no concrete plans about my future, I did have a very strict budget: $40 a week. I had no job—I was free! But then again, I had no job, so I was broke. After graduation I had gone home to Takoma Park briefly to stock up on the essentials: stolen toilet paper from my mom's stash, a floor-length bathrobe from my childhood wardrobe, and cheap canned goods, which I considered critical to my survival. (Once I got to New York I quickly learned they sell food there, too. These are the things you learn in the big city.)

I also brought the Stevie Nicks album my brother had given me for my birthday, which immediately became the sound track to my first summer in the city. Growing up I had never been a free spirit; I was studious and risk-averse. I liked to be prepared for any and every occasion, preferably with little index cards I could consult for guidance along the way. But I knew that was no way to live a twenty-something life. I was in Manhattan now, armed with a fresh beginning and a decades-old compilation CD. I was ready to embrace my inner gypsy.

I signed a lease on a two-bedroom apartment in the East Village with my friends Matt and Rakesh, which, if you do the math, is one fewer bedroom than roommate. But there was a 5 x 7-foot nook that jutted out from the back of the apartment, and, according to the real-estate agent, it could easily be converted into a third bedroom. The nook had three walls; all we needed to do was add a fourth. Between the three of us I usually had the least money, so I was given the "third room," which was also the cheapest. The plan was that until I got around to putting a wall up, I would sleep on a mattress on the floor, like a lady Jean Valjean.

We all agreed that this was a perfectly reasonable way to live. After all, we had more important things to focus on—like how we were going to make it in this city of eight million people. Matt, who had been a theater star at our college, read for parts on Broadway during the day and waited tables at night. Rakesh was looking for an internship in the TV industry, and he occasionally enlisted me to act in the parody rap videos he was making at the time. Nights when Matt wasn't working, we'd do line readings to help him prepare for auditions, and then we'd all curl up on the couch to watch *So You Think You Can Dance*, an activity made especially exciting by the fact that Tram's friend Liam was a contestant on it.

The three of us didn't share food, but when we were all home we cooked and ate our dinners at the same time, like the makeshift little family we were. I found comfort in this routine—the three of us, crowding in the kitchen, Rakesh grilling frozen chicken breasts on the George Foreman grill, Matt throwing together some healthy-seeming barley concoction, and me, boiling pasta on the stove—because it reminded me of home.

Every night growing up my mom had cooked dinner, and every night the family gathered around the table to eat it. Over two-crust spinach pie, or a broccoli and goat cheese quiche, my parents drilled us about school and discussed their own work—my dad's job on the Hill or my mom's at the magazine. My siblings and I, on the other hand, saw this time as an opportunity to torment each other, employing our food as weapons whenever necessary. My older brother Bennett was temperamental, prone to outbursts, and by the age of about six my little sister Devon had figured out how to best humiliate him. "A *minus*, huh?" eight-year-old Devon mocked one night, as Bennett proudly showed the family a painting he had done well on at school. His face turned bright red with fury and, as if in slow motion, he hoisted that night's dinner—a beautiful homemade artichoke-and-spring onion pizza, yet to be sliced—off its platter. Devon jumped out of her seat and started to sprint out of the room, squealing hysterically in triumph and terror as she attempted to escape our older brother's wrath. She was too slow. The pizza hit her square in the back.

Of course, dinner with my roommates was less dramatic. And I wasn't cooking the elaborate, well-balanced meals of my childhood. On my meager budget, the menu usually included some combination of whole wheat pasta, rice, tuna fish, canned chickpeas, lentils, and Trader Joe's frozen chicken breasts. When I was feeling flush, I'd buy a salmon fillet and make a variation on one of my mom's weeknight staples from the childhood table: salmon on rice with scallions and a pistachio aillade. Most nights I'd eat my food at the kitchen counter, shoveling it into my mouth as I hunched over a bowl, but that dish—the warm, fluffy rice; the rich, fatty salmon; and the bright, nutty sauce—was worth eating properly, with a napkin, in a chair (or at least on the couch in front of the television).

After stuffing the dinner dishes haphazardly in the dishwasher (a luxury we didn't yet realize was unique for our circumstances), Matt,

Rakesh and I would lie on the couch, guzzling wine from the cheap magnum we usually had around, talking about the new Zadie Smith book we were passing between the three of us, or the indie band one of us had discovered online. When we were sufficiently buzzed we'd head out into the East Village night and try to generate as much excitement as possible on what little money we had.

I was missing Tram that summer, but I told myself to be patient. She was going to join me in New York just as soon as she graduated from art school. In the meantime, I was lucky to have Matt and Rakesh as my surrogate brothers. Matt and Rakesh were handsome and charming, the funniest, warmest people, and they made friends everyplace they went. I was happy to tag along, lightly buzzed, to wherever the evening took us. Usually it took us to the bar—any of several low-rent places with names like "Cheap Shots" and "Plan B"—but occasionally we stumbled into wonderfully magical and unlikely scenarios. I have a hazy memory from a late night out that ended at an upstairs jazz bar in Alphabet City, a secret hovel of a place populated almost exclusively by kindly sixty-year-old former musicians; the next day none of us could remember exactly where it had been. Later I wondered if I had dreamed the whole thing, as occasionally happens on sitcoms.

I'd always call Tram the next day and recap the night before, playing up the romance factor and gliding over some of the sketchier details. I was constantly babbling on about which restaurant she'd love (I never mentioned that I myself had never eaten there—hello, I was on a budget!), and what neighborhood we'd want to live in, and the legions of eligible straight men who were just floating around Manhattan, waiting to be her boyfriends.

Those first few months in the city, I felt cozy and euphoric and safe. I had the occasional temp job and a little bit of additional babysitting income; I had Matt and Rakesh as my confidants; I had my near-daily phone calls with Tram; and I had a wonderfully romantic view of my purposefully aimless existence. Everything was going according to plan.

On phone calls home to Maryland, my mother would beg me to apply for one of the many full-time employment opportunities she regularly forwarded to me from a job listing website, but I had no interest in heeding her advice. Already I worried I was perilously at risk of turning into her. I had attended the same college that she had; I wanted to be a writer like she was; I, too, had a fondness for tiny cakes, high-waisted pants, and soft cheeses. The apple clearly hadn't fallen far from the genetic tree, but that only made me more annoyed when she tried to tell me what to do. I loved my mom and I respected her career. That did not mean I was ready to start living an exact replica of it. I had waited my whole life to move to New York, and I was not about to ruin those first few precious years with something so corporate as a real job. I certainly was not going to find a source of income on a website called JournalismJobs.com.

I wanted to be a writer. What exactly I wanted to write I wasn't sure, but I figured the only way to find out was through experimentation. I'd haul my old-school MacBook to the nearest coffee shop and pound away on one of dozens of half-conceived, never-to-be-finished projects. There was the package about Canadian bands for *Rolling Stone*'s website that I didn't bother finishing. There were short stories, screenplay treatments, and essays. In moments of deep uncertainty, I started haphazardly filling out grad school applications—just in case. I didn't accomplish much, but I had the vague notion that I was on track with the whole writing thing. I actually enjoyed doing it, for one thing, and that seemed like as good a sign as any.

And signs were all I was looking for that year. That, and money to pay the rent.

The slim wad of cash I had brought with me to New York barely lasted a week, and my temp jobs were sporadic. After a few weeks of playing it fast and loose with my overdraft situation, I came to understand that I would have to get a more reliable—if not more permanent—job. The goal was simple: I wanted to find some form of employment that brought in just enough money to prevent me from getting evicted while also keeping my pantry well-stocked with $7 bottles of wine. I wandered around downtown Manhattan, idly handing out my résumé at bars and restaurants along St. Marks Place and Ludlow Street, staring intently at the people I passed. How had they become themselves, these strangers with face tattoos and sinewy muscles and hardened attitudes? What were the chances that they had shown up in this city like I had, an innocent, dorky, suburban kid with ill-formed artistic dreams? I had never fallen in love or been dumped, I'd never gotten in a fistfight with anyone other than my brother, and the only drugs I'd ever done were of the plant-based variety. I didn't even own a single shawl.

After a few days of getting turned away from waitressing and bartending jobs, I lowered my standards considerably to the retail sector—which paid about forty times less than a proper restaurant gig would have—and put in an application at a shop that exclusively sold Brazilian cheese puffs and French cream puffs. I got the job on the spot.

"You're speaking to New York's newest Brazilian cheese puff seller," I told Tram on the phone, walking home after my first shift.

"What the hell is a Brazilian cheese puff?"

"I have no idea," I said.

The cheese puff shop was one of those specialty establishments so specialized that no one, including its employees, expected it to last the summer. When I went in to submit my job application, the store was empty—a state that was not, I would soon learn, unusual. But it was a nice walk across town, which was increasingly sun-dappled and tree-lined the further I got from my apartment, and I'd call Tram as I made my way west. Once at the shop I got paid $10 an hour to stand around gossiping with my pleasingly bohemian coworkers, most of whom were modern dancers and actors and painfully cool teens, while drinking free cappuccino after free cappuccino and covertly snacking on pastries. At the end of the shift, jacked up on sugar, I would load up my backpack with stale baked goods and haul ass out of there. At home with Matt and Rakesh, I'd spread the bounty out on the kitchen counter, and we'd sit around drinking wine and trying to discern what, exactly, made these snacks—basically cheesy bread, formed into chewy little balls and baked with a variety of herbs—"Brazilian." (One day at work, I asked my boss, who was not himself Brazilian—he was a former venture capitalist who had been to Rio once—and he told me: French cheese puffs, aka *gougères*, use all-purpose flour; the Brazilian version uses cassava flour.)

In a way, it was the perfect job. Low-stress, low-commitment—and I loved to bake. During breaks I'd go into the kitchen and badger the pastry chefs with incessant questions about their techniques and training. As I stood behind the cash register, I'd dream of myself in a cute little white chef's hat and a pair of fashionable clogs, conjuring up picturesque confections in the back of a fancy restaurant.

Then my shift would end and I'd leave and forget it all. I liked my job just fine, but the real action in my life happened at night. Before New York, I'd had a handful of short-lived boyfriends, but my dating track record was otherwise dismal. Now that I was here, though, I had discovered the ultimate early-twenties cruising spot—coffee shops— and I was not going to let the opportunities pass me by. After dinner at home I would head to the aptly named Café Pick-Me-Up, open my laptop to one of my vague writing projects, and scope out the scene for cute boys to make eyes at. My strategy was: stare them down until they asked me out. Much to my shock, this worked fairly regularly.

There was the waiter who told me of his plan to move to a cabin out west (no specific cabin, just "something rustic, maybe some horses") to write his collection of short stories. There was the roller-skating Frenchman who was on track to inherit his father's apple orchard right outside of Paris ("the son of an APPLE MOGUL!" I wrote to Tram in a characteristically unhinged e-mail). There was the white boy who worked at a Japanese news service, a guy who seemed promising until he tried to force me to order a blue drink at a crowded bar on a Friday night, for reasons he wouldn't or couldn't explain. "Blue drinks are not my thing," I said, much to his annoyance. I ordered a beer and that was the end of it.

But it wasn't until I started dating the guy who worked at my local coffee shop that things got complicated. This guy was a handsome film student, the son of a diplomat, and he had an identical twin. He lived with his brother about a block away from me, and because we dated only briefly, I never learned to tell the two apart. This became problematic after things between us inevitably fizzled out; I kept seeing one of them around the neighborhood, but I never knew if it was the guy I'd dated or his brother, whom I'd never actually met. One day I found myself hiding behind a stranger at the coffee shop to avoid having to deal with an unpredictable confrontation. Another time, I ducked into the corner bodega at the last minute to prevent a run-in with God-knows-who. Ultimately, the process of going to get my morning bagel became too stressful to bear. So I got a Mr. Coffee and a toaster. It wasn't the most bohemian move, but hey, I had to eat. Plus, I was still sleeping on a bare mattress in the living room, so my gypsy cred remained strong.

The no-wall lifestyle couldn't go on forever, though. Because I had turned my nose up at hiring a professional wall-builder—it cost about a thousand dollars, way out of my price range—I had no choice but to do it myself. So I bought a bunch of construction materials, which I then immediately abandoned in a heap on the living room floor. After a while my roommates, the most tolerant humans alive, started to grumble. They had come home to find me blasting "Gold Dust Woman" and dragging pieces of drywall around the room in a daze one too many times.

I knew I needed to figure out how to build a serviceable wall for my nook, but at twenty-one my most formidable talents were making pretentious book recommendations, getting in shouting matches about politics I knew nothing about, chugging wine, and writing dirty limericks over Gchat. Home construction projects were not on the list. *What would Stevie do?* I wondered while sweating it out in my unair-conditioned apartment. Then one day, as I lounged on a pile of couch cushions on the living room floor, it came to me. The goddess of leather and lace would not build a wall. She would make *a man* build her a wall. And that was when I thought of David Jones.

David Jones was a guy I'd gone to school with who was a friend of a friend and lived in the city. He and I had a fleeting romantic encounter at the end of college, and while I didn't necessarily see it going anywhere, I was open to the possibility of a fling. He had great hair. Moreover, upon moving to New York, he and his roommates had built a bunch of walls in their Williamsburg loft. Handy, cute, and familiar—why not? I figured asking David to help me build a wall would kill two birds with one stone: First, I'd have a wall. Second, I'd find out if he was interested in me. I mean, no guy in his right mind would put up drywall for a woman he didn't want to make out with, right? It was the perfect plan: I'd get my wall and trap a man.

So I called him. David agreed to assist me with the wall, which, as I assumed we all knew, meant that I would lie on the couch while he did all the work. In preparation, I put on a cute outfit and bought a six-pack. When he arrived, I used my best wiles to try to inspire some romance.

"Would you like a beer?" I asked as he cut a hole for the door with a saw. He declined.

"You're very good with your hands," I said from across the room as he struggled under the weight of a ten-foot piece of drywall.

I fanned myself seductively as he secured the door to its hinges.

And then, something mysterious happened. When the wall was all done, David . . . left.

"What happened?" I mused on the phone with Tram, whom I called immediately after the door clicked shut. "Did someone just build me a pity wall?"

Tram tried to soften the impact of David's lack of interest, but I felt brutally insulted. In addition to spurning me, David had built a wall that didn't reach the ceiling; there was a three-inch gap at the top. Also, the door didn't close all the way. Also, it didn't have a knob.

A few days later, my manager at the cream puff shop told me he'd have to cut my hours. The store just wasn't making enough money to keep a full staff, he said. But I'd been working only twenty hours a week to begin with, and I could barely pay my rent as it was. I certainly could not survive on ten hours a week of minimum wage.

And that was how, in my least ragtag turn yet, I ended up as the editorial assistant at a bimonthly Catholic magazine. Which I heard about via JournalismJobs.com.

Stevie Nicks would not have approved of a twenty-two-year-old working at a magazine that put out special issues about the Eucharist. My new life involved sensible flats and brown-bag turkey sandwich lunches. I could no longer stay out all night with Matt and Rakesh; work started at 9 a.m. sharp. And instead of being surrounded by America's most fashionable artisanal cheese puff sellers, I was now working with a small staff of mostly older men. We ate lunch together in the office each day, and watercooler chatter would often turn to the latest Catholic issues of the moment—the ramifications of the sex abuse scandal, the possibility of female priests, Pope Benedict's red Prada slippers. I longed for my wayward lifestyle and unlimited supply of Brazilian baked goods.

There were a few upsides to the gig, though. There was the steady paycheck. Also, Catholics tend to be very nice people, and many of them have martyrish tendencies, so even when my colleagues were working long hours trying to put an issue to bed, they never once asked me to stay a minute past 5 p.m. In fact, most of my coworkers were great. But that didn't make me feel any less wistful about the fact that my bohemian days were at an end.

When our lease ran out on the East Village apartment the following summer, Matt, Rakesh, and I decided not to renew it. For one thing, I'd made plans to live with my college roommate Ann, who was moving to New York that fall. I had been hoping that Tram would come with her, but she was still finishing school; next year, she promised.

The boys and I had no sense of what we were giving up. We didn't realize how lucky we'd been, with our decent, modestly priced apartment, our close, no-drama friendship, and our easily won, low-stakes jobs. *New York isn't so hard!* we had thought when we first arrived.

We were wrong. Almost immediately after leaving the apartment on East Ninth Street and Avenue C, I began to feel nostalgic for that carefree first year, when my biggest worries were whether the cheap wine would last us through the night; whether I could teach myself to be good at karaoke; and how long one could survive on a diet of cream puffs and cheese. Things got a lot more difficult for me after that. But I'd gotten my share of the New York magic. I knew where I was headed— sort of. And maybe selling out wasn't so bad after all. Even Stevie Nicks bought a house in Malibu and covered it in lace.

SEMI-BRAZILIAN CHEESE PUFFS

As much as I mocked the pastry shop for its hyperspecialized goods, I lived off those cheese puffs for months. They were delicious. The cassava flour creates a slightly chewy texture, so the puffs are denser than *gougères*, and they keep their shape for much longer. I love *gougères*, but you have to eat them right out of the oven or they deflate within minutes. These cheese puffs incorporate the best elements of both varieties. I used Gruyère to give them the nutty, earthy flavor I love about *gougères*, and cassava flour for a little added heft.

Makes about 20 cheese puffs
Prep time: 10 minutes; Cook time: 15 minutes

2 cups tapioca flour (also sold as cassava or manioc flour)

1 teaspoon salt

1 teaspoon ground black pepper

1 teaspoon finely chopped fresh thyme

1 teaspoon crushed red pepper flakes

1 cup whole milk

½ cup butter

2 eggs

1 cup grated Gruyère

1 cup grated Parmesan

Preheat the oven to 400°F.

In a medium-sized bowl, whisk the flour, salt, pepper, thyme, and red pepper flakes until they are evenly incorporated. In a medium saucepan, bring the milk and butter to a boil. Remove from the heat and add the flour mixture to the liquid, using a hand mixer to incorporate. Add the eggs and cheese and mix until the dough is uniform. Scoop little balls (about 1 heaping tablespoon each) onto a parchment-lined baking sheet. Let sit for 10 minutes, then bake for about 15 minutes, until the puffs are golden brown.

SALMON AND RICE
WITH PISTACHIO AILLADE

Growing up, my mom had a stable of weeknight dishes she could whip up in less than thirty minutes—many of which were improvised based on what she had sitting around in the pantry. This was one of

my favorites. Throw the rice on the stove, pop the salmon in the oven, grind up a few pistachios, and in a few minutes you've got a meal that's healthy, delicious, relatively inexpensive, and, most importantly, incredibly easy to make.

Makes 2 heaping servings
Prep time: 15 minutes; Cook time: 25 minutes

For the aillade:

¾ cup shelled pistachios, roughly chopped

2 large cloves garlic

½ teaspoon salt, plus more as desired

½ cup extra-virgin olive oil

⅛ teaspoon orange zest

For the salmon:

2 cups water

1 cup jasmine rice

Pinch of salt, plus more as needed

1 (10-ounce) skinless salmon fillet

Extra-virgin olive oil

Freshly ground black pepper, for seasoning

3 scallions, chopped

Preheat the oven to 350°F. To make the aillade, bake the pistachios for about 4 minutes, until fragrant. Remove from the oven and let cool. Using a mortar and pestle, pound the garlic cloves into a paste. Add the pistachios and salt and grind until they form a uniform paste. Stir in the olive oil and orange zest. Add additional salt if desired. Set aside.

In a small saucepan, bring 2 cups of water to a boil. Add the rice and a pinch of salt and reduce heat to low. Cover the pot and let simmer for about 20 minutes, until the rice has absorbed all of the liquid. The rice should be firm but tender. Turn off the heat and let the rice sit, covered, for a few minutes. Fluff the rice with a fork before serving.

While the rice cooks, turn the oven up to 425°F. Pat the salmon dry, top with a drizzle of olive oil, and season with a pinch of salt and pepper. On a lined baking sheet, bake the salmon for about 5 minutes per half inch, or until the fish reaches an internal temperature of 145°F. Remove from the oven and flake the salmon with a fork.

Stir the scallions, salmon, and aillade into the rice. Serve immediately.

5

Junk Food

Tram

We hung out maybe three times before Amy asked if I wanted to be her new roommate. At $250 a month, my share of the rent was ridiculously low, even back then. I thought I had hit the lottery: a cool new friend and a place to live that even I could afford. The apartment was carved out of an unused unit in an office building. The floor, black and white tiles in a checkerboard pattern, had severe water damage, so the place had sat unlet for years. Save for the fact that it was in Chicago, the loft was the sort of cool, bohemian space I'd always thought Lucy and I would share.

Amy's dad was the building manager, and he had somehow convinced the building's owners that it would be a good idea to let her live in the unused office for a nominal rent. Her father was also an architect, so just before she moved in he had installed a standard kitchen and a full bath. We had zero privacy; it was an open space with a sleeping loft that hung suspended from the ceiling, with just enough room for two beds. When the platform was first installed, Amy's cats couldn't quite figure out the ladder, so we rigged an elevator system that consisted of an Easter basket and a few scarves tied together. Sing Sing or Keanu would climb into the basket and wait for us to haul him up over the railing. I happily settled into my new home by painting the few walls we had and then hanging up flimsy curtains for the semblance of privacy.

I was bummed that Lucy was now living a thousand miles away in New York. I told her to wait for me, that I'd join her as soon as I'd saved up enough cash. In the meantime, Amy seemed like she could be the perfect temporary best friend replacement. She was small and elfin, with more than a passing resemblance to Björk. Amy was a former ballet dancer who, like me, harbored vaguely artistic aspirations. My new roommate and I didn't know much about each other, but we both loved the same bands and had a mutual admiration for the other's fashion sense. That seemed like a good enough reason to move in together. I just had a gut feeling it would work out. And it did, at first.

Unlike my previous living situation, the food thing wasn't an issue. I felt comfortable almost immediately, as soon as I saw Amy's rice cooker on the counter. Not that I was cooking much. Between my two jobs and peripatetic attempts at pursuing some kind of creative career, I didn't have much energy or the inclination to invest time feeding myself nutritious meals. I ate out pretty much every day: fried noodles drowning in brown gravy from Duck Walk; grinders oozing with melted provolone from Philly's Best; and thick slabs of greasy, Chicago-style pizza. When we did cook, dinner was usually ramen, which we'd purchase by the carton in Chinatown. We'd simmer the freeze-dried ramen noodles in the broth, drain the noodles, and stir-fry them with a bag of Jewel-brand "Oriental Style" frozen vegetables. If I was feeling more ambitious, I'd fry a Chinese sausage and eggs, and eat these with jasmine rice and a few slices of raw tomato. I'd sit down to my meal, do a little shimmy and think to myself, "Mmmm . . . sausage and peppers." Then I'd wonder what Lisa was up to now. Rounding out the rest of my sodium- and MSG-rich diet were the counterbalancing forces of coffee, Adderall, Tylenol PM, and cheap vodka.

To pay the bills I worked full-time at a women's clothing boutique with the unfortunate but appropriate name Tragically Hip. The store specialized in the best kind of disposable, polyester-blend clothing to wear if you were in the mood to make some questionable life choices. In addition to skimpy club wear, we sold spandex gauchos, sweater ponchos in every color your heart could desire, and other garments that would indeed be classified as tragic, if not so much hip. It was an easy, mindless job that did not require too much of me. I spent days drawing in my sketchbook, texting Lucy, playing solitaire on the computer, and crafting elaborate window displays devoted to the epic love of Whitney Houston and Bobby Brown. To make some extra cash, I started working at the sex shop next door a few days a week. The interview for the job was nonexistent, as the owners of the sex shop also owned Tragically Hip, so they didn't inquire too deeply into whether or not I had any experience with the merchandise. (I didn't.)

On the weekends, packs of spray-tanned orange bachelorette parties would come squawking in, searching for the vibrator that Charlotte owned on *Sex and the City*. Then the self-appointed Samantha of the group would look at me coyly and giggle. "We want... *The Rabbit*." I would roll my eyes and wave at the wall of silicone and plastic. "They're all called The Rabbit. Which one?" I'd show them a few models, and they'd titter some more, making a few lame Mr. Big jokes before finally deciding on the pink version, alongside some penis-shaped pasta and the other phallic-themed novelties that seemed to be a requirement for celebrating one's impending nuptials.

Most customers were more discreet, sidling in and carefully averting their eyes when I greeted them at the door. They would wander over to examine the hosiery, or spend an inordinate amount of time reading the condom box labels, and then orbit, in gradually smaller circles, around the display cabinets containing whatever item they had come to buy. Everything was behind glass countertops to deter shoplifters and to force the clientele to speak to us, thus providing an opportunity to upsell. It was surprisingly easy for me to not be embarrassed at the merchandise I was peddling, despite the fact that I was quite naive when it came to these matters. I had only the vaguest notion what any of this stuff was, or what exactly you were supposed to do with it, so I treated all that silicone and plastic the same way I would a pink-fringed poncho at Tragically Hip.

Early on, I remember helping one woman who leaned in to tell me, sotto voce, "I'm . . . shopping for a friend."

"Cool, what is your friend into?"

Her friend was a fan of lube, more specifically, cherry-flavored anal lube. I thought to myself, *Man, why would you ask your friend to buy you something so . . . personal?* It turns out, a lot of people do, because about half of my clientele just happened to be picking up, say, a new flogger, or a set of leatherette cock rings—always for a friend!

Perhaps it was the environment, or maybe my obvious guilelessness, but people tended to get incredibly personal very quickly. One woman came in and confessed that she'd been dating her boyfriend for seven months, and, "Everything's fine, he's fine. He's just . . . I'm just so . . . bored with him, you know?"

I nodded my head sagely, like I did know (I didn't), and showed her some of our most popular items. As I rang up the transaction and wrapped her purchases in tissue paper, she said to me, "Thank you. For being so discreet and for making this experience so much less awkward than it could have been."

I just shrugged and said, "No problem," having no idea what she was talking about. What was so embarrassing about buying glass beads?

Even after I figured out where exactly those glass beads were supposed to go, I got over my embarrassment quickly, because even the most extreme retail job is ultimately a retail job. It didn't matter what I was selling. I still had to deal with mind-numbing boredom and irritating customers.

*   *   *

After a few months of living together Amy and I were getting along fine, but things weren't clicking the way I'd hoped they would. I'd assumed that our relationship would evolve into something deeper, but so far there wasn't that magical alignment of temperament, or interests, or even humor that I'd thought would develop naturally. It wasn't effortless, the way it was when you met a kindred spirit.

On good days, we'd stay up all night listening to music and working on the millions of unfinished projects we had going at any given time. We talked about the clothes we'd make, the murals we'd paint, the screenplays we'd write—just as soon as we got around to it. There was always something more pressing that got in the way: day jobs, cute boys, and parties to go to. It felt profound, like we were baring our souls to each other, in the way that anything spoken at two in the morning feels like confession.

At the time, Amy and I were obsessed with this Japanese bubble-gum pop duo. I think we unconsciously took on those personas for a while—these plastic, cartoon people—because we were young and dumb and it was fun. I had always been an anxious person, worrying about things real and imagined: my health; the future; if the lack of a visible thigh gap was preventing me from having a boyfriend; or the threat of my little brother getting swept up with the wrong crowd and joining a gang.

Above all, the constant menace of impending adulthood loomed over me. I'd always thought I would pursue fashion as a career, but it seemed too unrealistic, too frivolous—so I abandoned that dream. And although I loved power suits, seamed stockings, and "executive realness," I could never actually see myself working in an office. My talents were grounded in the visual realm. I knew I wanted to be an artist, I just couldn't quite figure out how to get there. Overthinking wasn't working for me, though, so I took a sabbatical from my responsibilities. I did what I had to do—worked my two jobs, paid the bills—and the rest of the time I just turned my brain off and tried to have fun, with little regard for the consequences.

Even though the rock-bottom rent helped a bit, art supplies, other people's Adderall, ramen by the case, and handles of bottom-shelf vodka did start to add up. More often than not, I'd find myself wondering if I could put off buying a bag of cat food for another day; my next logical thought being—*would Sing Sing and Keanu eat ramen?* (They wouldn't.) Amy and I would scrounge together enough change for exactly two beers and a respectable tip, and just before leaving the house I'd down a few Tylenol Arthritis capsules to give me the most bang for my buck. We would sit at the bar, nursing our precious beers, and wait for someone to offer to buy us drinks. Usually, we didn't have to wait very long. Amy was really cute and outgoing. They'd buy me a drink, too, because I was part of the package, but I could tell they didn't relish having to deal with the standoffish friend. I didn't have a problem being an ice queen, a role that came naturally to me, while Amy lined up her next ex-boyfriend. I didn't see the point in doing the same. None of these guys were the real thing.

Working two jobs, my free time was fairly limited. I scratched my creative itch by wandering the streets before shifts and taking pictures of interesting-looking strangers. I'd always get permission first (I wasn't a total creep), and, surprisingly, not a single person ever said no to me. I am normally a pretty shy and quiet person. Never before would I have been able to work up the nerve to speak to so many people, but the camera gave me purpose. There was something about having that old Kodak around my neck that made me nearly invincible. That lens was my safety net, a barrier between me and the world.

I shot pictures of swaggering teenage boys, their clothes and egos too big for their coltish bodies; beautiful twinkly eyed babushkas who reminded me of my own grandmother; and the shoplifters I'd caught at Tragically Hip, posing with their purloined merchandise before the cops arrived. I remember watching in awe as an austere-looking gentleman wearing an ornate black floor-length cape drifted down the street, his heavy presence enough to part the sea of baby punks and Cubbies fans on Belmont. The man looked like he wouldn't be out of place in a Caravaggio painting. When I asked him if I could take his picture, he simply nodded and rested his steady, unnerving gaze upon me. Slightly unsettled, I snapped a few pictures. Afterward, he handed me a card. It was for his one man show, the story of how he had spent decades of his life in prison, wrongfully convicted for a crime he did not commit.

I loved that moment of vulnerability, when a complete stranger would look at me directly and all the artifice would fall away. I lived for small truths, like discovering that the menacing-looking goth dude I'd followed because I wanted to take a picture of his biker jacket turned out to be wearing a well-loved *Cats* T-shirt underneath all that leather. I proudly told him I'd learned to play "Memory" by heart in the fourth grade. Those flashes of realness felt to me like eating that first bite of a perfect summer tomato after months of nothing but processed garbage.

I was self-aware enough to know that I wasn't going to be the next Diane Arbus or Nan Goldin. I had a knack for getting strangers to open up to me, but I was actually a pretty bad photographer. I could never get a handle on the technical aspects of the art. My images would come out hazy and unfocused, or completely blown out because I didn't quite understand that whole aperture business, nor did I care to spend too much time trying to learn it. On very rare occasions, I'd take a good picture. But more often than not this was purely by chance, not by my own design. It's difficult to tell when you are learning a craft if your deficiencies are due to inexperience, or if you're simply bad because you have no talent for it. I enjoyed taking pictures, but I knew I fell into the latter category. I was fine with photography as a hobby, but it was a pretty expensive one. I was printing in a rented darkroom space, and film and photo paper were ridiculously pricey, so I turned my mind to other creative outlets.

I was increasingly dissatisfied with the shallow turn my life had taken. I was bored with my job, I wasn't making good work, and I had started to get fed up with my living situation. Some of it was the typical roommate domestic drama, but the lack of any walls and doors in our apartment meant that we never got a break from each other. I would sometimes find thinly veiled attacks (in the form of bad poetry) all over the apartment for me to read. All I wanted was a room with a door so I could lock myself inside. I'd cooled on the friendship after living together that first year, protecting my sanity by spending more time away from home. I crashed on other friends' couches for days at a time.

There were fundamental things between us that just didn't line up—our senses of humor, our political philosophies, and how we saw the world. I had mistaken our shared interests for a real, profound connection. Those things—the pop music, the shared wardrobe, the vague idea of wanting to do something creative with our lives—they were all surface. We never actually made any progress toward our futures because we were too distracted by the present. We had a lot of fun together, but perhaps there was never anything more substantive to our relationship.

When Lucy came to visit Chicago, we made plans to meet downtown, not too far from my place. We had been writing real letters to each other all year, but I felt oddly shy. Before she could see me, I spotted Lucy. There is a brief moment of panic in seeing someone you love after a long time—often the memory you've held in your head and the person standing before you don't quite line up. It takes your brain some time to reconcile this new stranger with the person you once knew. I worried that she had changed, and maybe I had changed a little. What if it wasn't the same between us? After an embarrassingly shrill, giddy reunion, with hugs and screaming, my insecurities dissolved into nothing.

What I had been missing, what I had been craving, was that easy, magical intimacy that happens with a friend who knows you almost better than you know yourself. Sometimes it felt like we shared a brain or, at the very least, custody of it on alternating weekends. Even with all those miles separating us, I barely needed to finish a thought before Lucy would pick up the rest of the thread. Sometimes all it took was a single word, a look, to make us collapse into a fit of giggles.

In college, I loved dragging Lucy to art installations or letting her press the latest Lorrie Moore story collection that she had read and cherished into my hands. Even though we didn't share the exact same taste in music or books, I still liked seeing what she obsessed over. I'd read her sharp, witty columns in the school newspaper, and tell her she was the second coming of Dorothy Parker, and she let me cajole her into modeling my final projects for a design class. It was the kind of mutually supportive friendship that I craved. Even if we weren't directly collaborating, I felt inspired to push myself further, just so that I could show Lucy something that I was proud of.

I felt a little bolder, a little more secure in myself with Lucy around. I was drunk on that extra bit of fearlessness that I always felt when I was with her. Amy and I had been trying to force something that was never there to begin with.

Hanging out in my apartment, the one we should have been sharing, I showed her my black-and-white photographs and the camera I'd since retired.

"Now that you aren't planning on following in the footsteps of noted fashion photographer Nigel Barker, what are you going to do when you grow up?" Lucy asked.

"I don't know. Sell furry handcuffs and tube tops until I die?"

"What about fashion design?"

"You don't think it's kind of frivolous? Makes me a bad feminist?"

"No, of course not. But who cares what I think. Do *you* think it's frivolous?" she asked.

I thought about it. Clothes could be stupid and shallow and crass, like the awful polyester nonsense that I shilled for a living. But there was beauty out there, too. It was the armor you put on to face the world. It was the internal self, made visible. I thought about the cloaked man who carried the weight of the world on his shoulders. The stranger whose tough leather exterior revealed a tender soul, soft as a kitten. It's almost an unconscious act, getting dressed in the morning. But I understood that something as small as the hem of a pant leg, or the curve of a seam, could speak volumes about a person. It's how we soundlessly communicate who we are, and the person we wish to be. My answer to Lucy was no, I didn't think so. Not the way I did it.

"So . . . when are you moving to New York? It's going to be perfect! We'll get an apartment together and you'll find a job in fashion in no time at all."

"Soon," I promised.

I had put the future on pause, drifting through my early twenties on a sea of fast-food wrappers and ephemeral pleasures. I filled the space where my brain should have been with nothing of consequence, because I found tackling the real question of what I was going to do with my life too daunting. Consuming junk food all day is fine for a time, but eventually you're going to want something real. I was ready to get serious about the future.

PHO-SPICE BRAISED SHORT RIBS

Amy and I often found ourselves drunk and hungry at two in the morning. We'd usually go to Flash Taco, because it was open all night and it was conveniently located right next to the Damen L stop. I'd always get the same thing: two dry, stringy chicken tacos that came with watery green and red salsas that tasted nearly identical to each other. I'd never had much experience with Mexican food, beyond the American facsimiles one would find at Taco Bell (also always eaten at two in the morning), so these "tacos" tasted divine to my indiscriminating palate.

One late night we were getting a ride from this guy Ralph. He asked us where we wanted to eat, and we answered, "Flash Taco!" without a second thought. He made a face and said, "Nah. Flash Taco is gross. I'm going to take you somewhere else." I was about to argue, but Ralph was a big dude, and presumably he knew what he was talking about. He was right. When I finally tried real Mexican food, or at least the realest Mexican food you could find in Chicago, I was in awe. Oddly enough, I was struck by some of the similarities between Mexican and Vietnamese cuisines—the brightness, the emphasis on contrasting flavors, and even some of the same ingredients.

Short ribs are wonderful, and so easy that even drunk twenty-two-year-old me could have managed them if I'd had a little foresight and planned ahead. These are braised low and slow in a pho-inspired broth, dark and complex with charred onion and ginger, cloves and star anise. I serve them in tacos, on corn tortillas, with bright quick-pickled red onions, cilantro, lime, and a healthy shot of sriracha.

Serves 6
Prep time: 15 minutes; Cook time: 3½ to 4 hours

---

3 pounds beef short ribs, bone-in
Kosher salt and freshly ground black pepper
2 tablespoons extra-virgin olive oil
1 medium whole onion, unpeeled
1 (4-inch) piece fresh ginger
3 cups low-sodium chicken broth
1 cinnamon stick
2 whole cloves
2 whole star anise pods
1 teaspoon sugar

Continued

2 tablespoons hoisin sauce
1½ tablespoons fish sauce
½ tablespoon sriracha
4 cloves garlic, peeled
2 medium carrots, peeled and cut into 2-inch chunks

Note: Short ribs are an excellent meal to prepare a day ahead. They reheat well, and one advantage of letting them spend the night in the refrigerator is that you can easily discard the layer of excess fat that will collect on the top.

Preheat the oven to 325°F. To prepare the short ribs, trim off any excess fat—or don't. I usually skip this step, because I am waging a personal war between my arteries and myself. Generously season the short ribs with salt and pepper. In a heavy-bottomed pot or 4-quart Dutch oven, heat the olive oil on medium-high heat. Sear the short ribs, about 3 minutes per side, until they are browned on all four sides. You may need to work in batches to avoid crowding the short ribs. Turn off the heat, remove the short ribs to a plate, and drain the excess oil from the pot.

Place the onion and ginger directly on the open flame of a gas burner or grill for about 15 minutes. With metal tongs, turn occasionally so that all the surfaces are charred. If you are doing this on the stove, you will want to open a few windows and get your exhaust fan going, because it smells amazing but will produce a lot of smoke. Remove the excess burned onion skin and rinse the onion and the ginger.

Using the same pot that you used to sear the short ribs, turn the heat up to high and deglaze the pot with the chicken broth, scraping with a wooden spoon to release any brown bits. Add the cinnamon, cloves, star anise, sugar, hoisin sauce, fish sauce, and sriracha. Stir to dissolve the sugar. Add the short ribs, onion, ginger, garlic, and carrots. Cover and bake in the oven for about 3 hours, until the short ribs are tender and pull away from the bone easily. Discard the onion, ginger, cloves, garlic, carrots, and cinnamon stick before serving.

SPICY LEMONGRASS CHILI CHICKEN WINGS

Sometimes, after a late night out, we'd stumble over to the twenty-four-hour Jewel-Osco and buy two boxes of frozen Hooters chicken wings. These were a little fancier than the more plebcian frozen wings because they involved a complex two-step process. You were supposed to bake the wings in the oven for what felt like forever, but was actually more like thirty minutes—an eternity when you are drunk. While the wings cooked, there was a little plastic tub of sauce that got zapped in the microwave until it had melted into a pool of neon orange with a thick layer of grease swimming atop it. We'd climb up to the loft and eat the wings with our legs dangling over the edge. The next morning, there would be a little tray of chicken bones at our feet.

I no longer engage in such slovenly behavior, but I still love wings. These are superior to Hooters frozen chicken wings in every way imaginable.

Makes 2 pounds of wings
Prep time: 15 minutes active time; 1 to 24 hours to marinate; Cook time: 45 minutes

---

4 tablespoons chopped fresh lemongrass (about 3–4 stalks),
    discard the tough outer leaves
3 cloves garlic, minced
1½ tablespoons sugar
1 tablespoon sambal oelek
1 tablespoon fish sauce
1 tablespoon toasted sesame oil
1 teaspoon kosher salt
2 pounds chicken wings
1 tablespoon extra-virgin olive oil

Preheat the oven to 450°F.

In a food processor, pulse the lemongrass, garlic, sugar, sambal oelek, fish sauce, sesame oil, and salt for about 2 minutes, until the mixture has formed a chunky paste. Pat the chicken wings dry with paper towels. In a large bowl, toss the wings with the lemongrass and garlic mixture, massaging the paste into the meat until every surface is covered. Cover the bowl and refrigerate for at least 1 hour or up to 24 hours.

Place a wire baking rack on a baking sheet and brush the rack with olive oil. Arrange the chicken wings on top of it. Bake for 20 minutes. Flip the chicken wings over and return them to the oven. Bake for an additional 20 minutes, or until the wings are crispy and golden brown in places and the internal temperature reaches 165°F. Serve hot.

6

Fashion Salad

Lucy

After I left the East Village, I moved into a one-bedroom apartment approximately the size of a large hot tub. The place Ann and I shared was a five-story walk-up on the Lower East Side, and even though we knew it was kind of a dump, we considered it—all three hundred fifty square feet of it—the price of doing business in New York City. At twenty-three, we felt lucky to have steady jobs to pay the rent. Ann worked for a clothing buyer, and I, in a stroke of good luck, had just scored a glamorous gig as an assistant at a fashion magazine.

We were living the dream, albeit with a few unfortunate drawbacks: Our backyard was infested with rats, but the dumpsters were also back there—so we simply never took out the trash. Once again I didn't have a bedroom wall, or a door, but Tram had sent me a cute curtain with pretty green leaf patterns on it, so I hung that up and went about my business. Ann and my paychecks were so meager that we were afraid to turn the heat on in the winter, but that wasn't a big deal either. One of us (we could never remember who) had inadvertently stolen a North

Face jacket from an old college acquaintance, and the two of us took turns wearing it to bed on cold nights.

It wasn't a perfect setup, but we were not especially deterred by the challenges; New York wasn't meant to be easy, was it? We were supposed to struggle. How else would we gather material for the novels and indie rock albums that we would one day hypothetically write? We felt invincible and optimistic. Our skin had the eerie youthful glow of a witch high on baby's blood. We were living in a city bursting with possibility—not to mention thousands of cute boys—and we were determined to capitalize on our fleeting youth.

Ann and I had already lived together in filth during college, and existing in a semisqualid state never bothered us much. For a while in New York, it still didn't. We'd invite guests over and pile onto "the couch" (my twin bed, with the curtain pulled back) for a feast of pesto pasta salad. We had a little television, but we preferred to listen to the drama unfolding in the apartment next door: The woman who lived there was our age, and her boyfriend, who was significantly older, had left his wife and kids to be with her. The two of them were constantly fighting about whether or not his parenting skills were up to par, which, of course, they were not. "How depressing!" I said gleefully to Tram on the phone, relaying the latest events over in 5C. "You go through all the trouble of getting a sugar daddy, and you still end up in a shithole like this!"

Our apartment was a mess, so Ann and I went out a lot. We had a little crew, a hodgepodge of people we'd collected over time—college friends and friends of friends and people we'd cried in front of at work—and we clung to each other desperately. There was so much we were unsure of that year; we relied on one another for constant advice and consultation. We ate dinner together every Friday night, and then we met up for brunch a few hours after we'd said good-bye. We talked incessantly about the boys who didn't like us, and the boys who were stringing us along, and the boys who did like us but who were too pathetic for words, and, in the case of one friend, the middle-aged foreign diplomats who were sending us inappropriate text messages. We bickered about which one of us deserved to buy that vintage dress we all had our eye on, and about who had drunkenly flaked out on the bill from the night before. We'd be mad for about ten minutes, and then we'd forget our gripes over a round of Bloody Marys.

This was long before any of us could afford therapy, or gym memberships, or even cable television, so alcohol seemed like a reasonable coping mechanism for dealing with our problems. We were consumed by stress from our jobs, overworked and in over our heads, and we had no one to guide us but one another. I was especially lost at my new magazine gig. I felt like it had fallen from the sky straight into my lap (which it kind of had; a babysitting client had put me up for it), and while I didn't want to blow the opportunity, I was having a hard time fitting in. Protocol at the Catholic magazine was straightforward: you went in, you did your work, you behaved politely, and at the end of the day you went home. But the fashion world operated under what appeared to be a complicated set of unwritten rules. And I could not figure out what they were.

It was not lost on me that I was clearly the wrong person to have landed this opportunity. My sartorial sense had evolved slightly from those first days of college, when I lived in oversized turtleneck sweaters, ill-fitting boot-cut corduroys and knock-off Birkenstock mules, but it was not *that* much better. My wardrobe consisted primarily of jeans and an endless variety of blue-and-white striped shirts. I understood nothing about designers and trends, and I knew even less about the people who supported them. Tram was the fashion person.

Still, I had been given an entry into the publishing world—at a national magazine, one that people had actually heard of—and I wanted to succeed. So I did my best to conceal my cluelessness and diligently attempted to find my place. I was perpetually trying to assess my actions from a bird's-eye perspective: Was I dressing right, talking too much, talking about the right things? Was I trying too hard or not trying hard enough? I called Tram to get her advice on which designers to name-drop in the event that someone asked me about my favorite artists and labels. She gave me a very cool, heavily Japanese roster of names, which I dutifully cited in casual conversation. I spent hours perusing the latest collections at Style.com—and then I studied the backstage pictures, to see who had been photographed at what shows and with whom. I trolled eBay and upscale consignment shops for hand-me-down Balenciaga and YSL, and I bought as much of it as I could afford. But even after months of my strict, self-imposed fashion education, I still felt like an outsider.

On the phone with Tram, I attempted to break down the mysterious sights I witnessed around me: this person's outfits, that person's seemingly miraculous ability to go out to the trendiest restaurants in town on what I had to imagine was a $24,000 salary.

"The intern just ordered Thakoon straight off the runway—from her boss's phone," I whispered to Tram one day in a covert call from my cubicle.

I couldn't afford any new designer clothing, so in addition to my consignment finds I supplemented my wardrobe with Tram's designs, which I begged her to let me buy. (She always sent them, but she never let me pay.) These were the only items in my wardrobe I could wear with total confidence, not least because people were always complimenting me on them. Tram was my only lifeline into this strange and indecipherable universe. She helped me navigate the fashion world as best she possibly could from eight hundred miles away. But even with her help, the constant self-doubt was exhausting. So after work, my friends and I went to the bar.

That was the year I learned how to do an Irish car bomb. One night I went out drinking with the fashion editors—a rare and flattering invite—and I woke up the next day fully clothed and clutching my cell phone so hard it was like I had died and my hand had gone rigor mortis

around my Nokia. Another morning (or, more realistically, midafter-
noon), I was walking to brunch after a night out when I felt a foreign
object in my purse. I pulled it out. It was a burrito, still wrapped.

I had no idea how it had gotten there. Neither did my friends. I ate
the burrito.

In the autumn this kind of behavior seemed acceptable, but as winter
rolled around, things in my life that had once felt fun and zany took on a
more sinister tone. It was too cold to leave the apartment, and drinking
at home felt somehow much worse than downing four vodka gimlets at
the bar. Plus, the novelty of the apartment itself had begun to wear thin.
Ann and I got in a note-passing war with our neighbors, because the girl
was waking up at 5:30 a.m. to do at-home aerobics, and the walls were
so thin that I could hear every heel-kick. Tram came to visit, and I realized that my slovenliness, once mild and tolerable, was now straight-up
disgusting. The place was so dank and grimy that any attempts to clean
it were futile. Getting through the layers of filth was like peeling back
an onion, where the center of the onion was hell. There were a bunch of
mice scampering around, but for the sake of our sanity we pretended it
was just one mouse; we called him Fievel and started taking an interest
in his life. At one point we became convinced that he was turning our
oven into some kind of makeshift rodent hostel. Considering the trash
situation, it was probably true. After that, I limited myself to using the
stovetop.

Once upon a time, I might have been the ambitious and resourceful
home cook who would use my dismal living circumstances as an excuse
to expand my stovetop repertoire. Constraints can be inspiring, and I
love a challenge. Also, I was a cooking nerd. I baked a Queen Anne's
lace cake for my sixteenth-birthday party. My mom and I used to hand-
make tortillas for family fajita night. Even in college, cooking was on
my mind. Like any future Big Woman on Campus, I had brought a rice

cooker with me to school, which I immediately dropped down the staircase in my dorm, shattering the top and spewing glass and rice everywhere. After moving out of campus housing and into an apartment, I started making food for myself and for my friends, throwing dinner parties and baking cakes for special occasions. When I arrived in New York with Matt and Rakesh, our modest but serviceable kitchen had been a site of respite for me: I was always in there experimenting with stews and broths and sauces, and when all else failed I ate whole wheat pasta with olive oil and some freshly grated Parmesan cheese. I was broke, but I had standards. I shopped for whatever ingredients seemed cheap and good at the grocery store or the farmer's market, and you could often find me in the kitchen, dressing up a bowl of lentils.

By that second year, though, I was getting tired of acting like the plucky and capable young lady I felt that I was supposed to be. Standing in my poorly lit kitchen pouring the gross chickpea syrup from the can into my stained sink, it would occur to me that I was not some sort of bohemian, rom-com-esque heroine. I was just poor. At the bars I'd laugh with friends about the mice that lived in my apartment, but at home alone with Fievel I felt depressed and a little alarmed by the seemingly boundless depths to which my standards had sunk. A proactive person would have called the exterminator, or at least the super, to get a handle on the rodent problem. The only time Ann and I tried to call the super it turned into an hours-long manhunt; he was incredibly elusive. We eventually found him nursing a stab wound in an apartment that was, miraculously, even crappier than ours. After a while I stopped trying to convince myself that my walk-up was part of some quirky, twenty-something adventure, and I started avoiding it—especially the kitchen.

It was easy to steer clear of the kitchen, because food was not a high priority for me at that moment. I was constantly on a diet. Not because I was overweight—by most standards I was on the small side—but because at the fashion magazine, anyone who wasn't rail-thin was considered at least kind of chubby. (Years later I would feel perversely validated when a former colleague referred to me, in those days, as the "fat, smart one.")

Being thin wasn't some sort of insane magazine-wide mandate; in fact, my boss, a kind, high-powered editor, led a healthy lifestyle and encouraged others to do the same. But it was difficult not to be influenced by my surroundings. My coworkers were effortlessly fashionable beanpoles, girls with legs as long as my entire body and not an ounce of fat in view. Many of them were naturally skinny, those infuriating model-types with horrible diets and racehorse metabolisms, who ate Butterfingers every afternoon as a pick-me-up. The rest of us were not so lucky. There were group-wide juice cleanses, and lunch was a daily exercise in competitive dieting. You compared salad notes to see who could survive on the closest approximation to a bowl of straight lettuce. There were people who were known specifically for "eating pasta sometimes"—in a bad way.

I loved pasta, but I had a reputation to uphold—so I started to eat a lot of salads. Because my boss needed me at my desk at all times, I got to expense my meals as compensation for not getting much of a lunch break. The corporate cafeteria had a decent salad station, so every day I trooped downstairs and got myself a hearty bowl of spinach, chickpeas, tofu, cucumbers, celery, cherry tomatoes, a hard-boiled egg, sunflower seeds, and olive oil. Or, as I came to call it: my fashion salad. As things that contain almost no calories or flavors go, it was not bad. It was not, however, in the least bit filling. Every day I ate my fashion salad, and every day by 2 p.m., I was starving.

Starving, but on a mission. Sure, I wanted to do well at my job, impress my boss, get my writing in the magazine. But what I really wanted was to be skinny enough that I looked leggy in a shapeless shift dress that barely covered my butt.

The problem was that after I polished off my free daily salad, my food options were limited. I was broke, and eating healthy can be pricey. If I'd had money, I would have signed up for one of those delivery services where they drop a little lunch bag at your doorstep every night, the bag containing a single pea, a sliver of ham, and a grape—"dinner"— for $50 per meal. But I could not afford that. Instead, I subsisted on diet egg omelets (fat-free "eggs" that come in a cardboard box), Zone bars, vodka, the hot cocoa they provided for free in the office snack rooms, and a fairly kick-ass Chinese stir-fry that I made every other night for six months.

Naturally, I did not lose a pound. One of several problems with subsisting largely on vodka was that it made me drunk pretty quickly, and then my meticulously planned starvation program went out the window. I would go out for cocktails and then on the way home, buzzed and ravenous, I'd hightail it to the local deli and scarf down a bagel with cream cheese and a pint of Ben and Jerry's. The result was that while my figure remained basically the same, I was also constantly hungry, freezing, and hung over.

When Tram came to New York for a visit, she and Ann had a little talk about whether or not to be worried about my newfound disinterest in eating. Food had always been central to our friendship, but when Tram opened the fridge all she found were the ingredients for the master cleanse, a bag of spinach, and Diet Coke.

"We eat out!" I explained to her when she eyed my empty fridge with suspicion.

Ann rolled her eyes.

Ann had plenty of reasons to complain about my disordered eating habits. The main one was that they rendered me completely insufferable. In most circumstances I had no willpower. Give me a single drink and I'd inhale two Cuban sandwiches. Leave a free cupcake on my desk and it was gone within seconds. But at my disgusting rat pad, my self-control was ironclad. I justified my behavior by acting superior— referencing my "health kick" as I sipped slowly on a $9 green juice, or talking up the probiotic benefits of a tub of nonfat Greek yogurt—but really it was my way of convincing myself that I was in control.

One night, when I was cranky and hungry and complaining about one of our friends, Ann lost patience with me.

"I'm probably just being a dick," I said phonily, expecting Ann to assure me that no, I was totally right.

"Well, maybe if you ate something other than a Zone bar every once in a while, you'd be less of a dick," she said.

I stormed off, furious—but after a moment of reflection, I had a disquieting realization. My lack of proper nourishment was making me act like an asshole, and my friends were not going to tolerate it. That was not good. My friends were all I had. Slowly, I introduced carbs back into my diet. Where before I would go out to restaurants and order salads, the new me would choose pancakes. I used real eggs—plus cheese!—to make omelets on our gross stovetop. It occurred to me that my staple order at Subway—the salad bowl—was disgusting, and then in a flash I understood that everything about Subway was disgusting and I never went there again. I was eating like a normal human, and the world did not end. My carb-face did not assume King Kong proportions and take over Manhattan. I started focusing on my work instead of my thighs, and I realized I'd likely gotten as much out of my assistant job as I was going to get. It was time for a new gig. And maybe a new apartment, too.

Things moved so fast in those days. Within a few weeks I was settled in at a different magazine job, and I had just moved to an apartment in Brooklyn. It was a spacious, beautiful place, with old bones and high ceilings and a rotating cast of roommates. Best of all was the kitchen. It was clean and cozy, with black-and-white tile floors and a window that looked out onto a beautiful backyard garden. As I made awkward small talk with my new roommates on that first night, I thought about the day not too long from then that Tram would replace one of them.

Later I was unpacking my things in my tiny new bedroom when I realized I had accidentally taken the North Face coat that Ann and I

had relied on to keep us warm the winter before. I was alarmed, almost worried for her safety. The weather was turning, and that apartment was cold as hell. Would Ann be okay without the coat for a week or two?

I texted her immediately: "Stole the North Face by accident, but no fear; will return ASAP!"

A few minutes later, I got her response.

"Don't worry about it. U know what I just found out? Heat is free in NYC!!!"

SZECHUAN TAKEOUT-INSPIRED CHICKEN STIR-FRY

I didn't discover Szechuan food until I moved to New York and my friend Steffie, a core member of my hodgepodge crew, took me to an old-school Chinese place she loved, a restaurant I would later come to live by. I was obsessed with the tingly, numbing flavor of the Szechuan peppercorns, but I could afford takeout only occasionally—so at home I tried to re-create the flavors on my own. I'd walk the few blocks south to Chinatown on Saturday and load up on peppercorns, Chinese broccoli, chili peppers, and cheap produce. This dish was one of the few that I felt was worthy of stepping into the kitchen for.

Serves 1 (plus leftovers for lunch the next day)
Prep time: 25 minutes; Cook time: 10 minutes

¾ pound boneless, skinless chicken thighs, cut into 1-inch pieces

2 tablespoons soy sauce

1 tablespoon sesame oil

1 cup roughly chopped Chinese broccoli

2 tablespoons peanut oil

Continued

2 teaspoons whole Szechuan peppercorns
About 15 dried Szechuan chilies
3 cloves garlic, minced
1 (1-inch) piece fresh ginger, minced
5 scallions, white parts only, chopped
⅓ cup unsalted peanuts

Marinate the chicken in blended soy sauce and sesame oil for at least 15 minutes.

In a pot of boiling water, quickly blanch the Chinese broccoli. Remove with a slotted spoon and drain.

In a wok, heat the peanut oil until hot and just smoking. Add the peppercorns and chili peppers and cook for about 30 seconds, until they are fragrant and blistered and have released their oils. Add the garlic, ginger, and scallions. Stir for a minute or two, until they begin to brown. Add the chicken and sauté, tossing frequently until cooked through, about 5 minutes. Add the peanuts and Chinese broccoli and cook for about 3 minutes more. Remove from heat and eat—everything but the chilies!—immediately.

WARM CHICKPEA AND ARUGULA SALAD

Sometimes after work, in moments of sheer desperation, I would open up some chickpeas and eat them straight out of the can, hovering over the sink and shoving them into my mouth with a fork. But when Ann walked in on me eating this way one day, I felt sheepish. It was okay to be disgusting alone, but it was better not to get caught. I decided it was time to class up the meal. I turned it into a proper salad and realized that, in addition to this being a more civilized way to live, the dish tasted much better with very minimal effort. The only drawback was that it did require a plate.

Serves 2
Prep time: 5 minutes

- 1 tablespoon extra-virgin olive oil, plus more to drizzle
- 1 (16-ounce) can chickpeas, drained and rinsed
- 1 teaspoon crushed red pepper flakes
- ½ teaspoon dried rosemary
- ½ teaspoon sea salt, plus more as desired
- ½ teaspoon freshly ground black pepper, plus more as desired
- 2 cups tightly packed arugula
- 1 tablespoon lemon juice

Heat the olive oil in a skillet over medium-high heat and add the chickpeas to the pan. Add the crushed red pepper flakes, rosemary, salt, and pepper and stir until the mixture is well incorporated and the chickpeas begin to crisp, about 4 minutes. Remove from the heat and, in a medium bowl, toss with the arugula. Drizzle olive oil and lemon juice on top for garnish. Season to taste with additional salt and pepper. Serve immediately.

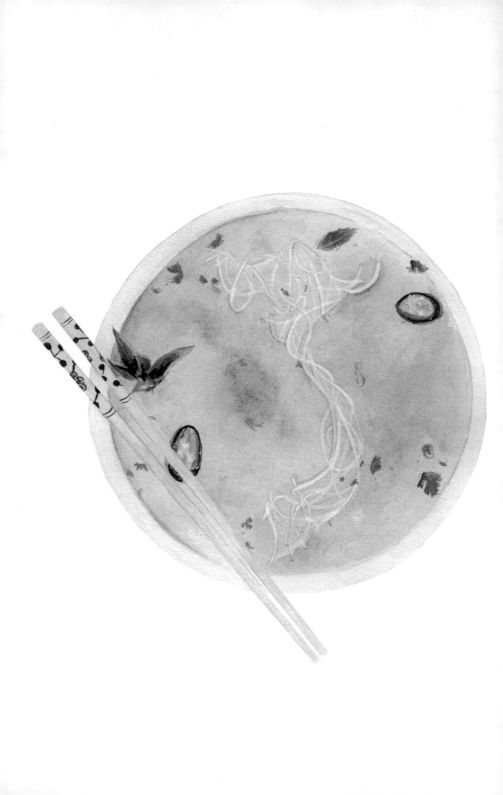

7

Romeo, Romeo

Tram

I had a date with a guy named Romeo. I knew that was his real name, because the night we met I demanded that he pull out his driver's license to prove it. Even in that dark bar, heavy with fog from the smoke machine and the atonal buzzing drone of an avant-garde noise band that I wasn't really into, I could tell he was way out of my league. He looked exactly the way you'd expect someone named Romeo to look, with the absurd bone structure and slightly sad, haunted countenance of an El Greco Jesus. I knew pretty much nothing about him, but in my mind the dark shadows under his eyes hinted at hidden depths, an artistic, tortured soul. I knew there was no way he could look like that, and be called Romeo, and not be a heartbreaker. I gave him my real number anyway and agreed to meet him Tuesday night for dinner.

Tuesday rolled around, and perhaps my subconscious was trying to sabotage this budding romance before it had even begun, because, as usual, I was running late. I had a good reason, though—I'd spent the last two hours on the phone with Lucy, telling her about the hot guy I'd met at a bar and obsessing over the degree of not-trying-too-much my outfit should broadcast. If I knew anything about guys, it was that they really cared deeply about what you wore. I mean, a misplaced bangle could be the one thing standing between me and true love. Pregaming before a date was a regular ritual for us, and I almost liked it better than going on the actual dates. The awkward dinners and drinks felt like a necessary formality to get to the good stuff, which was laughing about all the ways it went wrong the next day with Lucy on the phone. If, by chance, there was ever a second or third date, I could rely on her to provide insightful romantic advice. She was an expert at deciphering the millions of things a guy could mean when he texts "what R U doing" at two in the morning. And then a few weeks later, when I was single again, she'd remind me that it was a good thing. Guys our age were usually idiots, barely able to wash themselves and use punctuation correctly, much less be in a stable romantic relationship. Our twenties were for having fun, making mistakes, and getting our acts together. No sane person would consider settling down before thirty anyway. We had the rest of our lives for the right dude to come along, hopefully after we'd figured out everything else first.

This was in the early days of texting, before smartphones, back when we all collectively embraced the unique speech patterns of The Artist Formerly Known as Prince, so I tapped out a short missive on my RAZR: "Sorry going 2 B late C U soon." He did not reply.

This was not an auspicious start to what could potentially be an epic, earth-shattering, whirlwind romance. For a brief moment, just before I exited the train, I hoped he would not show. It would save me the trouble of sitting through what was surely going to be a terribly uncomfortable dinner—and, if I was really lucky, eventually getting my heart stomped on. But as I emerged from the station, I spotted my date leaning against a bike, dressed head to toe in...black spandex. Oh my God. To my absolute horror, Romeo was wearing some sort of snug, body hugging, cycling outfit that left nothing to the imagination. How drunk was I when I agreed to this? Did he expect me to ride to the restaurant perched atop his handlebars? And more importantly, was it too late to ghost?

My friend Tshaun once had a guy show up on a first date in a full camouflage outfit: camouflage hat, shirt, jacket, and pants. He wasn't in the army, nor had he recently returned from a duck hunt—this was just his look. Tshaun stuck it out, and the guy turned out to be a pretty decent boyfriend. I decided that I should give this Romeo the benefit of the doubt. Perhaps a heart of gold lurked underneath all that stretchy Lycra. If anything, it would make for a juicy telephone conversation tomorrow with Lucy.

After we exchanged an awkward hug, Romeo confessed that he had come straight from work and hadn't received my text; he thought maybe I had stood him up. He then asked if I'd mind going to his place so that he could change into real clothing and I gratefully nodded yes, making a concentrated effort to avoid looking at his groin area. We walked his bike the few blocks back to his apartment in awkward near silence, the sound of his funny plastic bicycle shoes clip-clopping like horses' hooves on the pavement.

He drove us (in a car) to a Vietnamese place in the Little Saigon neighborhood of Chicago. It was a shabby restaurant storefront with two stone lions standing guard at the entrance, and it boasted the charmless yet accurate name: Vietnamese Restaurant. I briefly wondered why on earth he would bring me here. Was he trying to introduce me to my culture? But I pushed the thought aside, too preoccupied with remembering how to behave like a human being. The place was completely deserted. Karaoke videos played in the background, and the scent of recently burned incense lingered in the air. The proprietor of this establishment, a skinny old Asian man, put down the cigarette he was smoking and silently gestured Romeo and me over to a sticky, vinyl-tableclothed table and placed two menus in front of us. Then he walked the ten feet back to the bar, picked up the cigarette, and stared.

Romeo seemed to be taking a long time to decide what to order, so I asked him if he needed help translating. He confessed that he was a vegetarian. My heart sank at this revelation. Romeo wouldn't be able to eat anything. Vietnamese cuisine is not particularly meat-heavy, but what we don't have in volume, we make up for in variety. My people like to sneak several different kinds of meat into every dish. It is not uncommon to find broth made from pork and chicken in the same noodle soup, topped with squid, prawns, tender meatballs made from ground whitefish, thick slabs of pork belly on top of that, and a few slices of offal if you're feeling festive.

Most likely, he would spend the rest of our date sipping weak black tea and silently scrutinizing and passing judgment on my dining skills. This relationship was clearly DOA. When the waiter returned to our table a few minutes later, eager to impress my date, I ordered lemongrass chicken in broken Vietnamese. The old man laughed at me, corrected my pronunciation, and informed both of us in English that I had just ordered "chicken grilled from a long distance." When it was Romeo's turn, he asked for the bok choy. A few minutes later, after consulting with the chef, our waiter came back.

"You want bok choy?" our waiter asked.

"Yes."

"Just bok choy?"

"Yes."

"It comes with just bok choy."

"I know."

"No meat?"

"I'm a vegetarian."

"What about pork?"

"I don't eat meat."

"You eat chicken?"

After a few rounds of this, our waiter shook his head, incredulous, and disappeared into the kitchen. Shortly after, he emerged through the double doors with our plates, placing them in front of us with a shrug. "Bok choy," he said skeptically. Romeo's bok choy was exactly that, an oval plate piled high with greens stir-fried in garlic (and probably oyster sauce, too, which is decidedly nonvegetarian, but I chose to not disclose that information). I couldn't help but notice that our waiter was now joined at the bar by two members of the kitchen staff, who wanted to see with their own eyes the hilarious white man eating just vegetables for dinner. I may speak my native tongue like a particularly unprecocious three-year-old, but I do understand everything that is said to me. Or rather, around me. We spent the rest of the date with this peanut gallery tittering a few feet away, puffing on Marlboros.

Miraculously, the rest of the date went well, and there was another dinner two days later. And the day after that. And the day after that.

I have no memory of this, due entirely to the four vodka tonics I had consumed, but apparently on the night we first met, I had mentioned to Romeo that my favorite food was Vietnamese. A friend had recommended this restaurant, and he just wanted to take me someplace I would enjoy. I was pleased to discover that he had a completely normal wardrobe, full of jeans and button-downs and other nonstretchy clothing. He was running late for our first date—hence the spandex getup. He hadn't frittered away two hours on the phone with his best friend discussing what shoes to wear. Romeo would rather arrive on time wearing an embarrassing outfit than risk letting a girl he'd just met think she'd gotten stood up.

I knew it was stupid and reckless and completely unlikely, but I was falling fast for this guy. He was kind and thoughtful, and he had a way of looking at the world that constantly surprised me. He called when he said he would, and for the first time I didn't find myself looking for an exit. As unlikely as it was, this new guy seemed to live up to his name. I did everything you're not supposed to do, and took it a few steps further than that. I found an Italian red wool cycling jersey at a vintage shop and thought that it would be a good idea to appliqué his name across the chest in pink letters, with hearts in lieu of *O*'s. Because that's what a fully grown, adult man wants to wear, right? When I explained this project to Lucy, she sanely suggested that I might want to hold off on giving Romeo this gift for a little while, until I knew him better. It could send the wrong signals, and I didn't want to come off as too aggressive. Better to take it slow and not rush into anything. Lucy was right, of course. I nodded enthusiastically in agreement, because this was smart, rational advice.

I put it off for a whole day. When I presented the jersey to him, like a proud house cat with a disgusting dead mouse in its jaws, he thanked me. When I pressed him further, he agreed to wear it in public. Just the once. He kept his jacket completely buttoned up to the neck the entire time, but still, I appreciated the gesture. If this was a test that my addled subconscious had dreamed up, he'd passed with flying colors. I liked Romeo so much, it didn't even occur to me to play it cool. On our third date, at a Mexican restaurant with the Cubs losing on a flat-screen in the background, I asked if I could call him my boyfriend. Romeo pretended not to hear me and changed the subject. And then two days later when I asked again he said okay.

I was a crazy person all through that fall and winter, walking around Chicago punch-drunk on dopamine and hormones. Lucy's sage advice to be careful and proceed cautiously fell on deaf ears, because it was already too late. All the love songs were about Romeo. My face, usually frozen in a natural permanent scowl, now hurt from smiling so much. At the sex shop where I worked, complete strangers coming in from the street would say to me, "You look so happy straightening those latex outfits!"

Some weekends, Romeo would surprise me by stopping by the shop with lunch, and the other girls I worked with would singsong his name and quote lines from a certain Shakespearean play. He'd take this in stride, used to it by now, after having had it repeated to him by literally every single person he'd ever met since birth. He'd give me a kiss and drop off a brown-bag lunch with my name on it. The contents were usually a healthy sandwich on wheat bread with sprouts, edamame for a snack, and a bottle of springwater, none of which I ever in a million years would have chosen for myself. I wasn't into a healthy, balanced diet, but I appreciated the gesture and always made an effort to take a small bite before magnanimously offering the rest to my coworkers.

In the middle of that frigid December, I moved into a studio apartment. I owned nothing, just the bare essentials and some books and art supplies. I didn't even have a bed; I slept on an old blue vinyl couch that a friend had given me. The best thing about my new place was the privacy. My old loft had no walls, so sleepovers had been out of the question. I could finally have Romeo over for a home-cooked meal and introduce him to my culture, on my terms this time. Our first date was not the ideal introduction to the food of my people. I wanted a do-over. I was certain that the best way to make him fall in love with Vietnamese cuisine, and by extension *me*, would be to cook the popular soup pho. It's usually made with long-simmered beef bones and thinly sliced flank steak, but my non-Viet friends always liked to order the chicken version, and so I set out to devise a vegetarian chicken pho.

I made multiple trips to various grocery stores on public transportation, picking up rice noodles, fresh herbs, tiny but deadly bird's-eye chilies, mung bean sprouts, and spices from the Vietnamese grocer, before heading to Whole Foods for the "vegetarian" component of the meal. After a long time spent staring at the fake meat options in the frozen foods aisle, I finally settled on Quorn, a chicken substitute that sounded pretty appalling, but from my experience, vegetarians didn't seem all that picky. I'd witnessed on multiple occasions my meat-eschewing friends going completely bonkers for hummus, which as far as I could tell was a bland, basement-y tasting bean dip with the consistency of wallpaper paste. If they could eat hummus, they could eat anything. I conveniently forgot that chicken broth is not actually vegetarian and threw a small carton into my basket.

Lack of experience never stopped me from doing anything most of the time. I once showed up at Lucy's apartment with a grocery bag full of ingredients for a salmon dish that I generously offered to teach her how to make, never mind the fact that I'd never cooked fish before in my entire life. That salmon turned out fine, overcooked and under-seasoned, but nobody got food poisoning. An undeniable success. My vegetarian pho would be no different. I'd seen my mother do it a million times, and she made it look effortless, or as effortless as any eight-hour process could be. With little evidence to support this notion, I was confident that I had inherited her culinary prowess. Perhaps it was poor time-management skills, magical thinking, or some killer combination of the two that led me to believe I could beat my mom's cooking time by seven hours. I started about half an hour before my new boyfriend was to arrive for what was to be a romantic culinary journey through Southeast Asia.

In my miniature kitchen, with just a two-burner stove and exactly six inches of counter space, I washed and prepped my herbs, laying them in a colander on the windowsill to dry. I dumped the chicken broth into a pot along with an onion, a carrot, and a handful of star anise and coriander seeds, and then filled another with water for the noodles. The water was taking too long to boil and my pot had no lid, so I improvised with a frying pan. *How clever am I! How resourceful!* I imagined a future me, at the advanced age of, like, twenty-eight, when I would finally have my shit together and would prepare meals in my own enormous kitchen with perfectly patinaed white marble countertops and a fancy French stove. I would look upon these salad days with fondness. Around an enormous reclaimed-wood dining table, Romeo would tell our incredibly photogenic biracial children about the time their mom cooked vegetarian pho, the perfect union of our two food cultures.

After dreaming up the most pretentious baby names imaginable for our future progeny, I took out the box of Quorn. It was frozen solid, and my running it under a lukewarm tap was ineffectual. I didn't own a microwave, so I had no choice but to try the neighbors, with whom I usually tried to avoid making eye contact. I mean, what kind of lowlifes would live in a building such as this?

I stuck my rice noodles in the now-boiling water, turned the heat down just a bit, and set out to find a microwave. I knocked on one door after another, until finally a lady at the end of my hall waved for me to come in. I sat there making small talk with my neighbor, looking around at her palatial one-bedroom and noting that although it was much bigger, it was just as crappy as my studio. It took about fifteen minutes to get that frozen block of processed fake meat to defrost.

By the time I returned to my place, the highly sensitive smoke alarm, the only thing that worked in that shitty apartment, was wailing, and the noodles were now stuck to the bottom of my pot. At five foot three, I was too short to reach the alarm. Jumping didn't help, not even with a running start. I tried dragging the couch over, and yet I still couldn't reach it. I had a few empty cardboard boxes left over from my move, so I stacked them as high as I could. Not thinking too much, I scrambled up the boxes, and *BOOM!* I collapsed right through them. But I had in my possession the offending alarm. I pulled out the batteries and threw them across the room.

This is how Romeo found me. I sheepishly showed him the bland chicken broth, the burned, congealed mass of noodles, and the Quorn, which, to be fair to me, was disgusting all on its own. He reached up and replaced my smoke alarm like it was no big thing. Then he took me out to dinner.

BOK CHOY IN OYSTER SAUCE WITH CRISPY GARLIC

Makes 2 side servings
Prep time: 5 minutes; Cook time: 15 minutes

8 ounces bok choy (broccoli or rapini may be substituted)
4 cloves garlic, thinly sliced
4 tablespoons extra-virgin olive oil
3 tablespoons oyster sauce
1 tablespoon toasted sesame oil
1 teaspoon soy sauce
½ teaspoon sugar
Sesame seeds, lightly toasted

In a large pot of salted boiling water, blanch the bok choy until it is just barely tender. Drain and transfer to an ice bath. In a small saucepan, fry the garlic in the olive oil over low heat, stirring frequently and taking care to not let the garlic burn. Cook until the garlic is golden and crispy, about 2 minutes. Remove the garlic with a slotted spoon and reserve. To the garlic-scented hot oil, add the oyster sauce, sesame oil, soy sauce, and sugar. Stir, over low heat, until the sugar is completely dissolved. Drain the bok choy thoroughly and then transfer to a plate, spooning the sauce and sprinkling with the crispy garlic and toasted sesame seeds just before serving.

ACTUALLY DELICIOUS VEGETARIAN PHO

Serves 2
Prep time: 15 minutes; Cook time: 1 hour

For the broth:

    1 large whole yellow onion, unpeeled

    1 (2-inch) piece fresh ginger, unpeeled

    1 cinnamon stick

    1 star anise pod

    1 whole clove

    ½ teaspoon coriander seeds

    1 (3-inch) square of kombu

    1 (8-ounce) daikon radish, cut into 2-inch pieces

    3 medium carrots, peeled and cut into 3-inch pieces

    4 ounces shiitake mushrooms, sliced

    5 cups low-sodium vegetable broth

    1 tablespoon soy sauce or fish sauce (the fish sauce makes this not strictly vegetarian, but it adds a wonderful depth), plus more as desired

    1 tablespoon butter

    8 ounces wide rice noodles (also called "banh pho")

    4 ounces sliced firm tofu

    ½ red onion, sliced paper thin

    1 scallion, chopped

    ¼ cup chopped cilantro

For serving:

    Few sprigs Thai basil

    Handful mung bean sprouts

    1 jalapeño, sliced

    Lime wedges

Hoisin sauce
Sriracha
Freshly ground black pepper

Roast the onion and ginger directly on a gas burner, using tongs and turning frequently until they are partially blackened, about 7 to 10 minutes. Alternatively, you can roast them for 7 to 10 minutes in the oven on an ungreased pan, under the broiler set on high heat. Rinse the onion and ginger, removing the charred bits, and reserve.

In a large stockpot, toast the cinnamon, star anise, clove, and coriander seeds on medium-low heat for about 1 minute, until fragrant. Add the charred onion and ginger, kombu, daikon, carrots, shiitake mushrooms, vegetable stock, and soy sauce or fish sauce. Bring to a boil and then reduce heat to low and simmer, covered, for about 45 minutes. Using a slotted spoon, carefully remove the mushrooms and reserve. Strain the broth and return to the pot. Add the butter and more soy sauce or fish sauce to taste.

Just before you are ready to eat, in a separate pot boil water and cook the noodles according to package directions until they are al dente. Drain the noodles thoroughly, rinsing under cold running water to stop the cooking process. Divide the noodles evenly between two bowls, top with some tofu and mushrooms, and garnish with sliced onion, scallions, and cilantro. Ladle broth onto the noodles and serve immediately. At the table, include a platter of herbs, sprouts, jalapeño, lime wedges, the different sauces, and ground black pepper, so that people may customize their bowls according to their individual preferences.

8

From Scratch

Lucy

Can you take the trash out again? Thanks."

Garbagewoman wasn't something I thought would be part of my job description at twenty-six years old. Then again, it wasn't technically a job. It was an internship. After several years of working at various fashion and art magazines, I was restarting my career. I was ready to get serious, to take charge of my professional life. And yet here I was, four years out of college, a full-time, unpaid intern at a political blog. Taking out the trash.

Even so, I would not be discouraged. The stakes were high. I had quit my job for this unpaid position, and I was counting on it to lead me to success. If the trashcan was full, I would empty it. If the water-cooler bottle needed to be switched out, I would replace it. (Well, me and two other women, because I was not strong enough to hoist the jug by myself, and none of the guys would lower themselves to the task.) No responsibility was too menial, no request too debasing. I was the Tracy Flick of over-the-hill interns, and I was throwing myself into the role at full force.

For once in my career, my hard work had a purpose. Until this point I had worked mostly as a low-level editor at glossy magazines, a position that had never quite clicked for me. After leaving my job at the fashion magazine, I worked for a while at an arts and culture monthly, where I spent much of my time trend hunting. My job was to find the bands you didn't know you needed to listen to, or the actors you weren't yet aware you were going to fall in love with. I wasn't great at it, but I was good enough. When the magazine introduced a page dedicated to discovering New York's arty "it" kids, my bosses made me its editor. I was encouraged to wander the streets of Brooklyn and downtown Manhattan, to go to wild warehouse parties and tap into my young-person network to find up-and-coming artist types who were talented enough for our consideration.

At the magazine we all laughed about this outrageous new role I'd taken on. "You're like Carrie Bradshaw," my boss said to me one night as I was scanning clothing racks in the office, looking for something acceptable to wear on a scouting mission (i.e., a night at the bar). "Except..." We looked at each other. We both knew I was no Carrie Bradshaw. A fashion editor walked by and assessed my outfit critically. "You should probably wear a thong with that skirt."

"Your life is so glamorous!" Tram said on the phone when I told her about this new part of my job.

"This is not what I envisioned when I pictured a career in journalism," I said.

I should have been having fun with this new column, but instead it made me feel like I was falling behind schedule. I was jealous of the kids I was routinely "discovering," and not just because one of the scouting prerequisites was that they be attractive enough to double as models. I envied them because, at twenty-one or twenty-two, they knew what they wanted to do with their lives. They had five-year plans they'd started executing at seventeen. I shared their ambition, but not their direction. I'd always had a difficult time pinning down my goals. As a kid, I wanted to try everything: every sport, every language, every instrument, every extracurricular activity, every candy bar. Who knew what I might miss out on if I didn't sample it all? I wasn't known for my natural grace, but perhaps ballet classes would reveal some hidden genius. I was quiet and hated public speaking, but surely I should give student government a go. What if there was some untapped potential, sitting latently in my fingertips, waiting for me to realize it? I was eternally indecisive, unable to choose a path, afraid that to do so might preclude me from unearthing some other, slightly more exciting talent.

This uncertainty stayed with me as I grew up. I changed majors four times in college. Months before graduation, my mom suggested I apply for fellowships or full-time office positions, but that felt like too big of a commitment, so I distracted myself by reading novels instead. Once I got to New York, I bounced between jobs for a while—first at the cheese puff shop and then at a number of basically random publishing gigs—because I needed to pay my rent. Plus, I figured, writing was writing. But I had no strategy. One job turned into another, and years went by before I even realized that I was adrift.

By the time I was in my mid-twenties, the nondecisions I'd made at twenty-one were calcifying around me in a terrifying way. I felt haunted by my aimlessness. It didn't help that the publishing world was changing. The economy had crashed and magazines were folding left and right. I started to feel like I had inadvertently set myself down a long and winding path to unemployment. I knew it wasn't too late to change direction, but I also knew that if I was going to do that, I had to do it with purpose. No more drifting, no more hoping that good opportunities would just present themselves to me. I needed a well-thought-out plan that could carry me through the rest of my life. No pressure!

Night after night, I'd go home to my apartment in Brooklyn and attempt to imagine my future over a big pot of soup. My mom had given me an immersion blender for Christmas the previous year, and it had led to all sorts of experimentation in the kitchen, not to mention protests from my roommates about the stray ham hocks I kept leaving in the fridge. As I zipped my little handheld blender soothingly over a Moroccan red lentil soup, or a Russian borscht, or a butternut squash purée, I dreamed of moving to Argentina to work at an English-language newspaper. I thought about going to Kenya and trying my hand as a foreign correspondent. I started filling out the application for a Fulbright to study politics in Venezuela. I came dangerously close to moving to Portland, Oregon, basically to do nothing. I would have gone almost anywhere to escape the stultifying frustration of my life. But one day, hunched over a cutting board, it struck me that all of these glamorous plans I'd dreamed up had one thing in common: in order to execute them, I would have to be a reporter.

And so, over a steaming bowl of mushroom soup, I decided I was going to learn how.

I had always thought of reporting as a respectable way to make a living. Unearthing important stories, speaking truth to power—a high-risk, high-reward enterprise for people who weren't afraid of anything. And it was in my blood. My mom is an editor at a financial magazine, and my dad was a foreign policy journalist earlier in his career. My maternal grandparents met as reporters at the *Kansas City Star*. As children my siblings and I were taught to appreciate the profession: When my dad went on a reporting trip to Guatemala in the late '80s, my brother and I crafted a scrapbook commemorating his adventure. I loved the glamorous photos my mom showed me of my grandparents' early lives in the field: my young and beautiful grandmother, the first-ever woman to be a full-time reporter on the daily paper, calling in a story from an airplane hangar; my grandfather, tall and dapper, walking away from a crime scene, steno pad in hand, dead body in view. When I was little, I was obsessed with cheesy TV news heroines like Murphy Brown and Lois Lane. I wanted to be bold and fearless like they were. At twenty-six I wasn't sure that was still possible, but I figured it didn't really matter.

Even if I didn't break my generation's Watergate scandal, I'd at least pick up a marketable skill.

It was a good plan. The problem was, no one would hire me. I applied for entry-level jobs at local newspapers all over the country, but I had no experience, and the editors—mostly crusty, salt-of-the-earth types—were not impressed by my fashion cred. For months I was in limbo, sending my résumé to newspapers in Newark and Phoenix and Dallas, never hearing back, becoming increasingly depressed about my prospects.

One day, after getting another e-mail rejection from a small-town newspaper I didn't even remember applying to, I called Tram to vent on the walk home from work. I was upset, freaking out about my seemingly endless stream of career failures. I wanted advice; I wanted the person I trusted most in the world to help me figure out how to fix my life.

"No one is ever going to hire me," I said. "I'm going to be an assistant editor forever."

"Everything is going to work out, I promise," Tram told me. "You're such a good writer! Anyone who doesn't want to hire you is crazy."

I knew Tram was being supportive—what else could she say?—but her pep talk only made me feel worse. I no longer believed that my life was going to miraculously self-correct. Doubt had been creeping into my mind for months. What if I was too late to fix my mistakes—or worse, if I simply didn't have any talent? I was becoming concerned that the last four years, maybe even my whole life to this point, had been a waste of time. In the face of so much rejection, I was second-guessing every choice I'd ever made. I had zero faith in myself, or my capabilities, or in the idea that everything was going to be okay just because I wanted it to.

"Thanks," I said. "Maybe."

Tram meant well, but her words rang hollow. It felt like she was just being polite, paying lip service to her annoyingly depressed friend. And that was fair. I was being a drag at a time when things were going really well for her. She was in love. She was making art she cared about, and she was starting to have success as a fashion designer. I was proud of her, I really was. But I was also a tiny bit jealous. I was eternally single and professionally flailing; she had this great new boyfriend, someone she could talk to anytime, day or night, about her career, her anxieties, her struggles. She had focus and drive; she knew what she wanted to do and she was going after it. She was just like the people I was putting in my little section of the magazine. In fact, if she had lived in New York, I would have featured her in it.

But Tram wasn't going to move to New York—I was pretty sure of it. She hadn't told me yet, but I could sense that she was laying the groundwork to let me down gently. For years we had talked about New York with the incessant enthusiasm of dippy teenagers; now on our phone calls she was vague when I raised the subject. She was even different when she talked about her work. It used to be that we would go on for hours about whatever projects we had going on, my writing and her art, down to the most minuscule details. But she didn't seem interested in doing that now. When I asked what she was working on, she would gloss over the specifics or change the subject entirely. She had also started to make offhand comments about moving in with Romeo—which seemed odd to me if she was still planning to head back east. I hadn't even met this guy; she'd been dating him for only a couple of months. But already she was choosing him over me, and our plans, and, if you asked me, her career, too.

The reality was starting to sink in. Tram was going to stay in Chicago to be with Romeo. They would have a grown-up apartment with, like, a KitchenAid mixer and an espresso machine and matching white plates—the gleaming trappings of settled adult life. Meanwhile, I'd be in New York, a washed-up spinster cat lady, pathetically chasing after young, beautiful, talented people who, unlike me, still had promise.

"Lucy, are you there?"

The line had gone quiet for a moment.

"Sorry, yeah. But I have to go. I just walked in the door and I have to feed the cat."

We hung up, and I looked out over the glittering black expanse of the East River. I was halfway over the Brooklyn Bridge. I loved New York, even though the relationship lately was feeling one-sided. The city was beautiful and thrilling, impossible and inspiring, packed to capacity with millions of interesting and talented people. But right now I felt alone.

Tram and I still talked regularly over the next few months, but our conversations made me anxious. I was dreading the inevitable—her announcing her decision to stay in Chicago. In an effort to be less of a downer, I was also trying not to talk so relentlessly about my catalogue of boring problems, but I was consumed by them, so I didn't have much else to say. When she asked how the job hunt was going, I'd rattle off some vague platitudes in an effort to stay positive, but the reality was that I still worked at the arts magazine, I was still unhappy, and I was no closer to executing my escape plan.

Then one night in the dead of winter, while I was attempting to dull my misery at a bar in the East Village, a friend told me about a blog she knew of that was hiring interns. It was a small but reputable political site, she said, and they often promoted underlings because the company didn't have the money to employ people with actual qualifications. It seemed perfect. I'd put in a few months of unpaid labor to learn the basics, I would dazzle the editors with my talent, and at the end of the run they would have no choice but to hire me as a reporter. I went home in a whiskey haze, optimistic for the first time in what felt like a year, and started crafting my cover letter over a gooey late-night grilled cheese.

For once, things went as planned. I applied for the internship and I got it. A few weeks later, I put in my two weeks' at the magazine. I was about to start my new career. Better late than never.

I had never been an intern before, and those first few days were strange and unsettling. For one thing, there were as many interns as there were actual paid reporters—which seemed to me like a lot of free labor. And as interns we were a wildly overqualified bunch. Among us were PhD candidates, recent J school grads, and even a full-blown journalist in his forties, trying to break into the national scene.

At first, it appeared that this reporting internship did not include much in the way of instruction on how to be a reporter—which, obviously, was what I was there to learn. For the most part, we were expected to find and crop photographs for the staffers to use to accompany their pieces. The company used Skype for all its communications, and as a result the office was eerily silent. We sat in rows at long, white, cafeteria-style tables, silent but for the clacking of keyboards, speaking only via instant messenger. There was a very kind and talented editor whose job, among many other things, was to wrangle us, but he was obscenely overworked, so his attentions were divided. And recognition, of course, was what we were angling for.

All of the interns had something at stake. Several of us had quit our jobs for this opportunity. I had sacrificed my income, my job security, my dignity—all for a shot at getting hired when the three-month program ended. I had taken on a handful of outside freelance projects to supplement my salary of zero, and at night I'd go home and try to scrape together the energy to write celebrity profiles, or do market research, or transcribe other people's interviews—whatever would bring in a couple hundred bucks.

But I refused to get discouraged. Instead, I applied every ounce of my diligence to becoming indispensable at the office. I tethered myself to my computer and did everything in my power to stand out among my peers. I had never been the smartest person in the room, or the most charming, or the most fashionable, but I have a competitive streak that is difficult to counter. I was in my element here. I woke up early to comb through the Internet, scrolling through thousands of local news items and wire stories hoping that something might spark a story idea in my mind. I bought a 1,000-page political almanac and studied the name of every senator, every congressperson, every committee. I learned Photoshop with the intensity of Serena Williams on the losing end of a match. I asked my editor out to coffee, and I began to pitch and write stories. All this, plus the trash.

It was a strange but exciting time. I was stressed to the point of mania, and I felt as outraged about my exploitation as I was thrilled by the challenge of the work itself. In spite of it all, I was learning something. The extreme circumstances of my situation—a dwindling savings account, an uncertain future—propelled me into survival mode. I had to succeed, so I made certain that I did.

When I started the internship, I had no idea how things were going to turn out. I thought there was a strong possibility that I'd end up moving back home with my mom—a failed late-in-life intern who lived in the basement of her childhood home. I would be the creepy recluse that neighborhood children were afraid of. I would wear my hair in a long braid down my back and train Dizzy, my cat, to give me foot massages.

But after a few weeks, I was starting to gain confidence. I had written a few features, and I was proud of how they had turned out. The editors were responding well to my work, too. I could almost remember what success felt like. I was still scared and alone, but I no longer felt like I was falling through the sky without a parachute.

Anyway, I was working too hard to feel lonely. I would come home from the office with long, unfinished to-do lists, interviews that needed to be transcribed, stories that I had to write up for the next morning. The prospect of a night of homework was exhausting, but the kitchen calmed me down. I'd pack myself a grown-up lunch for the following day, a gourmet sandwich and one of my dad's trademark chocolate chip

orange juice cookies—the same ones I remembered him baking fresh in the mornings and slipping into my lunch bag right before I left for school—and then I'd make some soup.

My kitchen was bright and comforting, with great light and beautiful old-fashioned fixtures. Each night after I returned home I'd settle onto a stool by the stove, luxuriating in the smell of garlic and onions. An hour later, relaxed by a little distraction and recharged from the food, I was ready to get back to work.

After the internship ended, the political blog did offer me its coveted fellowship, but the financial compensation was meager—so much so that I wouldn't have been able to survive on it. At around the same time I was offered a more competitive salary for a job at a national news organization. I turned down the fellowship at the political blog, but with sadness at leaving the place behind. This had been my first home as a reporter. The editors had challenged me, and I had proven myself. When I got home from work at the end of my last week, I flopped down on the couch and picked up the phone to call Tram. But I hesitated. Things had been a little weird between us lately. I would call her later.

WILD MUSHROOM SOUP
WITH PISTOU

I've always loved soups, but I really went crazy for them when I was on my super-stringent intern budget. I had saved up a little money to quit my job at the magazine, and that pitiful fund had to last me indefinitely. Possibly, I thought, for the rest of my life. Soup, conveniently, is both delicious and very inexpensive. One double batch can get you through a full week. On a cold winter night there's nothing so calming as a steaming, earthy bowl of wild mushroom soup.

Mushroom Soup

Serves 8
Prep time: 20 minutes; Cook time: 51 minutes

About 0.4 ounces dried wild mushrooms, such as porcini
4 cups hot water
1 large white onion, diced
4 cloves garlic, chopped
2 tablespoons extra-virgin olive oil
2 cups cremini mushrooms, roughly chopped
4 cups button mushrooms, destemmed and roughly chopped
2 cups shiitake mushrooms, roughly chopped
4 tablespoons butter
2 bay leaves
2 sprigs fresh thyme
2½ teaspoons salt
1½ teaspoons freshly ground black pepper
3 cups chicken stock
½ cup heavy cream

Steep the dried mushrooms in the hot water for 15 minutes. Strain out the mushrooms and reserve the water. Discard the dried mushrooms.

In a large pot, sauté the onion and garlic in the olive oil over medium-high heat until soft, about 6 minutes. Add the chopped mushrooms, the butter, the bay leaves, and the thyme. Sauté until the mushrooms are soft and brown, stirring occasionally, about 15 minutes. Stir in the salt and pepper. Add 2 cups of the reserved mushroom water and the chicken stock. Simmer over medium-high heat, partially covered, for 30 minutes. Add reserved mushroom water as needed.

Remove and discard the thyme and the bay leaves. With an immersion blender, purée the soup until smooth. Stir in the cream.

Pistou

Serves 8
Prep time: 10 to 16 minutes; Cook time: 10 minutes

8 slices bacon, roughly chopped
1½ cups chopped walnuts
1 cup chopped flat-leaf parsley

In a cast iron skillet over medium-high heat, fry the bacon in its own fat until brown and crispy, about 6 minutes. You may need to do this in 2 batches. Remove the bacon from the pan and set aside on a plate lined with a paper towel.

Spread the walnuts out in a separate skillet and toast over medium heat for about 4 minutes, until brown and fragrant.

In a small bowl, stir together the parsley, walnuts, and bacon. Serve with the mushroom soup.

CHRIS MADISON'S CHOCOLATE CHIP ORANGE JUICE COOKIES

Makes 3 dozen cookies
Prep time: 45 minutes; Cook time: 15 minutes

2¼ cups all-purpose flour
1 teaspoon baking soda
1 teaspoon salt
2 sticks butter, softened
1½ cups tightly packed brown sugar
1 teaspoon vanilla extract
2 large eggs

Continued

½ cup freshly squeezed orange juice

1 (12-ounce) bag semisweet chocolate chips

1 teaspoon grated orange zest

A few pinches of sea salt to sprinkle on top of cookies

Preheat the oven to 375°F.

In a medium bowl, mix together the flour, baking soda, and salt. In the bowl of a standing mixer, using medium speed, beat the butter and brown sugar until fluffy, about 3 minutes. Add the vanilla. While the mixer is still running, add the eggs one at a time, mixing until fully incorporated. Alternating between the flour mixture and the orange juice, gradually sift in first the dry ingredients and then the orange juice, incorporating each until combined. Mix until the dough is uniform, about 4 more minutes. Fold in the chocolate chips and the orange zest.

Cover and refrigerate for 30 minutes.

Scoop the dough in small balls, about 1 tablespoon each, and place on a parchment-lined baking sheet, leaving about 2 inches of space between them. Flatten each dough ball slightly with the heel of your hand and sprinkle lightly with sea salt.

Bake for 12 to 15 minutes, or until golden brown. Remove from the oven and cool on wire racks. If you are too impatient to let the cookies cool, that's okay. If you can read this, you are old enough to indulge in a fresh out-of-the-oven, moist, crumbly, piping-hot cookie every once in a while.

9

Changing My Mind

Tram

In high school, I picked up a curious book at the library with an elfin man in a fur trapper hat on the cover. Its title, scrawled across the front in black marker, was promising: *Confessions of a Window Dresser: Tales from a Life in Fashion*. It was Simon Doonan's first memoir, chronicling his unlikely journey from an impoverished childhood on a council estate in Ireland to his then position as creative director of Barneys New York, one of the most glamorous companies on earth. It was my first glimpse into a world that existed outside of the beige, comfortable suburbs of Washington, DC. I knew I could never be as funny or outrageous as Doonan, but I completely identified with his love of fashion, his craftiness, and his desire to get the hell out of his hometown. The book was also my first introduction to Barneys, which sounded like the most dreamlike, wondrous place. Years later, when I found myself employed with the company, my opinion remained untarnished.

I got myself a job in the men's department, selling fancy clothes to finance guys, sneakerheads, and the occasional dandy. I loved coming to work, because it never felt like I was actually working. I was basically getting paid to hang out with a group of fashion-obsessed oddballs for nine hours a day. We were a little makeshift family of aspiring artists, musicians, designers, and writers; so young and full of such optimism that we believed anything was possible. Like me, they saw clothing as a medium for creative expression. It didn't matter what labels you wore (but of course, a fancy designer name didn't hurt—we did have that nice employee discount, after all). It was not unusual to find my friends dressed in something self-designed and whipped up over a long week-end, handcrafted baubles around their necks, or some fabulous thrift store schmatta that they'd picked up on a lunch break.

Before I started working at Barneys, I was intimidated by the staff. They seemed like the coldest, bitchiest people in the world. It wasn't until after I was hired that I realized the blank looks on the sales associates' faces didn't signify indifference or snobbishness—it was utter boredom.

My Barneys was the bad Barneys, ranked second-to-last in the country after the Detroit location. In any retail job, there are long stretches of time when the store is empty, and sure, you could probably use that time to do something "productive." But if you were like us, you would find better ways to entertain yourself. We prank-called celebrities, gave one another haircuts in the stockroom, and traded outfits in the middle of our shifts. I started the tradition of theme days, where, to the cha-grin of management, the entire staff would dress up like lumberjacks, homecoming queens, or pregnant ladies. The store manager declared a moratorium on theme days after the infamous "Hip Hop Day," when half the men's floor got sent home for showing up for work looking like reject members of Bone Thugs-N-Harmony.

Mostly, though, our diversions were food-related. The moment I walked through the front door, I would focus my thoughts on what I'd be having for lunch. If it was a weekend, there was a never-ending potluck happening in the break room. It didn't matter if there were homemade baked goodies, cold pizza, or Thanksgiving leftovers—if you left food in the back, it would get eaten. The girls in the women's department once found a chicken salad that a customer had forgotten in the dressing room, and, naturally, they devoured the whole thing. When the woman returned a few minutes later to retrieve her leftovers, Jenny and Kristin spent a good ten minutes helping her comb through the store looking for that Styrofoam container, scratching their heads when the search turned up empty. It was a really good salad.

To pass the time between clients, I used my on the clock hours productively by making darling Twiggy-esque shift dresses from garment bags. And when my coworker Kenneth arrived at work one day with an unfortunate haircut, I remedied the situation by cobbling together an ingenious birdcage hat from gift boxes. My trilby would have dazzled master haberdasher Philip Treacy himself, and was complete with a tiny paper starling with wings that fluttered when you moved a lever.

I'd read in an interview that Phillip Lim got his start in the business by working part-time at the Barneys in Beverly Hills. He was unpacking boxes one day and saw the address for the designer Katayone Adeli on the packaging. He applied for an internship, worked his way up to design assistant, and over the course of many years managed to build a brand that was not only beloved by fashion critics but was also a huge financial success. I latched on to this Cinderella story because here was a designer that I greatly admired who had worked his way up with nothing but sheer talent and dedication. If he, a kid with an immigrant background similar to my own, could achieve this level of success, what was stopping me?

I'd been slogging away toward the goal of being some kind of working artist for what felt like an eternity with very little to show. For a while, it was okay to be in a dead-end job, because everyone I knew was in the same boat. But my friends had begun to move on to more serious employment that offered things like health insurance and Roth IRA accounts. The ones who wanted to stall a little longer went to grad school. Even Lucy wasn't shilling cheese puffs anymore. She worked absurd hours at a fashion magazine, and she suddenly seemed so incredibly grown up. It scared me sometimes, because I worried that I was getting left behind.

We still talked constantly and e-mailed even more. Sometimes, the conversation would turn to what I was working on, but my little projects sounded so lame and inconsequential in comparison to the glamorous life Lucy was leading. I knew that she wanted me to move to New York. That had been the plan since high school; the two of us, living in the same city, in the same apartment. To entice me, she'd tell me about the amazing stylist assistant job that I'd be perfect for, the contacts I could make, or the fashion-y friends she was sure I would love. It sounded alluring, but also, maybe too good to be true. Lucy had always been supportive of my little projects, greeting everything with the same interest. But in recent months, I thought maybe her enthusiasm sounded a little forced. She'd asked me again when I was moving to New York, and I skirted the subject. Things were finally happening for me in Chicago, and I wasn't quite ready to uproot my life and start over again. I felt a little bad after these conversations, and I promised that I'd have something more concrete to tell her the next time we talked.

It was a creative, inspiring time for me. Dealing firsthand with high-end, high-concept clothing at Barneys gave me the opportunity to reverse engineer garments. I examined the seams and the stitching of dresses that cost more than what I paid for a year's rent to learn how they were constructed. I woke up early to make clothes before work and often couldn't wait to get back to my machine after a long shift. On my days off, I would be seized with such youthful zeal that I'd cut and sew for fourteen-hour stretches at a time, often forgetting to eat or drink anything. I dreamed of the day that my clothes would be hanging on the racks, sold alongside the designers I so admired. For the first time in my life, it felt like the creative career I had dreamed of was within my grasp. I was still making only incremental progress, but it felt like progress nonetheless. I was no longer surviving on ramen, finally able to make a decent living at Barneys. I loved my day job, the friendships I'd made, my cozy studio apartment, and the new life that I shared with Romeo.

The thought nagged at me, though, that if I wanted to get serious about fashion, I needed to go to New York. To test the waters, I flew out to visit Lucy with my friend and coworker Tshaun, who happens to be the worst person in the world to fly with. We spent an extra twenty minutes going through security because he kept setting off the alarms with all of his accessories. And then he feigned surprise when the TSA agents informed him that no, he couldn't bring those empty bullet shells that he'd been wearing as a belt on the plane. When we landed, we went straight from the airport to the intimidating glass-and-steel monolith where Lucy worked, dragging our vintage suitcases with us like we were ready to move in. We poked around the office, took selfies to post on Tshaun's blog, and then Lucy left us in the beauty closet where we helped ourselves to all the fancy shampoo, French lipsticks, and bottles of Chanel nail polish we could fit into our carry-ons.

Tshaun stayed with his friend Momo at her beige parent-subsidized apartment in Midtown while I spent the week with Lucy and her roommate, Ann, in their fifth-floor walk-up on the Lower East Side. They had a miniature kitchen they never used, a mostly empty fridge, and a stove they were afraid to turn on—lest they disturb the little Russian mouse they'd dubbed Fievel who had made a comfortable home inside the oven. They ate all their meals out. There was no food in the house save for a bag of coffee in the freezer and some sad-looking energy bars. It cost too much to heat the apartment in winter, so that evening, we all huddled together underneath a blanket on Lucy's twin bed to watch *Working Girl* on Ann's twelve-inch television. After the movie was over, Lucy handed me a North Face puffy jacket before putting on a fleece. Ann burrowed under a pile of clothes on the bed in her room to keep warm. We quoted lines from the movie ("I've got a mind for business and a bod for sin!") all night to one another until we fell asleep. To me, it all seemed impossibly glamorous; this wonderful, bohemian lifestyle.

When I got back from my trip, my life continued on as it always had. I folded cashmere sweaters and bullied dozens of clueless men into abandoning their terrible boot-cut jeans. Tshaun choreographed and taught me elaborate dance routines to celebrate Black History Month (the "Harriet Tubman" was a big hit). But there were only so many dances I could perform and birdcage hats I could make before management took notice and put an end to all of my extracurricular activities. I was bored out of my mind with Barneys, even though I loved my coworkers. Something had to change, but I still wasn't sure if I was ready to make the leap to New York.

In art school, a few of my teachers had encouraged me to show my work in the student showcases at the end of the year. As a proud inhabitant of emotown, I would shrug my shoulders and screw my face up in distaste. What was the point? They'd argue that the point of any of this was to share your art with the world. I disagreed vehemently. For me the point was the work itself. I aspired to be like famous recluses Henry Darger and Vivian Maier, people who toiled in obscurity, their talent unacknowledged until decades after their passing. I wanted my art to be squirreled away in an attic, only to be discovered and exploited years later by an opportunistic blogger. It seemed to my naive, idealistic mind that the process was somehow more pure if the final product was created for an audience of just one. I wasn't interested in the victory lap on the runway at the end of a fashion show. I rolled my eyes at my fellow amateur designers, who seemed interested in fashion only as a means of bolstering their fragile egos.

My own fragile ego was content to sit in my corner, stitching my garments without a purpose, but Lucy knew that this was no way to behave if you wanted to have a successful career. She had always been my constant champion, strategically wearing the dresses I had designed in front of influential people, slipping photographs of my garments into meetings at the magazine where she worked. Lucy called me immediately after an editor for a high-fashion glossy complimented a frock that

I had sent her, cooing over it and asking, "Cute! Is that Marc?" I tucked that throwaway comment away in my pocket to save for a later time, when I could take it out and examine those words over and over again. Apparently I did care about what other people thought. I felt validated that a little dress I had sewn had fallen under the scrutiny of knowledgeable fashion-types and had passed for something by a real designer. With Lucy's encouragement, and the gentle push that I needed, I started doing shows in small art galleries.

That's how I landed myself an interview with a national arts organization that was looking for up-and-coming designers for their fashion program that year. There was a lot at stake. The foundation provided funding, business mentorship, a partnership with a PR company to promote your line, and a spot in a professionally produced fashion show. It was a huge platform, the kind of audience that seemed nearly impossible to reach on my own. The program had helped launch the careers of Rodarte and Proenza Schouler, current darlings of Anna Wintour who had gone on to win critical acclaim, commercial success, and awards from the Council of Fashion Designers of America.

After I got the initial call, I hemmed and hawed for days, waffling between panic and manic euphoria. I briefly toyed with the idea of dropping out of consideration completely, but I couldn't say no because I knew Lucy and Romeo would murder me if I didn't at least throw my hat in the ring. I'd been making clothes for a decade at that point, but most of my technique was self-taught from a set of vintage sewing books I'd picked up in a thrift store. I knew I possessed only a tenuous grasp of standard pattern drafting and clothing construction practices. Compared to past designers, I was severely underqualified. But what I did have was intuition, a strong creative drive, and the confidence in my ability to bluff my way through almost any situation. After a period of creative impotency, during which I procrastinated by moaning over the phone with Lucy, I finally had an eleventh-hour breakthrough. The night before my meeting, I threw together a mood board with inspiration imagery and a few fashion illustrations. I didn't have a clear concept, just a fuzzy idea, the inchoate semblance of a thought, but I knew I could make it look good.

The day of the presentation, as the unsmiling staff in their black clothes gathered around me like a murder of crows, I did what I always did, which was bullshit. *I've been working on my spring collection for months; of course it would be done in time for the show. Of course my line is carried in multiple stores,* which was technically true. In the months since I'd returned from New York, I'd managed to talk a few independent boutiques in the Chicago area into carrying my line. If anything, I knew my illustrations looked great. Digging myself the deepest, darkest, most pretentious grave ever, I namechecked my favorite industrial designers and heard myself uttering the words "postmodern" and "street-level surrealism"—all in reference to some hypothetical quilted party dresses. They thanked me and let me know I would be allowed a weeklong, torturous braise in my own self-doubt and insecurity before they'd get back to me with the inevitable rejection.

To my utter shock, the program director called me the next day. I had been selected as one of their designers. Only a year earlier, I had crashed this show with Tshaun and Lamond because we were too cheap to pay for tickets. We parked ourselves at the open bar, a free blood orange martini in each hand for maximum efficiency, and made pithy, catty remarks about the looks walking down the runway. I never gave a single thought to the poor designer who had been sweating over this collection for many weeks. And now I was going to be the opener.

I spent the next few months churning out patterns and samples, feeling like I'd developed a permanent hump on my back, hunched over like Quasimodo at my sewing machine. But stitching clothes in your bedroom—finishing a dress at two in the morning, feeling proud and accomplished—and putting them on a model in real life are two very different things. I kept mostly to myself at fittings, listening as the other designers talked about their sample makers; trips to the Garment District in New York to order bolts of expensive organic cottons, gossamer-light silks, and buttery suedes; the fancy showrooms in multiple cities that carried their lines. I had no showroom and no sample maker. I drafted my own patterns and cut and sewed every single stitch in my collection. The clothes were constructed from simple unbleached cotton muslin. Through the entire process, I felt like a complete fraud. I feared the moment that I would be unmasked, revealed as the amateur I knew I was. They would all laugh, but this time my humiliation would be televised, with a live audience.

The thing most people don't realize about fashion shows is how quickly they go by. There are weeks and weeks of pushing every single aspect of your life that is not fashion to the wayside. Months of buildup, anticipation, tears, shitty fast-food meals that you scarf down when you remember to eat, sleepless nights, and panic attacks. The day of the show arrives and your models walk. You plaster a smile on your face and wave at the audience and then it is over. I huddled with Tshaun and Lamond backstage and we all cried together. We got drunk at the after-party, but I couldn't even enjoy it. I was in such shock. The following morning, nursing a killer hangover, I wondered what the hell I was supposed to do next. I had spent so much time thinking *I just need to get to the show. I just need to finish.* I figured everything else would sort itself out.

Because of the opportunities the program offered me, I quit my job at Barneys and started selling my line in nicer boutiques in the city. I dutifully attended meetings with business mentors set up by the city's fashion incubator. I got recruited for a fashion design competition reality show. I could see myself being the girl who cried all the time, threw up frequently from nervousness, and then got sent home the first day. Auf Wiedersehen, loser! I was getting calls from shops in places as far off as Bogotá and Berlin, inquiring about carrying my dresses in their stores, but I didn't know the first thing about shipping internationally, including the tariffs involved. What would my recourse be if they failed to settle their accounts? I couldn't exactly show up on their doorsteps with a blackjack demanding payment.

That winter, I carefully packed up a few samples to send to a major national women's magazine located in the very same building that Lucy worked in. A few weeks later, I flipped through the pages until I found a silk blouse that I had designed, patterned, cut, and sewn. Next to it, in tiny black letters, I saw the name of my label and a credit for where you could buy the garment—a shop that carried some of the same designers Barneys did. I had done what I'd set out to do, technically.

It should have been a triumph. But I realized that this small victory was ultimately meaningless to me. I had complained loudly to Lucy about how stressed out I was at the time, but the happiest I'd ever been was when I was making my collection. The joy for me, the thing I craved more than anything, was that transcendent state psychologists call flow—the feeling when you are utterly and completely engrossed in an experience. There was a reason I'd built my collection from the humblest of materials, unbleached cotton muslin. Fashion was alchemy. It was magic. And there was nothing better than transforming raw materials into something beautiful.

Putting a price tag on it tarnished the entire process for me. Despite my stint in high-end retail, I was deeply conflicted about selling my own clothes. I understood the necessity of constantly churning out new collections, the manufacturing of desire for fickle customers, but I bristled against the garment industry ouroboros. Oscar Wilde, the Simon Doonan of his time, once said, "Fashion is a form of ugliness so intolerable that we have to alter it every six months." I believed that if things were beautiful, they remained beautiful, you didn't burn them after a season. I knew then that I didn't want to sell my clothes. I didn't want my "art" to be my livelihood. I would make a living doing something else.

I had been working toward becoming a designer my entire adult life. Why had it taken me so long to figure out that it wasn't what I actually wanted? The hardest part to admitting that I didn't want fashion as a career was all the people I would let down. Romeo had built me a professional website and had held my hand through all these months of self-doubt and fear. Lucy had gone out on a limb for me so many times; she had agreed to sit through countless photo shoots and flown to Chicago for my dinky amateur shows. Why couldn't I have had my annoying Stephen Dedalus moment years earlier? I could have been a dentist by now, like my mom had suggested, the good Vietnamese daughter she could be proud of.

Along with fashion, I realized that I didn't want New York either. Chicago was small and provincial in comparison. It wasn't nearly as exciting, but it felt like home. It had its own charms: the good friends I'd made, enormous apartments, and a slower pace of life. I liked going out, but not as much as I liked staying in and spending hours cooking something delicious and sharing that meal with Romeo. Despite the uncertainty of the future, for the first time in a long time, I felt secure and happy. I was no longer convinced New York could offer me what I already had. It looked like the last chance Lucy and I would ever have to live in the same city again had passed. I was a little melancholy about letting that dream go, but after all these years I was certain that our relationship would remain unchanged. She'd still be a constant voice in my head, the ever-present bass line, punctuating my every mood.

During a phone call late that winter, I confessed to Lucy that I was abandoning fashion as a career, and that, honestly, I just wanted to be an artist. I cringed as the words left my mouth, because they sounded as hokey spoken aloud as they did in my head. But Lucy didn't laugh at me, or berate me for wasting her time, Romeo's time, everyone's time. She got it. Because she felt that way, too; not about making clothes, but about creating work that was personal and meaningful. I finally broke the news to her that I wasn't moving to New York either. She didn't sound too surprised. I thought she seemed okay with my decision. I hung up later, feeling for the first time in a long time that I had made the right choice. I didn't know what I would do next to pay the bills; I just knew that fashion, as a career anyway, was over for me.

PISTACHIO ORANGE BLOSSOM PANNA COTTA

My coworkers and I used to get lunch at a terrible Greek restaurant across the street from Barneys. The food was pretty awful; salads consisted of a wedge of iceberg lettuce, thick slices of raw red onion, and a few bruised kalamata olives; the burgers were always burned and came with a slab of feta slapped on them between two slices of white bread. But we went there regularly because we were incredibly lazy and because the creepy old lecher who owned the place would sometimes hook you up with free food if you were a cute girl. Who were we to turn down a free meal? If we placed a phone order, we'd send out Anna from the women's department, with her Bambi-like features, to pick it up because the owner adored her. On a good day, she'd come back carrying a whole rotisserie chicken, which the staff would tear into like a pack of rabid hyenas. Usually, though, it was just an aluminum tin of baklava. I tried it only once but never touched it again, because I found it so cloyingly sweet.

Years later, I went to pick up an order at my favorite Lebanese falafel joint. The spot was bare-bones, minimally decorated with a mural of date palms painted on the cinder-block walls, but it was always hopping because the food was good and cheap. When I came home, I found that the owner had slipped in a little pan of homemade baklava. I thought to myself, *What a nice gesture. Too bad baklava is disgusting.* I polished off my lamb shawarma sandwich and more than the lion's share of Romeo's Vegetarian Platter #1, but I found that I was still hungry. So I took a tiny nibble out of a corner of baklava. It was revelatory, that combination of honey and orange blossom and crushed pistachios. The sweet floral aroma took me back to my childhood summers, the scent almost exactly the same as the night-blooming jasmine my mom grew on our back deck. It's never too late to change your mind. I'm still very particular about sweets (and pretty much everything), but the one thing I can almost never turn down on a menu is panna cotta. In this recipe, I've combined two of my favorite desserts, the delicate floral-scented flavor of baklava, infused into a silky pistachio milk panna cotta. It's so elegant and sophisticated, your friends will overlook the fact that it is basically fancy Jell-O.

Serves 4
Prep time: 5 minutes; Cook time: 25 minutes, plus 3 hours to chill in the refrigerator

---

  2 teaspoons gelatin
  3 tablespoons cold water
  1 cup pistachios, shelled and unsalted (about 10 ounces unshelled)
  2 cups whole milk
  1 cup heavy cream
  3 tablespoons honey
  ½ teaspoon almond extract
  ½ teaspoon orange blossom water
  Pinch of kosher salt

In a small bowl, sprinkle the gelatin into the water and stir to dissolve. In a food processor, pulse the pistachios for 2 to 3 seconds, until the nuts are finely chopped. Alternatively, you can grind them in a mortar and pestle or chop them with a knife.

In a small saucepan, heat the milk and pistachios on medium until the mixture comes to a low boil, about 5 minutes. While the milk is heating, whisk continually and keep a close eye on the pan so the milk doesn't scald. When it has come to a boil, turn off the heat and let the milk rest for 15 minutes. Strain through a cheesecloth or a fine-mesh sieve, discarding the pistachios. Return the milk to a clean pot and heat on low. Add the heavy cream, honey, almond extract, orange blossom water, pinch of salt, and the now-bloomed gelatin. Whisk until the mixture is uniform and the gelatin is fully dissolved, about 1 minute.

Divide evenly among four half-cup ramekins or small wine glasses.

Transfer to the refrigerator, cover with plastic wrap, and chill for at least 3 hours before serving. The gelatin is ready to serve when it is just barely set.

STRAWBERRY ROSE WATER CREAM PUFFS

My favorite thing to bring to the never-ending Barneys potluck was a plate of cream puffs; they are the perfect thing to hide behind the register and are easy to stuff into your mouth between clients. The puffs are only a little tricky to make, they're quite impressive, and they will please a crowd that is not so indiscriminate in its tastes as the Barneys staff.

Makes about 20 cream puffs
Prep time: 45 minutes: Cook time: 30 to 40 minutes

For the pastry:
  1 cup flour
  1 tablespoon sugar
  ⅛ teaspoon kosher salt
  1 cup water
  1 stick unsalted butter
  3 large eggs

For the filling:
  1 cup strawberries
  2½ tablespoons sugar, divided
  Few drops of rose water
  1 cup heavy cream, very cold

  Confectioners' sugar, for dusting (optional)

Preheat the oven to 425°F.

  In a medium bowl, whisk together the flour, sugar, and salt. In a large

saucepan, bring the water and butter to a simmer and then turn off the heat. Let cool for about 5 minutes. Add the flour mixture to the pan, stirring quickly with a large spoon until the dough mixture is smooth. Transfer the mixture to the bowl of a standing mixer fitted with the regular paddle attachment and beat the dough on medium speed. Crack in the eggs one at a time, waiting about 30 seconds for each egg to be fully incorporated. Beat an additional 1 to 2 minutes, or until the dough is uniform and glossy.

Line a large baking sheet with parchment paper. You can use either a pastry bag or a freezer bag fitted with a ½-inch round or star tip. To pipe your cream puffs, fill the pastry bag about one-third full with the dough, taking care to not overfill. Give it a little shake to remove any air pockets. Squeezing gently at the top with a smooth and steady pressure, pipe small spirals about 1½ inches wide. They should look like the tops of soft-serve ice cream cones. Leave at least half an inch of space between the puffs. Press down the tips of the pastry dough with your finger, as these can burn easily in the oven. Bake for 10 minutes. Reduce the heat to 350°F and bake for 20 to 30 minutes more, or until the pastry is golden and slightly crispy. Remove to a wire rack to cool.

While the pastry is baking, mash the strawberries and toss with 1 tablespoon of the sugar and a few drops of rose water to taste. Using a standing mixer or a handheld mixer, beat together the cream and the remaining 1½ tablespoons sugar on the medium speed setting until stiff peaks form. Fold in the strawberries, cover, and chill before using.

When you are ready to serve, cut a small ¾-inch X on the bottom of each puff. Fill a pastry bag, fitted with a ½-inch icing tip, with the strawberry cream. Insert the icing tip into the base of each puff and pipe full with cream. If this is too fussy for you, you can simply slice the tops off the puffs and pipe the cream between the layers like a sandwich. Arrange the pastry into an adorable, flimsy pyramid, and dust with confectioners' sugar, if desired. Serve immediately.

Variation: In lieu of strawberries and rose water, add 4 teaspoons cocoa powder and 1½ tablespoons Kahlúa for cocoa cream puffs.

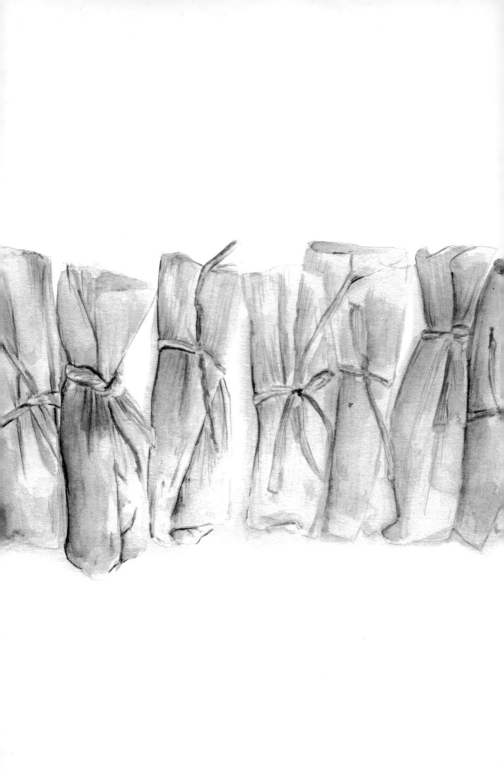

10

Thanksgiving Tamales

Lucy

It was Election Day, 2008. America was about to make history, and, more importantly, a cute boy was about to get my number.

I had spotted him from across the room at my brother's election night party. He had blond hair, a friendly smile, and he must have just cracked a joke, because everyone around him was laughing. I recognized him as someone my brother Bennett had tried to set me up with a year ago, back when he was concerned about my marriage prospects and kept threatening to unload me on one of his straight male friends. But it turned out he had only two of those, and one, he said, was a bit of a dud. The other was this guy. I was pretty sure his name was Ron.

They worked together writing cartoons at an animation company, and Bennett, generally a critical person, had only nice things to say about him. "Sounds great!" I'd said. "Hook it up!" But my brother, true to form, never got around to it, and the guy eventually left for a better job. They saw each other infrequently. After awhile I forgot all about it.

Now, a year later, he was sitting on my brother's couch. It was destiny. Or maybe it was just that my brother had really padded out the invite list to this party. Either way, I'd take it.

But as the night wore on and Obama inched closer to victory, the blond guy made no effort to introduce himself. Sure, one of the biggest elections of our lives was in progress, but still! Why was he even here, if not to pursue me? Did he not know that he'd tacitly committed to a lifelong relationship a year before, when he'd told my brother "I love sisters!" after being presented with my photo?

I noticed that my friend Jared was sitting on the same couch as Ron, and there was an open space between the two of them. This was no time to be demure. I plopped myself between them and started talking to Jared. Still nothing from the handsome, elusive man. So I turned to him and stuck out my hand. "Hi. I'm Lucy."

"Rob."

Ten minutes later Obama won Ohio. Everyone at the party walked over to Union Square for vague celebratory reasons. We were high with relief and drunk on champagne. We high-fived strangers and cheered people hanging off lampposts. Tram called me from Grant Park in Chicago, where she'd just seen Obama and his family stand before 240,000 people. "This is the most amazing thing I've ever seen!" she said, screaming through the din of the cheering crowd.

"I just met my future husband!" I yelled back, without irony. At the end of the night, Rob got my digits and said he'd text. *He probably won't*, I told myself, trained to cynicism after several years of dating in New York.

A few days later, he did.

Rob was a comedy writer at a late-night television show, and for our first date he invited me to the studio to watch from backstage. What did one wear to an event like this? I wanted to call Tram, ever my fashion guru, who usually advised me to "show three different types of cleavage at all times." But we were talking less and less since she'd decided not to move to New York; I never knew when our conversations would be normal and when they'd feel a little uncomfortable. It wasn't that we were mad at each other. We had just drifted apart. I kept telling myself that this was natural, that it happened with friendships, but that made me sad—I didn't want to think about it. So instead of calling Tram I tried to channel her, assessing my wardrobe as I imagined she might.

Watching from the writer's room that night, I was so nervous that I barely registered the actual TV show. Rob had to work, but he popped in periodically to say hi, and he made sure to sneak me downstairs to watch the musical guest perform. I was so tense that when I brushed past Beyoncé in the hallway, I didn't even notice her. At the after-party, I accidentally dropped and shattered my beer bottle in full view of several people. I was mortified. But at around 4 a.m., I finally started to relax. Rob was easy to talk to, and he made me laugh. I had been nervous about trying to keep up with someone who told jokes for a living, but it wasn't so intimidating after all; I was making him laugh, too.

At the after-after party, when he went to use the bathroom, the girl sitting next to me leaned in.

"I can tell Rob likes you," she said. "You guys have a good thing going."

"Yeah? How can you tell?" I didn't tell her this was our first date.

"I just can," she said sagely, with an air of mystery.

Surely this was a good sign. Who better than a close confidante to notice that her good friend Rob was super into his date? The girl got up to leave, and when Rob came back I asked who she was.

"The girl to your right? I think it was my coworker's girlfriend," he said. "I've never met her before."

So she wasn't a close friend of Rob's. Even better. Clearly she was a *mystical love oracle*. Our lifelong future together was sealed.

We stayed out until 5:30 a.m. and then Rob, like a true gentleman, put me in a cab. A few blocks later, I asked the driver to let me out at the subway station, because I didn't have enough money in my account to pay for a whole ride to Brooklyn. By the time I got off the train it was 6:30 a.m., the sun was rising high against the hot-pink sky, and I was grinning from ear to ear. Hope and change. For once, it seemed possible.

Over the next week, Rob and I corresponded sporadically. I spent hours laboring over each text and obsessively tried to parse the meaning of his opaque responses. We scheduled another date, but at the last minute he said he was sick and canceled. This was a red flag. Canceling on a second date was a classic *I-changed-my-mind-about-you* tactic; I knew this because I had used it myself. I let the disappointment sink in. I had been wrong to get my hopes up. Rob had obviously decided we were a bad match and planned to let me down gently through a series of elaborately constructed lies.

I couldn't blame him. Rob was handsome and funny and kind. His life seemed pretty stable. I, on the other hand, was a basket case. I had finally started to figure my career out, but my finances were no better than before. My credit card had recently been declined while I was buying a $2 granola bar. It could never work between us. Rob insisted we would reschedule, but I wasn't counting on it. To distract myself from the blow, I finally decided to confront a task I'd been neglecting for weeks: preparing to host my first Thanksgiving dinner.

When I was a kid, my family spent every Thanksgiving at my grandparents' place, a sprawling farmhouse in Ruckersville, Virginia. The family called it Hannah's Rest because, according to family lore, a dead woman named Hannah was buried in the backyard. Ruckersville was true country. There was a video store twenty minutes away, but otherwise the local entertainment consisted of staring at the neighbors' cows. Every year on Thanksgiving my family would gather at Hannah's Rest and gear up for a huge, butter-laden feast. We did Thanksgiving old-school, with all the trappings: a golden turkey, carved with exactitude by my grandfather; stuffing that had been cooked in the bird; a thick, gibletty, piping-hot gravy; canned cranberry sauce; buttered Parker House rolls; and the ancestral green bean recipe. My grandmother brought out the good silver and her best china, and we'd say grace and give toasts and then gorge ourselves until we couldn't move. After dinner, the adults went to bed at an absurdly early hour and I'd go up to my aunt's childhood bedroom and read old-timey novels until the cows started mooing for breakfast.

My grandfather died when I was a sophomore in college, but we carried on the routine for a few more years. It wasn't just that this ritual meant so much to us, although it did; it was also the only one we had. There was no backup plan. But eventually my grandmother Gummy moved to Maryland to be closer to my parents, and from then on when Thanksgiving rolled around, we found ourselves floundering. We dutifully tested out potential new traditions, celebrating with various friends in Maryland or relatives from my dad's side of the family, but it never felt right. A few times my siblings and I just spent the holiday at college, with our friends.

At some point during this window of time, I moved to New York. Traveling to and from the city around Thanksgiving is hellish, a nightmare of traffic and ten-hour bus trips. This year, my brother demanded a change. "You come to us," he told our parents. Bennett, who once chained himself to the fridge with my bike lock in order to avoid going to Sunday school, can be very persuasive. Our parents and Gummy agreed to the plan. Bennett's apartment was too small to fit the whole crew, but my place in Brooklyn was capacious by New York standards. And so it was resolved that I would host my first Thanksgiving.

The only problem was that I'd never really liked turkey, and I had no interest in cooking it. To me turkey was dry and bland, good only for its crispy skin. It also seemed like a huge pain in the butt to make. If we were reinventing family traditions, why not do the same with the food? Why not replace the turkey with something less traditional and more exciting? Something so unfamiliar to my loved ones that they wouldn't know if I screwed it up? This was how I decided to serve Thanksgiving tamales.

To be clear, I didn't know how to make tamales any more than I knew how to make turkey. But I had recently eaten some delicious ones, and the idea of serving tamales on Thanksgiving seemed like the height of wit—the kind of original idea that would send poor old Hannah spinning in her grave. About a week before the holiday I googled "most authentic tamale recipe" and glanced at it briefly. I noticed that the recipe was long, but I wasn't worried, especially since I was preoccupied with Rob, who had finally texted me back about a second date.

A few days before my family was set to arrive, I took a closer look at the tamale tab—and this time I paid closer attention. I got a little scared. This process seemed...complicated. Plus, a few of the ingredients were available only in specialty Mexican grocery stores. I started hunting around online to see where I could find pork lard and corn husks and Maseca corn flour. I discovered a few options, including a couple of places located in Brooklyn and one in Staten Island. In order to get to Staten Island from my neighborhood, I'd have to take several trains and then a ferry. *Sounds authentic!* I thought.

Rob and I had rescheduled our second date for two nights before Thanksgiving, and the evening of the date was also my only opportunity to go tamale shopping. No problem. Being not very skilled in the art of dating, I decided a Staten Island adventure would be just the second-date anecdote I needed to impress Rob. "What were you up to today?" I imagined he'd ask over dinner. "Oh, not much, just a brief trip to my favorite Mexican bodega in Staten Island to pick up the ingredients for Thanksgiving tamales," I'd reply sexily.

The night was a misty one, and as I rode the ferry across the Upper Bay, I pictured myself as Melanie Griffith from *Working Girl*, a lady with big dreams and bigger hair, on a mission to do important things with her life. Things like make a hundred tamales in one night. Once on the island, I walked a mile to the "specialty grocery store" I'd looked up online. Suddenly, I felt foolish. It was more or less a bodega. I had come all this way for a deli? Inside, however, I quickly realized that my instincts had been correct. The store had everything I needed: corn husks, Maseca flour, pork lard, and a million types of dried chiles. As I was selecting my ingredients, the woman who worked there offered to help me out. In my unpracticed Spanish I told her about my tamale experiment; a minute later, she had written two salsa recipes on the back of a receipt. *This is, without a doubt, the most authentic Mexican grocery store in all of the five boroughs,* I thought. A few minutes later I was lugging a tub of pork lard, a sack of flour, and a pile of corn husks back to the ferry.

As I made my way back to Brooklyn with several huge grocery bags, my satisfaction shifted to anxiety. I was nervous about my date. I was into this guy. I was so into him that a few days before, I'd sold my last remaining designer clothes so I'd have enough cash to pay for dinner. This made my affection feel terrifyingly quantifiable: apparently I liked Rob more than I liked a Marc Jacobs coat. (Purchased off eBay and slightly too big, but still.) In the past I'd had no problem playing it cool with guys. In fact, that was usually the problem. I could hardly bring myself to text them back, much less sell my clothes and travel across three boroughs for the sake of a cute little anecdote.

I met Rob at a tapas place in midtown, and my nerves disappeared as soon as we started talking. He cracked me up with stories about his high school theater embarrassments. Over the panini-and-sangria special—half price!—I regaled him with wild tales of my former job chasing down fashionable teens. I tried to impress him by mentioning the Susan Sontag book I was reading, but he didn't seem to know who that was. I gave him a pass. The night had gone so smoothly. I felt totally comfortable around this guy. For once, being on a date hadn't felt like work. It was fun and easy. I didn't want it to end.

After talking for an hour with empty plates in front of us, however, we finally did summon the check. I pulled out my wallet, which was actually just a leather pouch stuffed with useless cards, old ticket stubs, foreign coins, and, let's be real, straight trash. But where was the cash? I had pocketed more than $80 at the consignment shop—more than enough for my sandwich—and now it was nowhere to be found. Could I have spent it all on tamale ingredients without even realizing it? Eighty dollars for tamale flour? Was that even possible?

I rifled through my little garbage purse, panic rising, aware that you have only so long to dig through your wallet before it looks like you're trying to avoid paying. After a few more seconds, my time ran out. I took out my debit card, knowing that my account was already wildly overdrawn, and I calmly placed it on the check. It was like making a huge bluff in poker, except that's not how bank accounts work.

The waiter took the bill. And then two seconds later, he returned.

"I'm sorry, ma'am, but this card has been declined," he told me. I looked at Rob in feigned surprise: *How can this possibly be?*

"Ma'am?"

"Oops, I must have given you the wrong card," I said, phony smile plastered across my face. The bluff continued. I started taking out old business cards and receipts, pretending as if each one could be the magical second card that I didn't possess.

"I've got it," Rob said. The waiter looked at me sadly and left. I tried to explain myself, but what was there to explain? "Sorry I couldn't pay for dinner, I sold all my clothes in order to scrounge up cash, and then I spent it all on a tamale-related lark—date me, please!"

Thankfully, Rob interrupted me before I could dig my hole any deeper. "It's not a big deal," he said. He didn't sound like he was lying, but how could that be? In the early stages of dating, you are not supposed to reveal that you have less than $20 in your bank account. Rob wasn't supposed to find out about my "quirks" until at least the sixth date. I sat there, not knowing how humiliated to be, until he changed the subject and moved on completely. I tried to contain my shock as it registered that he really didn't care. He was not going to hold this incident against me. I knew this, because by the end of the night we'd made plans to hang out again, after Thanksgiving.

I was still swooning when I started slaving over the tamales the next day. Rob and me at the movies, brushing hands in the nacho container. Rob and me, riding a tandem bike down the West Side Highway. Rob and me as a pairs figure-skating team, winning Olympic gold in matching spandex outfits. When Thanksgiving came, I served my tamales with great success. The bodega lady's salsa recipes also yielded delicious results, and my fried plantains were a huge hit. My first Thanksgiving went off with only a few minor problems (a small fire in the backyard, a squabble over the dishes), and we resolved to do it again the following year. A few days later, I found that errant cash scrunched up at the bottom of my wallet, buried beneath a handful of defunct health-care cards. By then, however, Rob and I had already gone out again. The past was behind us. The Bush era was over. The future was looking up.

100% AUTHENTIC STATEN ISLAND TAMALES

Once, when I was stressed out by finals in college, my mom sent me a funny little care package: a huge box of frozen tamales, kept cold with big chunks of dry ice. She'd had them shipped from some artisanal tamale company in Texas just so that I'd have something delicious to eat while I studied. It was a weird present, one of my favorites, and I have loved tamales ever since.

When I decided to make them for Thanksgiving dinner, I didn't realize that tamales are actually perfect to serve the night *before* Thanksgiving. They're a huge pain in the ass to prepare, but they freeze really well and require little effort to defrost; you can keep them stockpiled in your fridge and reheat them for guests. Then you'll be free to spend your time prepping the next day's feast. These days I serve more traditional Thanksgiving

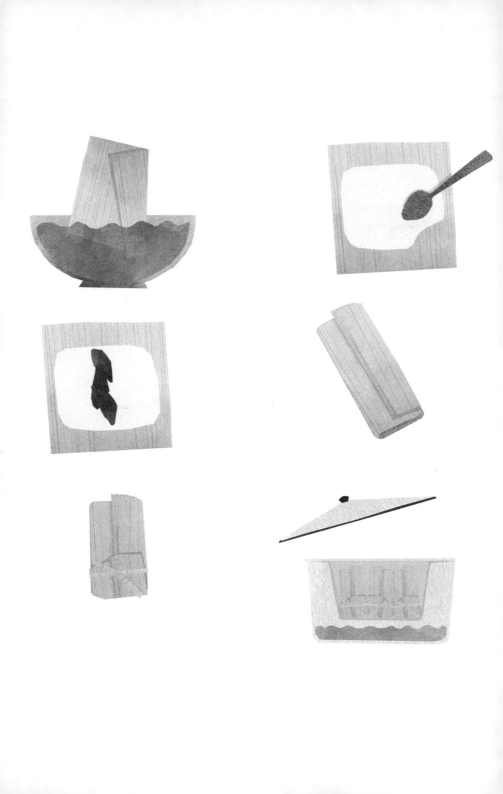

fare (although I do not cook the turkey; I outsource that job), but the night before is reserved for my annual family tamale party.

Makes about 24 tamales
Prep time: 1 hour; Cook time: 4 hours and 45 minutes.

Special equipment:
   Large steamer pot with a lid

For the filling:
   1 (3½-pound) whole pork butt
   1 large onion, roughly chopped
   4 cloves garlic, minced
   1 teaspoon salt
   1 teaspoon pepper
   10 cups of water
   ½ cup Salsa Roja (see recipe on page 157), plus more as desired
      and for serving

For the dough (masa):
   About two dozen dried corn husks
   6 cups Maseca corn flour
   1 tablespoon baking powder
   1 tablespoon salt
   1⅓ cups pork lard
   2 tablespoons Salsa Roja, plus more for serving
   6 cups reserved pork stock, plus extra if necessary
   Salsa Verde (page 159), for serving

Start by preparing the pork butt. Fill a large pot with the pork, onion, garlic, salt, pepper, and the 10 cups of water. Cover the pot and bring the water to a boil over high heat. Reduce to a simmer and let cook, still covered, for about 4 hours. You'll know the pork is done because it will be super tender and falling off the bone, with an internal temperature of at least 160°F.

When the pork butt is cooked, remove it from the water—now a lovely pork broth—and shred it with two forks. Toss the fatty parts. Let the broth cool and reserve. In a large sauté pan, heat about ½ cup of Salsa Roja over medium-high heat and add the shredded pork. Mix this together for a flavorful but not overwhelmingly spicy pork filling. Add more salsa roja if you'd like additional heat, but be mindful of any eighty-seven-year-old grandmothers you have coming to dinner. Refrigerate the pork until you're about to construct the tamales.

Right before you're ready to make the dough, soak about 2 dozen corn husks in a bowl of warm water for 20 minutes.

Whisk together the corn flour, baking powder, and salt. In the bowl of a standing mixer, beat the lard and the salsa roja on medium speed for 30 seconds. Gradually sift in the flour mixture and blend for several minutes more, until the dough is uniform. While the machine is still running, slowly drizzle in the pork stock, adding more if necessary to reach a doughy consistency. Beat until the dough is light and fluffy.

Drain the corn husks and wring them dry. You are ready to construct your tamales. On each husk, spread a thin ¼- to ⅛-inch layer of masa. Leave a 2-inch border on the top and bottom of the husk, and a ½-inch border on both sides. Then spoon in about 2 tablespoons of the pork filling so that it makes a vertical line up the center of the masa. Fold the sides of the husks together so that the masa just meets, then fold them both to one side. Fold the bottom of the husk up. Strip a small piece of corn husk off an extra soaked husk and tie it around the bottom flap of the tamale pocket, like a cute little belt.

Once you've constructed your tamales, put them in a steamer pot, standing upright and leaning against the side, and steam for 40 minutes to an hour. You'll know they're done when the masa is firm to the touch. Just open a cornhusk flap and peek inside a tamale to check.

If you're not eating these immediately, pop them in the freezer and then steam them again later for 20 to 30 minutes to defrost and heat. Serve immediately alongside the red chile salsa and the salsa verde.

Immediately forget what a hassle they were to make and resolve to repeat the process again soon.

SALSA ROJA

This salsa is incorporated into both the dough and the pork filling; I also use it as a sauce to serve alongside the tamales. But a word to the wise: It's spicy. Another piece of advice would be that you not put your contacts in directly after making it because, for instance, if you happen to be headed to a wedding later on in the evening, you will almost certainly show up looking like you just got stung by a bee in the eyeball.

Makes about 2½ cups
Prep time: 35 minutes; Cook time: 2 minutes

About two dozen dried red chile peppers (pasilla or New Mexican chiles work well)
2½ teaspoons ground cumin
5 cloves garlic, minced
1 teaspoon salt
1 teaspoon ground black pepper

Carefully stem and seed the dried chile peppers. Toast the chiles in a dry skillet over high heat for a minute or two, until fragrant. Once toasted, soak them in a bowl of warm water for about 30 minutes, until soft. Strain the peppers and reserve the water. In a food processor, blend the chile peppers with the cumin, garlic, salt, and pepper. Gradually add in about 2½ cups of the chile water. Ideally, your salsa will be the consistency of a smooth tomato sauce. If needed, add additional chile water to achieve this consistency. Once puréed, taste the salsa and add additional spices, if desired.

SALSA VERDE

Makes about 2 cups
Prep time: 10 minutes; Cook time: 15 minutes

16 ounces tomatillos, husked and with the stems removed
2 jalapenos, stemmed and seeded
6 cloves garlic, peeled
1 medium white onion, chopped
½ cup roughly chopped cilantro
2 teaspoons kosher salt
2 teaspoons lime juice

Set the broiler to high and layer the tomatillos, jalapeños, and garlic on an ungreased baking sheet. Broil until the tomatillos are juicy, brown, and blistering, about 10 minutes. Remove from the oven and let cool for 10 to 15 minutes. In a blender, purée the tomatillos, jalapeños, and garlic. Transfer to a medium-sized bowl and mix in the onion, cilantro, salt, and lime juice. Serve with the tamales.

11

Born to Run

Tram

My mother is the kind of crafty person to whom all the women in her social circle would turn if they needed help with a tricky task. She has the power to resurrect plants from the dead, cook unforgettable multicourse meals from scratch, and in a pinch, she can whip up a set of matching mother-daughter palazzo-pant jumpsuits on the sewing machine. She didn't know how to turn on a computer until I was in high school, when she discovered online dating. But within weeks, she had a snappy screen name ("Mother Hen with Two Chicks") and had figured out on her own how to hook up our stereo to the PC so she could sing karaoke on the Internet.

Guys in real life were always trying to date her, too, but she'd shrug them off. There was one particularly persistent suitor who badgered my mom for months. Finally, one sunny day in July, she told him he could come over to our house for lunch. He arrived the next day at noon, dressed in neatly pressed chinos and a nice lilac button-down. After introductions had been made, my mother walked him to the back of the house, where she handed him a shovel and told him to dig.

From the comfort of our air-conditioned home, my brother and I watched in amusement as the man struggled in the heat, finally stripping down to his undershirt, which was now completely soaked through with sweat. He came up the deck stairs, gasping and asking for water, which he swallowed down in big, greedy gulps. The poor sap labored out in the yard for at least two hours, until he had dug a hole deep and wide enough for a respectable koi pond. After my mom had deemed the work acceptable, she nodded and invited him in to eat. We never saw him again. The lesson was that men were unnecessary—good for digging a new home for your prizewinning carp in the backyard, but that was pretty much it.

With the exception of manual labor, I learned early on that if I wanted to get something done, I had to do it myself. My mom had enough to think about, so I didn't bother her with things like permission slips and parent-teacher conferences. I took the liberty of signing all the school paperwork myself as soon as I learned to forge her signature.

In fourth grade, I had to get permission to participate in a sex ed class. Thinking it would be in the best interests of all parties involved if I spared my parents the awkwardness of the birds and the bees talk (which I had given myself a few years earlier anyway, with a stolen copy of *The Thorn Birds*), I signed the paper myself. We operated on a symbiotic system of benign neglect—as long as I got good grades, took care of my little brother, and never exhibited any signs of being in a gang (gang affiliation, of course, was signaled by the wearing of baggy jeans), I was free to come and go as I chose. I decided that anything I didn't know I could figure out on my own or learn from a book. Parents, like my mom's suitors, seemed unnecessary.

After the divorce my dad was out of the picture, and with no positive male role models around, I assumed the responsibility of teaching my little brother how to be a man. I picked up a book called *Dressing for Success*, a guide to men's fashion that was published at a time when flared trousers and muttonchops were de rigueur. Sure, it was a little dated, but I so desperately wanted my little brother to be a success, I devoured it cover to cover. I learned the ins and outs of menswear: the history of the Windsor knot, the difference between tattersall and gingham, and the correct footwear to pair with a seersucker suit in the summertime. I taught Jimmy how to tie a tie and expounded on a few theories I'd developed on my own, such as the appropriate time to wear French cuffs (never) or a three-button suit (only if you are a time traveling basketball player from the '90s).

My first year in Chicago, it was a novel feeling, having to take care of only myself for once. I still worried about my mom and Jimmy, and I felt pangs of guilt about not being as heavily involved in their lives. If my tween brother was acting up, my mother would ask me to talk some sense into him, but my lectures had little effect over the phone. I had a choice: I could either make myself sick with anxiety or hope that they'd be okay on their own. It was easier to pick the latter. The comforting thing, though, about having someone to worry over is that they will worry about you in return. If I fell ill with the flu, there was no one in Chicago to scold me for being too vain to wear a winter hat and getting sick in the first place. I'd have to drag myself, shivering and weak, to the Jewel-Osco and back, and then microwave my sad little bowl of canned soup. Whenever I was feeling especially self-pitying, I reminded myself that I had survived my formative years with minimal guidance from my parents. I never needed anyone before; adulthood would be no different. If the trade-off for a little loneliness was independence, it was almost worth it.

Sometimes, though, books failed me, and my own self-guidance was not enough. Being directionless and dreamy young people, in college Lucy and I read Susan Miller's horoscopes with religious fervor. But for the serious stuff, we knew we needed to consult a real psychic, face-to-face. Of course, we knew it was all baloney; these were scam artists who preyed on the feebleminded, gullible saps who had no control over their lives and so looked for answers in some imaginary higher power. People like us, basically. One especially sketchy psychic we visited answered the door in a knockoff Juicy Couture tracksuit. I paid her, and then she took my hand, examining my palm.

She traced my love line with a long, French-manicured talon. "You will have just one great love in your life."

Seriously? I thought. I wanted to be the romantic hero of a Bruce Springsteen song, not the girl waiting on the porch for words that he ain't spoke. I'd always hoped for the wild, shambolic lifestyle of a Cat Power or a Courtney Love, burning so brightly, just teetering on the brink of destruction, but without the substance abuse, of course. Even this stranger I'd just met confirmed what I already knew: I would never be good at the casual relationship thing, despite my postfeminist ideals. Like Cher Horowitz, I could never bother with anything or anyone I wasn't completely infatuated with. She rattled off a few more ambiguous predictions, and just as our five minutes were coming to a close, she took both my hands in her hands and said in a voice dripping with concern: "When I look at you, I see a black aura."

"What?"

"You have a black aura. I will pray for you. But you need to buy these special candles. They cost $10 for every year of your life."

I burst into tears because I did not have an extra $200 to spend on magic aura-cleansing candles, and I wouldn't for the foreseeable future. Did she take credit cards? I did not understand exactly what having a black aura meant, but it sounded awful. I emerged from the room, sobbing, and broke the bad news to Lucy. She responded by taking me out for steak and plying me with malbec. At dinner, I laughed about it eventually, but part of me wondered if there was any truth to the psychic's words. Maybe there was something seriously wrong with me. Perhaps it was as obvious to other people as it was to this complete stranger.

The main reason I didn't date seriously in my early twenties, besides the black aura, was because I spent most of my free time hanging out in places that straight men didn't typically congregate. On Tuesday nights I had a standing date with my friends Tshaun and Lamond, whom I'd met in a 3-D design class. Our bond was cemented when (to the instructor's exasperation) we all made clothes hangers for our final projects. We hit up gay bars with punny names like Cocktail, Man's Country, and The Anvil, where we'd detail our exploits from the weekend before. Afterward, we'd stumble home on the Red Line. They'd walk me to my apartment first, even though it was out of the way, just to make sure I got in safely.

The guys I was meeting in Boystown weren't into me for obvious reasons, but I wasn't having much luck finding a boyfriend outside the gay bar scene either. My romantic ideal at the time would have worn his inner damage on his tattered vintage shirtsleeve like a badge of honor. He was preferably an artist, a little tortured, a little unhinged, and free of the burden of a fully developed prefrontal cortex.

This was great in theory, but the problem was dating a self-styled tortured artist in real life. There was the Polish photographer, who worshipped at the altar of Terry Richardson. In addition to being a skilled documentarian of scantily clad women, he also made angsty Photoshop art. Much of his work at the time was devoted to the Iraq War. One piece that he was particularly proud of featured a sad-eyed moppet with what looked to be a lone red teardrop running down his dirt-streaked face. If you looked really closely, that tear would reveal itself to be one of Saddam's elusive WMDs. I humored him for a while, because he was kind of okay-looking and it was summer. When I stopped returning his calls, he texted me: "I guess you just don't like Polish people."

My one consistent suitor in those days was my friend Liam, who claimed to be a professional skateboarder/DJ/beatmaker/rapper/b-boy/bar mitzvah dancer. Everything he did was annoying, but kind of sweet at the same time. He would steal my iPod, and then it would reappear a day later, with obscure soul groups from the '70s that he knew I would like slipped onto it. He had been nursing the biggest crush on me for a long time, a fact that he was not shy about communicating. Liam would have been a devoted boyfriend but there just wasn't that spark for me.

I was mostly okay with never dating anyone seriously because I'd seen what happened to people who fell in too deep, too early. My old roommate Donna got pregnant and didn't end up with the guy. Amy would be deliriously happy for a few weeks, convinced that things would be different with each new boyfriend. And yet, without fail, she'd spend most of her time either fighting with the guy or in a constant state of tears. I knew that these relationships never lasted. Why focus all your energy on a soon-to-be ex when you could be investing in your future and having fun? It helped that Lucy was pretty much in the same boat as me. She dated a lot of guys but was never head over heels about any of them.

I wasn't expecting to meet Romeo. He was not in my plan, not for at least a decade. Romeo possessed none of the qualities that I thought I wanted in a guy. He was a grown man, with all the signifiers of adulthood: a graduate degree, a real job, and an apartment with walls that were lined with serious artwork, which he had paid someone to professionally frame. He had already gone through his emo phase, wrestled his demons, and done the tortured artist thing. He had opinions on wine that went beyond, "Um, the one with bubbles?"

I was completely obnoxious the fall that I met Romeo. I would spend hours with Lucy on the phone, only half listening to a story about her latest professional crisis, her dating life, or the crazy roommate who was trying to steal her cat. Her problems, my problems—they didn't really register anymore. My brain was as soft as an overripe peach that season, and I had emoji hearts emanating from my eyes. I gave terrible advice. A guy is giving you the runaround? Tell him you love him! Don't know what to do with your career? Don't worry! Everything's going to work itself out! I sincerely believed those words, because for so long

I'd been hopeless about my romantic prospects, and out of nowhere a real-life Romeo had fallen into my life. Anything was possible. Besides, Lucy had always been a million times more poised and together than I was. She would be fine. Mostly, I waited for the perfect segue to bring the conversation back to my new boyfriend. I was absolutely certain she would want to know all about what Romeo liked to eat for breakfast, or the terrible Prada shoes that he loved but that I hated and was trying to casually transition out of his wardrobe. I was self-aware enough to end every conversation apologizing profusely to my friend for being so insufferable and gross. Still, it never stopped me from doing the exact same thing the next time we spoke.

Romeo and I decided to share an apartment after our respective leases ended. When I told my mom I was moving in with my boyfriend, I was prepared for some kind of outrage, ready to face the surprise conservative values, previously hidden to me, that would suddenly emerge. Instead, she just said, "Good. It's not safe for a girl to live alone." Surprised at her nonreaction, I asked for her recipe for *bo luc lac*, which translates to "shaking beef," a wok-tossed steak dish that is a favorite of mine. She inquired about my moving day preparations, and I told her I didn't have much furniture, not even a bed, just a vintage blue vinyl couch that a friend had given me. And then, as if it had just occurred to her, my mom asked, "Tram, where will you sleep?"

Even as I was moving in with Romeo, I was thinking about all the ways I could leave him. I could just pack up my big cardboard box, hop in a cab, and live with Tshaun or Lamond for a while until I found my own place. Or maybe, if she'd have me, I'd finally move to New York and rent a bachelorette apartment with Lucy. It wasn't too late. Either way, when I inevitably found myself alone again, I'd be just fine.

By this time, I had cleaned up my act. I was eating real food, riding my bike everywhere, and doing yoga. Without a twenty-four-hour Jewel-Osco at my doorstep, I had to plan my meals in advance. Eating a box of frozen Hooters wings feels more like a lifestyle choice when you are deliberately putting them in your shopping cart, as opposed to a drunken mistake made at three in the morning. I had to ask myself, *Do I really want to be the most disgusting person on the planet?* And the answer was no, especially now that I had a new boyfriend to impress.

Romeo's diet was practically monastic in its austerity. In the summer, he survived almost entirely on tomatoes, olive oil, and bread. I found this absolutely appalling, but as long as he didn't make me eat it, it was fine. Not that I didn't love vegetables, I'd just prefer them in a stir-fry, with some kind of seasoning, aromatics, as part of a well-balanced plate. What I craved most was the Vietnamese food that I had grown up with. I worried that if I ate what I considered home cooking, I'd disgust him. It was that old fear again, picked up in the school lunchroom. I didn't know if I could let go enough to allow him to see the real me—an ugly uncouth carnivore, with strange food, and a black aura.

Whenever Romeo left town, I'd spend hours cooking dishes that I had craved for weeks. There were thick slices of indulgent pork belly, simply poached until tender and eaten with steamed jasmine rice and sweet Chinese pickles. The rich, velvety broth needed little seasoning, beyond a dusting of sea salt, finely chopped fresh cilantro, scallions, and a grind of black pepper. I marinated cubes of steak in minced garlic, sesame, honey, chiles, and oyster sauce overnight. The next day, I turned my gas burners as high as they could go and tossed the beef in a sizzling hot wok until it was lightly caramelized on the outside and perfectly medium rare on the inside. I roasted whole chickens brined in white wine, and then boiled the bones for hours until I had a silky homemade stock, which I'd hide in the back of the freezer for another lost weekend and a delicious noodle soup.

A few hours before Romeo was due to arrive back home, I would hastily straighten up the apartment and dump all the meat in the garbage. Once, when he went to take out the trash, he saw evidence of that weekend's activities atop the refuse heap. "Looks like you had a good time." He just smiled and took the bag out to our garbage chute. When he came back, I asked sheepishly if it grossed him out, preemptively feeling the sting of rejection. "No," he said. "Why would it?"

I cooked my mom's "shaking beef" in Romeo's presence and the world did not end. In fact, his favorite thing to do was to argue with me over the best method for cooking steak, purely theoretical, of course, because he's never actually eaten a steak. I would ignore his trolling, because what sane person would take advice on cooking meat from a vegetarian? For dinners together, I would make us the few Vietnamese vegetarian dishes that I knew, improvising new ones as well. I taught Romeo to hold his chopsticks properly, so that my family would not laugh at him at dinner. Not about his chopstick-holding technique, anyway.

I remember walking down State Street during my first few months in Chicago and seeing the stores lit up in all their holiday finery. The view was almost perfect save for the scaffolding and signs of construction. I thought to myself how beautiful this city would be when it was done. It didn't occur to me until much later that the city was a living, breathing, ever-evolving organism. It never would be done. I was always biding my time for the long-awaited day, far into the distant future, when I would be complete as a person. By then, I would have smoothed out my rough edges and conquered my insecurities. I couldn't imagine any worthwhile guy wanting to dive into a serious relationship with me in my current soft, unfinished state. Sometimes I would look at Romeo and wonder how this feeling could possibly last. Because I knew I couldn't think clearly or see clearly when it came to him. I was addicted to that sickly sweet jolt of dopamine that my deceitful brain received when we were together.

We had fights, big ones and stupid small ones, the same fights every couple has. I was certain there would be a bad day, or an argument, that would spiral out of control and reveal the quicksand on which we had built this relationship. I waited and I waited, but the doomsday scenarios

I'd predicted never came. All these beliefs that I'd held as absolute truths for so long were suddenly called into question. I had always been fine with being alone. I told myself that I didn't need anyone, especially not a man. But now I found that I welcomed Romeo's steadying presence in my life. It scared me how quickly I had acclimated to being part of a couple. I always thought it was dumb to fall for the first acceptable guy who came along. You fell for the sixth or seventh one. Only after you'd made your mistakes and become the best version of yourself were you capable of a real relationship. But what if I had found him already? Was I going to sabotage it because of some stupid self-fulfilling prophecy?

It took me a long time to realize that the way I felt about Romeo, well, he felt that way about me, too. I found his food strange and hated his ugly Prada shoes, but I didn't like him any less. When I confessed to him what the psychic had told me years earlier? He laughed, and then he reassured me that I'd never had a black aura.

For years, I had clung stubbornly to my shitty Sony Ericsson bar phone. Romeo urged me to abandon this dinosaur so that he could reach me in an emergency. He suggested upgrading to something with GPS so that I'd never be lost again. But I secretly liked being inaccessible. If I had a fancy gadget that actually worked, I wouldn't have any excuse for ignoring Romeo's calls when I didn't feel like talking to anyone. Finally, my sad little bar phone sounded its death rattle, dropped its last staticky call, and died. I toyed with the idea of just not having a phone. I'd go off the grid entirely, and even the Department of Homeland Security wouldn't be able to listen in on my deepest, darkest secrets anymore.

"Why don't you just get an iPhone? We can join a family plan together," he said.

Family plan; iPhone. He'd tossed out those three little words like they were nothing. We'd been living together for a while. We'd dropped the L-bomb weeks into the relationship. But this, *a family plan*, this felt like too much commitment, too soon. There would be a legally binding contract, with our signatures on it, chaining us together for at least another year. Maybe two if we wanted to take a real gamble. I just didn't know. Even if I were to leave him, he could still call me. Or text.

The fear that he would break up with me had been replaced with the fear that we'd stay together. In a short period of time, my life had changed dramatically. Instead of spending my Saturdays recovering from the night before, I was in the kitchen perfecting my Neapolitan-style pizza dough recipe or baking peach pies from scratch. While my single friends were at the bars looking for boyfriends, I was trolling the antique malls searching for the perfect midcentury modern credenza.

I was still mad about Romeo, but I'd awoken from my romantic haze to find that I wasn't the only one who had changed. For the first time in our long friendship, conversations between Lucy and me were strained. The period when I was a drunken love fool on the phone was short-lived. I knew she was disappointed that I had decided not to move to New York, but I didn't see why anything between us should have to change.

Her name was still at the top of my speed-dial list, but I suddenly found myself hesitating to press the call button. I used to speak to her multiple times in one day, about everything and nothing, but now there would be long stretches of silence between us. I assumed these lulls in the conversation were because I bored her. I was practically a married old lady now. I didn't have any crazy dating stories, and the new domesticity that I loved seemed dull in comparison to what she was doing in New York. I felt awkward and self-conscious. I'd stutter and revert into myself, widening the gap between us even further.

I knew Lucy was busy with her own life, trying to make it as a political reporter. She was dating a new guy, too, who had great hair and good taste in shoes. It just made sense that she wouldn't have as much time for me anymore. All through our relationship, Lucy called me for advice that, in my opinion, she didn't really need. Most of the time, I'd just tell her things she already knew. Or I'd give some glib answer to make her laugh and she'd figure it out on her own anyway. I had to accept that she'd finally outgrown our friendship. It saddened me a little, but we weren't teenagers anymore. It was inevitable that our relationship would have to evolve. I was certain that Lucy would always be a presence in my life, but what shape that would take I wasn't so sure of anymore.

I'd come into my young adulthood with so many preconceived notions of the person I was, and a plan for how I'd conduct my life. I had been wrong about everything: New York, my fashion career, my love life, and maybe even my relationship with Lucy. If I signed that contract, there was no guarantee that Romeo and I wouldn't break up a month later. But no matter how much the uncertainty of the future scared me, the depth of my feelings for him outweighed any fears. I didn't need him to dig holes in the backyard, or mow the lawn, or perform any kind of manual labor. I didn't need him for anything. I realized that I liked the idea of being tied to Romeo. I wasn't looking for an escape route anymore.

That stupid psychic had been right about one thing: I'd never been the girl to date around, or to waste my time with a guy I wasn't crazy about. I'd tried casual dating and I sucked at it, because I am not a casual person. Even Bruce Springsteen was never that lonely drifter he'd romanticized in his songs. He was a dad of three now, with an embarrassing soul patch, and a wife he'd been married to for a million years.

A man as old as my grandpa, wearing a fanny pack and pleated corduroys, set up my shiny new iPhone. After we'd both signed our names on the dotted line, Romeo said to me, "Welcome to the twenty-first century."

FRIED TOFU WITH TOMATO AND BASIL

Although we weren't vegetarian, my family loved tofu growing up. There's nothing better than homemade soybean curd, and there are a million things you can do with it. The method for cooking tofu is similar to that of many fresh cheeses like paneer or ricotta. Depending on how long you press it, the bean curd can run the gamut in texture from as light and silky as a panna cotta to firm and almost meaty.

This tofu and tomato stir-fry is a traditional Vietnamese dish that is a regular fixture in my home. It's deeply satisfying and healthy but takes very little time to prepare. I prefer medium tofu, which is solid enough to hold its shape and becomes wonderfully custardy when cooked, but firm tofu is good as well. In the winter, when I can't find decent fresh tomatoes, I substitute with the whole canned variety.

Serves 2
Prep time: 10 minutes; Cook time: 25 minutes

---

14 to 18 ounces medium or firm tofu

2 tablespoons peanut oil, plus more for deep-frying

1 large red onion, sliced ¼ inch thick

12 ounces small tomatoes (campari or plum varieties are good here), sliced ¼ inch thick

2 teaspoons soy sauce, plus more as desired

½ teaspoon kosher salt

¼ teaspoon sugar

2 scallions, thinly sliced

Few sprigs basil (discard the stems)

Freshly ground black pepper

Drain the tofu. Cut into 1½-inch cubes and pat the cubes as dry as possible with paper towels. Fill a medium heavy-bottomed pot with 1 inch of oil. Heat on medium high until the oil reaches 360°F. Use a candy thermometer to monitor the oil temperature. Working in small batches to avoid crowding the pot, gently slip in the tofu cubes. Cook for 4 to 5 minutes, turning occasionally, until the tofu is golden brown. Transfer the tofu pillows to a wire rack or a stack of paper towels to drain.

In a wok or a large skillet, heat the 2 tablespoons of peanut oil over high heat. Add the onion and sauté 5 to 6 minutes, until soft and lightly brown in places. Add the tomatoes, soy sauce, salt, and sugar and cook for 5 minutes more, stirring frequently, until the tomatoes have broken down into a thick sauce. Add the fried tofu and cook for 2 minutes more. Fold in the scallions and basil. Remove from the heat and season to taste with soy sauce and pepper. Serve immediately.

STIR-FRIED WATER SPINACH
WITH GARLIC

Water spinach is also often referred to as ong choy, morning glory, and kangkong, among other names. It's an invasive species that is banned in many parts of the United States because of this very quality. My mother grows it in her backyard (as does pretty much my entire family). The long, tender green leaves are mild in flavor, similar to spinach. Because it is a semiaquatic vegetable, the stems are hollow and retain a nice crunch even when cooked. It can usually be found in Asian grocery stores, sold in large bundles. Look for the water spinach with young stems, the skinnier the better.

You can do a lot of things with water spinach. I like to dress the leaves with a light vinaigrette and eat them raw, simmer them in a broth to make a healthy soup, or simply blanch the leaves and season them with a shot of soy sauce and a squeeze of lemon. My absolute favorite way to eat this versatile vegetable is stir-fried, with a little bit of chopped garlic and fish sauce. If you're having a hard time tracking down ong choy, you can substitute regular spinach in this recipe.

Serves 2
Prep time: 10 minutes; Cook time: 10 minutes

---

1 pound water spinach (also called ong choy, morning glory, and kangkong)
2 tablespoons peanut oil
4 cloves garlic, roughly chopped
2 tablespoons fish sauce, plus more as desired
½ cup water
Freshly ground black pepper
Lemon wedges, for serving

To prepare the water spinach, pluck off the leaves and snap the tender stems into 6-inch lengths. Discard any tough, older stems. Wash the leaves and stems and place in a colander to drain. In a large skillet or wok, heat the oil on high. Add the garlic and cook until fragrant and just barely golden, about a minute. Add the water spinach. You may need to do this in batches; just keep adding more as it starts to wilt. When all the greens have been added to the wok, add the fish sauce and water. Cook until the stems are tender, about 2 minutes more. Season to taste with more fish sauce if necessary. Serve with a few grinds of pepper and a squeeze of lemon.

SIMPLE WHITE WINE ROAST CHICKEN

This is the chicken recipe I tried (and failed) to make when I first moved to Chicago. With more experience under my belt, I've learned a few things. It doesn't take much to cook delicious food. You just need

to start with good ingredients and know how to treat them well. A meat thermometer is not a bad idea either. In this recipe, I spatchcock the bird, which cuts down the cooking time dramatically and results in a remarkably moist, evenly cooked chicken with wonderfully crisp skin.

Serves 3 to 4
Active prep time: 10 minutes; 2 to 24 hours to marinate; Cook time: about 40 minutes

---

2 tablespoons kosher salt, divided, plus more as desired
½ cup dry white wine
1 (3½- to 4-pound) chicken (preferably organic and air-chilled)
2 tablespoons butter, softened
Freshly ground black pepper

In a large bowl, dissolve 1 tablespoon of the salt in the white wine. Using kitchen shears and with the chicken breast side down and the legs facing you, cut along the spine to remove it. You can save this piece for stock if you prefer. Add the chicken to the brine and, using tongs, flip to coat. Cover with plastic wrap and marinate in the refrigerator for at least 2 hours and up to 24 hours. A few times during the marinating process, turn the chicken over so the bird is evenly coated in the brine.

At least 45 minutes before cooking, take the chicken out of the refrigerator so the meat can come to room temperature.

Preheat the oven to 450°F.

Pat the outside of the bird and the cavity with paper towels so that they are as dry as possible. Discard the brine. With the bird cavity side down, press down hard on the breasts to flatten the chicken. Cut a little slash in the thickest part of the legs so they will cook more quickly. Rub the outside of the chicken and the cavity with butter and a generous amount of kosher salt, about a tablespoon. Season with pepper. Arrange a wire rack atop a roasting pan or a large baking sheet. Put the bird on the rack breast side up and roast in the center of the oven for about 40 minutes. The chicken is done when the skin is golden brown and crispy and the internal temperature is at least 165°F. Take the bird out of the oven and let rest, lightly tented in foil, for at least 10 minutes before carving.

12

Love and Turkey Burgers

Lucy

Rob and I were having The Talk.

We had been dating for six months, but for most of that time our relationship felt like it was still in the very early stages. Rob had a crazy work schedule, so we saw each other only about once a week. When he came up in conversation, I never called him my boyfriend. He was "this guy I'm dating." I had been more or less okay with that, but after several months, some of my friends were starting to raise questions.

"Does 'this guy' you're dating actually exist?" Sarah asked during a very important book club meeting we had convened to discuss the *Twilight* series. "Nobody's ever met him."

"Maybe he's dating multiple women," Steffie piped in. "You never asked him not to."

"Think about it: You see him once a week. What's he doing all those *other* nights?" said Elana.

It was a good question. What *was* he doing? Rob and I always had a great time when we were together, but he wasn't the best about corresponding in between dates. Once, I almost ended it completely because he had taken thirty-six hours to respond to a jokey text message I sent him. He would act cagey about scheduling hangouts, so the ball was constantly in his court. I didn't like that, but at first I figured Rob was just a flake. When I considered the alternatives—that he might be dating other people, or that he saw me as a casual fling—I started to worry.

Over the course of the next few days, I let my anxiety fester. I became convinced that Rob was a womanizing dirtbag and that, in addition to dating dozens of women besides me, he probably had a pack of towheaded kids stowed away somewhere on the Jersey Shore. Technically this was acceptable—because we had never laid out any ground rules.

I had no idea what I was doing in this relationship. I had dated plenty in the past, but usually things fizzled out after a month or so. My interest followed a reliable schedule—after five weeks, a switch would flip in my head and I would get bored and stop texting the guy back. I thought it was possible I had some sort of psychological problem; at one point I tried to force myself to make it past the two-month mark with someone I didn't especially like, purely as an experiment. But I only managed to hold out for six weeks. When I was younger I had taken it for granted that I would meet someone to spend my life with, but over the past several years I had come to terms with the fact that I simply wasn't cut out for a serious relationship. And I didn't need to be. It was a relief to know that I could take care of myself, that I was fine on my own.

Then I met Rob. At first I thought I would get sick of him, too. But five weeks came and went, and I was still interested. Maybe his playing hard-to-get was part of the appeal, I thought, that I would back off the moment he declared himself definitively. That was part of the reason I didn't push for anything concrete. I liked this feeling, the rush of excitement when I heard from him, the anticipation before a date. But over the course of several months, I realized the real problem was that I didn't know how to talk to him about what I wanted. I had never felt this way before. It scared me. I was so afraid of pushing Rob away that I didn't draw any lines or make any demands. I had let him dictate the terms of our relationship. But that had gone on for far too long.

What was I going to say? I knew I had to walk away if he didn't want to make it official, but I didn't want to come across as hostile. After all, he *probably* didn't have a second family. I didn't want to go in with guns blazing until something bad had actually happened.

I needed advice, and the person I most wanted to call was my best friend. But Tram and I weren't speaking much—which made it awkward when we finally did get on the phone. I didn't want to call her just to complain about my problems, nor did I want to reach out exclusively when I had good news, lest I sound braggy. So more often than not, I didn't call her at all. It was strange having this hole in my life for the first time in more than ten years. It was like having a phantom limb; I still felt the itch of her presence, but I couldn't access her. Now I was falling in love for the first time, and Tram barely knew anything about it. It felt weird and wrong. I missed her.

My finger hovered over the call button. I hadn't ever been able to figure out why Tram had been keeping her distance. Was she upset that I had tried to pressure her to move to New York? Did she think my life here was vapid and empty? Had I changed too much, or maybe not enough? Was she just sick of me? It hurt to know that she had been fine without me, even when I still needed her. I felt my pride surge and I put the phone down. Then I picked it up again. If I didn't talk to her now, the space between us would only grow wider. I tried to put myself in her position. If something were going on with Romeo, or with her family, wouldn't I still want her to call? The answer was yes. I dialed.

"I need some advice," I said. "I think have to break up with Rob."

"Oh my God, why?" she asked. "What did he do?"

"Nothing, exactly. It's just...we don't hang out that often. I don't know what he does with his free time. I think he's probably been seeing other people this whole time."

Tram paused for a moment.

"How sure are you?"

"I'm not. But we never set any rules," I said. "Technically he can do whatever he wants."

"Are you okay with that?"

"No, obviously not."

"Then why don't you just tell him what you want?" Tram asked. "You deserve to be with someone who treats you as you want to be treated."

"I know. I have to talk to him. But I'm afraid that what *he* wants is to be single," I said. "And then I will have to dump him, which I really do not want to do."

"It might not come to that. But you're never going to know until you talk to him. It'll be okay either way."

I promised Tram I would tell Rob how I felt. Then, as I was about to hang up, I paused. I was sick of the distance. I wanted a clean slate between us.

"I don't even know if I should bring it up, but I was nervous to call you earlier," I said. "Things have felt a little awkward between us. For a while now, actually."

"Yeah," Tram said after a moment. "I've been thinking that, too."

It had been about a year since she had decided to stay in Chicago. During that time I had felt wounded and rejected, and more removed from her than ever before. But finally it felt like we might start to breach the wall that had crept up between us.

I apologized for acting so weird and remote. Things had been really bad for me, I told her; I was depressed and lonely. I had expected her to move to New York to pick me up out of my slump, but I knew now how unfair that had been.

"I'm sorry, too," she said. She had been avoiding me because she thought I had outgrown her, that I had judged her decision to stay in Chicago, and she didn't want to be a drag on my life.

We had always been so close—often it felt like we could access the other's brain, read each other's minds. A shared look was enough to convey a private joke. When I called Tram and said, "Guess what?" she usually knew what I was going to say next. At some point over the course of our friendship, we settled into this idea that we didn't have to tell each other what we were thinking or feeling—we were so fluent in reading each other, our emotional shorthand was so strong, the other person would just *know*.

I realized how naive we had been. I had been projecting my own feelings onto Tram's silences, and she had been doing the same to me. We were our own people. It was ridiculous for me to think that I could accurately guess what was going on in her head. I suddenly felt a wave of regret. We had wasted so much time and emotional energy feeling hurt and confused, when we could have cleared it all up with a single conversation.

"We should try to talk like this more often," I said. "But in the meantime, I'm glad to have you back."

A few nights later, when Rob came to my neighborhood for a low-key dinner, I felt cautiously optimistic. Talking openly with Tram had solved everything between us. Maybe that was the approach I should have taken with Rob all along.

It was a beautiful spring evening. Sitting outside at my favorite French restaurant, we drank Côtes du Rhône and devoured perfectly seasoned roast chicken while I told him about the congressman I had interviewed that day. By now we were so comfortable with one another; it seemed impossible that he didn't think we were together. Back at my apartment, bolstered by confidence from my conversation with Tram—plus the wine—I went for it.

"So . . . what do you see happening with this?" I asked vaguely.

"What do you mean?"

"I guess what I'm wondering is . . . are you seeing other people?"

"Oh, no, I'm not," Rob said. "Are you?"

"No," I said, relieved. My friends had been wrong. Rob and I were on the same page after all. "So does that mean we're, like, official?"

I was expecting Rob to respond with a laugh—of course we were official! But instead, he paused.

"Well…"

He tried to explain himself while I sat there, heartbroken. He told me he had been in long-term relationships for most of his twenties, and he hadn't planned to date anyone seriously for at least another couple of years. He said he had to think about it.

He has to think about it? What's to think about? Either Rob loved me or he didn't. If he had to think about it, I already knew what the answer was.

I almost broke it off right then, but I couldn't bring myself to physically say the words. Instead I told Rob to let me know when he'd figured out how he felt. I thought it would be quick—one day, two days, maybe four. But days turned into weeks. Was he planning to put me off indefinitely? I texted him. No response. I tried him on Gchat, and he immediately went offline. *Oh, I see,* I thought, *not only is he going to dump me. He's going to be a dick about it.*

Finally I was done waiting. I called Rob and demanded to meet. We were going to break up, but at least it was going to be on my terms.

That night after work, I steeled my nerves at drinks with colleagues. "Excuse me," I told my friends after gulping the last of my wine. "I have to go break up with someone who isn't even technically my boyfriend."

Outside, I called Tram for a last-minute confidence booster.

"No matter what, it's better to know," she said.

Uptown at Rob's place, I was all business.

"Look," I said, halfway through the door. "We don't want the same things—"

"Really?" he cut me off. "But I want to be with you."

"I mean, like, *officially*. Boyfriend-girlfriend. Strings attached."

"That's what I mean, too," he said.

I paused. This was not what I was expecting.

"I don't understand why you had to consider it for so long," I said. "This isn't something you should have had to think about at all."

"I know it sounds stupid, but I had no idea what you wanted until you brought it up," he said. "You were playing it pretty cool."

But, I argued, if he liked me—*really*—I should have been on his mind regardless.

"I'm very literal sometimes," he said. "I'm good at compartmentalizing. I didn't really know where things between us were going, I just knew I was happy when I saw you. Once I had two seconds to actually consider it, there was no question. I really like you."

"*Really?*"

"Really."

It was nice to hear, but it took me a little while to trust Rob again. I thought maybe he told me those things because he didn't have the nerve to break up with me—at least not in person. Even so, I let myself proceed. I didn't know what would happen, but what was the point of turning back now? That would hurt as much as anything else.

But one day, a month or two in, I discovered that things between us had changed. It no longer felt like he might suddenly drop off the face of the earth. In fact, he stopped flaking out entirely. I had acted like we were in a relationship from the first moment we met, but apparently the label meant something to him. He was around all the time now, supportive and reliable, bringing me take-out soup when I was sick and helping me navigate the politics of work. We developed routines: omakase dinners at the Japanese spot we loved on Forty-Third Street; lazy Sunday afternoons in Brooklyn, browsing the bookstore on Court Street and grabbing decadent biscuit egg sandwiches for lunch in Red Hook. The uncertainty of the last six months had disappeared, and now I was able to enjoy our time together without the stress of not knowing where we stood. Was this what a relationship felt like? Over bagels at his place one morning, I decided that it was.

*   *   *

I wanted to celebrate, so I decided to embark on what I considered a critical early relationship milestone: the romantic homemade dinner.

I was aware going in that Rob didn't really know his way around the kitchen, because when we had first started dating I had asked him if he liked to cook.

"I make great pot stickers," he replied.

I had been impressed. Dumplings were pretty high-level, as bachelor food went.

"It's easy," he said. "All you have to do is dump them out of the bag and put them in the microwave."

So Rob wasn't a top chef. It made no difference to me, because when I imagined a romantic homemade meal, I assumed I'd be the one preparing it. But when I raised the idea, he was skeptical. His "housewares" collection consisted of two salad plates, two bowls, one eight-inch skillet, and a comically small pot. He had a spatula, a ladle, and a plastic slotted spoon. Until a coworker gifted him some hand-me-down forks and knives—presented to him in a shoebox—he hadn't had any of those, either. He didn't ever cook, so he didn't really get why I would want to stay in and do something that he viewed as housework when there were plenty of great restaurants in the neighborhood.

But I insisted. I communicate through food. I show off with food. How was I supposed to impress my new boyfriend if not by preparing him a lavish meal?

"We'll go to the grocery store and pick up a few ingredients, and then I'll throw something together at your place," I said, dramatically underplaying the amount of effort to which I planned on going. "I'm sure your roommates have some pots and pans we can use."

I called Tram to consult. If there's anything I love as much as cooking, it's calling Tram beforehand to discuss possible menus. First there's some catching up, then I mention my dinner party, and then I throw out a completely outrageous, incredibly elaborate idea for what to serve at it—at which point Tram tries to talk me down from the ledge. Her success rate varies. I am famous among my friends for aiming way too high with my dinner party ambitions. I know you're supposed to make your most tried-and-true dishes, but nothing excites me like a challenge, and there is no challenge greater than making enchiladas for the first time while fifteen hungry people sit in your living room and watch you funnel homemade chile salsa through a tea strainer. I love having a house full of people who think I'm out of my mind so that I can eventually prove them wrong. Which I do at least 60 percent of the time.

The phone call with Tram went as expected. We exchanged personal updates, and then I mentioned the insanely complicated fish recipe I was planning to prepare for Rob. Tram, ever so gently, wondered if it might be stressful to cook a whole sea bass, stuffed with prawns and baked in puff pastry, while making dinner together for the first time. I said no, definitely not.

I printed out the recipe and trekked over to Rob's. As usual it took forever to get there, and by the time I arrived it was already late. But it wasn't until we got to the grocery store that my plan officially fell apart. That was when we learned the fish counter was closed.

I froze. *What else do people eat?* I was unable to think of an alternative.

"So what should we make instead?" Rob asked. He was looking around the store, oblivious to the fact that I was breaking out in hives. Then he saw me.

"It's no big deal. Let's just do something easy," he said. "What do you usually make for dinner?"

My everyday cooking repertoire was pretty straightforward. There were noodles. There were proletarian soups. There was roast chicken. The food tasted good, but it was simple. It was nothing I would ever serve to company. Certainly nothing I would serve to my newly minted boyfriend. (Little did I know that Rob would have been impressed with anything; months later, he raved over a tossed-together late-night snack. "This is the best thing I've ever eaten! What is it?" he asked. I paused. "Um, buttered noodles?")

"I . . . I don't know what I usually make."

"Hm . . . we could just bail on cooking and go out to dinner?"

"No."

In fact, that was exactly what I wanted to do. I was already exhausted, and I hadn't even stepped into the kitchen. But I was too stubborn to admit my failure.

In the years since that night, Rob has weathered a number of my food-related freak-outs. Once, I had a fit because he'd failed to anticipate that I would want a tuna sandwich the moment I stepped off a two-hour bus ride. But this moment, at the grocery store, was Rob's first taste of my hypoglycemic meltdown behavior. To his credit, he knew exactly what to do.

"We'll make turkey burgers," he declared. "I have a George Foreman grill."

Turkey burgers? On a George Foreman grill? This was not the romance-inspiring, picture-perfect menu I'd been envisioning. Who eats turkey burgers on a date? But I had no other ideas, and in the time I was considering an alternate proposal, Rob had walked over to the meat aisle and picked up a pound of ground turkey.

"Do we need a side?"

"We could do . . . couscous," I suggested, the blood slowly returning to my brain.

He grabbed a box of the instant stuff and marched to the checkout line before I could object.

Rob and I went back to his house and enjoyed a lovely dinner of turkey burgers, instant couscous, and Bud Light. It wasn't the five-star fare I'd envisioned, but it turns out that didn't matter at all. We were figuring out how to be together, to compromise some of the rigidity of our strict personal agendas. It was a good thing, I determined, as I sipped my canned beer and let him do the dishes. Sometimes the best-laid plans were never that good to begin with.

ORECCHIETTE WITH PARMESAN CHEESE, SLOW-POACHED EGGS, AND CRISPY PANCETTA

I used to think you shouldn't serve pasta to anyone you were trying to impress, because it's so easy to make. *Too* easy. I thought you had to really sweat it out in the kitchen in order to earn your accolades—the closer to death you came, the more praise you deserved. But then I recognized that no one cares what you cook for them as long as it tastes good. For me, pasta is also the ultimate comfort food, which actually makes it the ideal thing to eat on dates. The date itself might be stressful, but the food will calm my nerves.

Here is a dish that is quite simple but sure to impress your shiny new boyfriend (provided he's not, like, an expert chef). Let's be real, it's very similar to a carbonara, at least in terms of its flavor profile. But the slow-poached egg—the yolk of which is deliciously velvety and rich—makes it even more decadent. It will also look extremely impressive atop your mound of orecchiette. The basil balances out some of the richness and adds a fresh note. The only tricky part of this recipe is slow-poaching the eggs; for that, a sous vide cooker is ideal. Otherwise, you absolutely need a candy thermometer. That said, if you're lazy, a poached egg will do just fine. The texture is only a little different, and it speeds up the process significantly.

Serves 2
Prep time: 10 minutes; Cook time: 1 hour

---

2 eggs

6 ounces orecchiette

2 ounces pancetta, diced

⅓ cup grated Parmesan, plus more for serving

2 tablespoons chopped basil

1 teaspoon crushed red pepper flakes

Salt and freshly ground black pepper

Fill a medium saucepan with water. Add the eggs and attach a candy thermometer. Bring the water to 140°F and cook for 45 minutes at a steady temperature. Monitor this temperature closely, and if the water gets too hot, add a few ice cubes to cool it down. After 45 minutes, remove the eggs from the hot water and place them in a bowl of ice water. Do not drain the water from the saucepan.

Cook the pasta per the instructions on the package.

In a cast-iron pan, cook the pancetta over medium-high heat to render the fat for about 6 minutes, or until crispy. Remove the pancetta and discard the fat.

Drain the pasta and combine in a bowl with the pancetta, Parmesan, basil, and crushed red pepper flakes. Season to taste with salt and pepper. Divide into two bowls and top with a decorative sprinkle of Parmesan.

In the warm water you reserved from slow-poaching your eggs, briefly reheat the eggs until warm. Peel them and add one to each pasta dish. Slash the egg and watch smugly as yolk oozes out like a Cadbury Creme Egg. Stir to combine and eat.

HIGH-CLASS TURKEY BURGERS

Turkey burgers are a humble food, but it is possible to class them up. That night at Rob's, thanks to my total cognitive paralysis, we kept it simple: our burgers consisted of ground turkey, salt, pepper, and possibly a shot of A1 sauce. They were totally fine. But now when I make them I like to pump up the flavor with fresh herbs and a sprinkling of cheese—which I put in rather than on the patties. (I've never loved the sight of huge globs of melted cheese dripping down my food.) With a few add-ons and fluffy brioche buns, these burgers are both delicious and ever-so-slightly sophisticated.

Serves 4
Prep time: 15 minutes; Cook time: 10 to 12 minutes

1 pound lean ground turkey
2 chives, finely chopped
¼ cup chopped flat-leaf parsley
¼ cup grated Parmesan
¼ cup panko bread crumbs
½ teaspoon salt
½ teaspoon pepper
¼ teaspoon garlic powder
¼ teaspoon onion powder
1 tablespoon extra-virgin olive oil
2 brioche buns (or any other type of buns you prefer)
Fresh lettuce, for garnish
Sliced red onions, for garnish

In a large bowl, combine the turkey, chives, parsley, Parmesan, panko, and seasonings and knead with your hands until well incorporated. Form into 4 large patties.

In a large cast-iron skillet, heat the oil over high heat. Add the patties and cook until lightly browned, about 6 minutes per side. The burgers are done when the internal temperature reaches 160°F. To cook on the grill, heat to medium high and cook for 5 minutes on each side. Serve warm on buns with lettuce and onions for garnish.

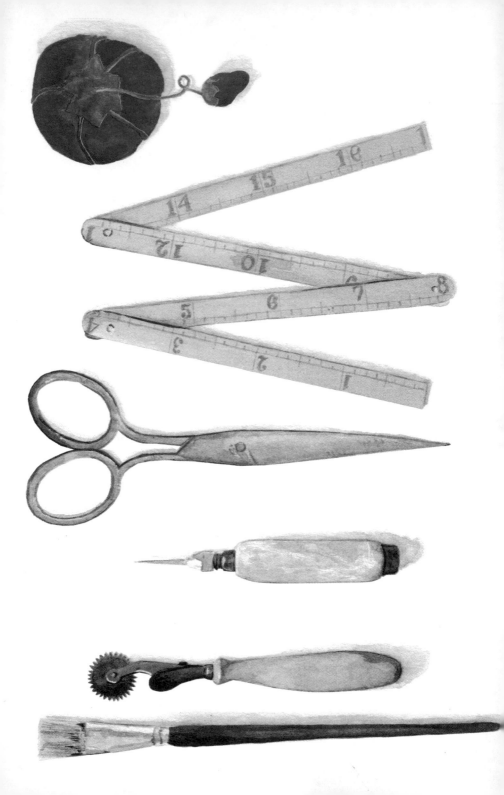

13

Craftwork

Tram

Romeo has a picture of me curled up into a tight ball, fast asleep, lying beneath a giant foam arm that I'd built from scratch, the hand as wide as my entire body. My jaw hangs slack in a deeply unattractive fashion, and there may have been some drool involved. This was how he found me in the living room after I had worked through the wee hours of the morning in a mad dash to meet a deadline. My dear sweet boyfriend took a moment to snap this incredibly unflattering picture and posted it to Instagram before waking me and leading me back to bed.

I had been working as a costume designer for several years, and on this occasion I had been commissioned to build a ten-foot-long arm for a performance artist. It was part of an installation exploring midwestern archetypes that included sleazy motivational speakers, spray-tanned bodybuilders, and a gospel choir. The prop was to be covered in fake hair, fingers clenched into a fist, with a lovely red rose tattoo painted on the forearm. In the center of that rose would be a beautifully rendered, anatomically correct vagina, with the name "Chrissy" in italic script underneath, topped off with a golden halo around the *C*.

I'd spent the past few weeks doing sketches and making scale models to prepare, and now it was time to build it. Every night, I laid down a plastic drop cloth and opened all the windows in our place to let in the frigid winter air. I donned my work uniform: a fur-trimmed parka; a *Food Party* apron that Lucy had gifted me; latex gloves; paint-splattered Forever 21 sweatpants; and a full-face respirator—the exact kind that a meth cook might sport. I sat for hours slathering toxic glue onto industrial-strength latex foam. I wanted to cry because it was three in the morning; I'd been working on this for weeks, and this thing that I was building in no way resembled a human appendage.

I had been so excited about the prospect of taking on such a project that, in a fit of manic overconfidence, I agreed to do it without fully comprehending just how complicated it would be. But after weeks of wallowing in the chaotic foam shit show that I'd built for myself, doubt started to creep into my mind. I was behind schedule and over budget, and besides, I'd never made an arm before. Livers, hearts, and spleens, yes. But a ten-foot arm? I didn't actually know if I could pull it off. After weeks of struggle, I e-mailed Lucy about the mess I'd gotten myself into, again. I wondered aloud if I might be bipolar. It was the only rational explanation for these irrational patterns of behavior.

"I am no psychiatrist, but I have seen *Homeland*, and I am pretty sure you are not bipolar," she wrote back.

I wasn't entirely convinced.

After I'd abandoned fashion as a vocation, I set about finding a new job that catered to my very specialized skill set (i.e., birdcage hats, panic attacks, and the ability to quote *Sister Act 2: Back in the Habit* from memory). I applied for dozens of jobs and sat through multiple interviews, only to be told I wasn't what they were looking for. I was getting desperate. My savings were dwindling down to next to nothing, and I didn't know how I was going to make my half of next month's rent. Then I saw a listing on a job board for an assistant designer at an independent costume production shop. I didn't know the first thing about building puppets or mascots, but I figured that I could just watch the first half hour of *Labyrinth* on YouTube and improvise the rest.

The costume shop was in a two-story loft strewn with dislocated furry body parts, like some kind of macabre Muppet slaughterhouse. There were shelves of retired NBA animal mascot heads, tails nailed to the mezzanine like trophies, and what looked like an elderly man's chest, pinned to a chair. (I found out later this was part of a costume for a male enhancement drug—rejected because it didn't look virile enough.) In the kitchen, there was a Freudian Christmas card from Cynthia Plaster Caster on the fridge. Pot leaves seemed to be a dominant decorating motif.

The owner of the shop had an impressive résumé. She had won major awards on Broadway and had thirty years of experience under her (figurative) belt. Waving at her brown crushed-velvet tunic and matching bell-bottoms, she told me that she never wore pants without an elastic waistband, because life was too short to be uncomfortable. This was about as far away from the fashion industry as I could possibly get. The shop specialized in the unusual: custom mascots and props for commercials, film, theater, and live appearances. She looked through my portfolio and at the garments that I had brought to show her. She turned everything inside out to examine the seams and the finishing. After an hour of scrutiny, my face beginning to hurt with the effort it took to look outgoing and upbeat, she told me that I was hired.

I spent the first few months of my employment in constant fear of being defrocked—of failing to perform a very simple task that would reveal my complete ignorance to the other employees. Every single day at work was an exercise in avoiding embarrassment, scrambling to correct my mistakes before my boss discovered them and chewed my head off. I'd text Lucy on my lunch break: "I think I'm getting fired today." And she'd remind me that I'd said the exact same thing the previous week, and here I was, still employed. Despite what the extensive tie-dyed wardrobe might suggest, my boss was not laid-back. She had exacting standards; "close" was not good enough. The job was not for everyone, she warned.

I spent a lot of time trying to keep up with the work. My boss hadn't built a thriving business in a competitive field by being lackadaisical. Something as small as a sloppy seam or a poorly placed stitch was a catastrophic error. The clients would never know if a button was a quarter of an inch off, but she would, and that, she told me, was what separated her work from the amateurs'. My coworkers would emerge from the bathroom, faces splotchy with angry tears. I'd watched more than one person disappear on his lunch break, never to be seen again. I'd go home and replay that day's mistakes over and over in my head. My evenings were spent studying pattern books, but there was nothing in them that could teach me how to construct a respectable habanero pepper from stretch velour.

I'd arrive every morning at work praying that this day might go better than the last one had. I'd come home and call Lucy. She'd tell me about her job as a reporter for a respectable news organization. She was finally living out those Lois Lane fantasies, chasing down political scandals and trying to squeeze information out of hacks and PR flacks. Then I would tell her about the latest mascot crisis. One year, a national organ transplant foundation rejected the purple velour lung we made for them due to its overwhelming resemblance to a diseased smoker's lung. An emergency meeting was called because the ad agency that had commissioned human-sized ballpoint pens thought that the tall, cylindrical costumes we'd constructed looked too phallic. Over the years, I built every animal imaginable, as well as hip-hop granola bars, chocolate chip cookies, and video-game babes for Comic-Con. The best thing about my job was that every project was different. We were reinventing the wheel each time.

There is something magical about the process. It starts out as a pile of garbage: bolts of synthetic fabrics, sheets of foam, thread, and buckets

of paint and glue. It's too much to wrap my head around the whole costume at first, so I start with something small: a paw, a belly button, or
the inside of a shoe. Weeks pass with my head bent over a table in a
fluorescent-lit room. I sew until I can't see straight. I lose track of all
the times I've accidentally stabbed myself with an X-Acto knife. My
coworker stitches right through her fingertip on the heavy industrial
machine, so I yank the needle tip out with tweezers, dump a bunch of
peroxide on her finger, and hope that she's up-to-date on her tetanus
shots.

After hundreds of hours of painstaking labor, it all comes together. A
face begins to emerge. Someone gets roped into trying on the costume,
and all of a sudden, Alexei the Hemophiliac Dog is standing before you.
After months of hard work, all that glue and thread and foam and fake
fur have been transformed into a plucky yellow dog with spirit, who
won't let a rare blood disorder keep him down!

I don't know exactly when it happened, but one day I walked into
the studio and I realized I no longer felt like I was on the verge of a panic
attack. I was completely at ease on the set of a commercial, secure in
my ability to put out any fires that might arise. I started doing freelance
work, designing and building costumes from my home studio, growing my own client base. I could negotiate budgets and manage a project
from concept to completion. I knew how to build giant cartoon shoes
from scratch, manipulate tricky materials, and make the scary industrial machines sing. More importantly, when I made mistakes, I could
reverse engineer exactly where I went wrong. It was no longer just blus-
ter; now my confidence was backed up by actual skills and experience.

I had heated arguments with my boss over an eighth of an inch and
other esoteric details that no one else cared about. Both of us were absolutely certain that if we did not have it our way, we might as well throw
the costume in the garbage and set it on fire. After our respective tan-
trums, we'd laugh and she'd tell me I'd been working for her too long.
It might have been the first time I'd felt comfortable enough around a

boss to scream right back at her, but the thing was, I'd always had that inside me. My obsessiveness over details, something that often manifests itself as controlling behavior, is a trait I've undeniably inherited from my mom.

My mom is a complete nut about food. Growing up in Vietnam with such a large family, food scarcity was a real problem. I can still feel a palpable sense of reverence in the way my family prepares meals. I was lucky to have grown up ignorant of want; I took it for granted that our fridge would always be full. I was always a slow eater, even as a child. After the dinner hour had passed, the dishes cleared, I would have barely made a dent in my bowl of rice. My mom would tell me in her usual cool, conversational tone that if I did not finish my dinner, after I died, in hell (I would be in hell, obviously), all the uneaten grains of rice would swell into fat white maggots and I would have to swallow them whole. To this day, I always clean my plate.

When I was growing up, she spent weeks obsessed with perfecting her rum cake recipe, going through an entire handle of booze in a month. Because we were little brats, my brother and I would show the near-empty handle to visiting cousins when my mom wasn't looking, hinting in hushed tones at my mother's drinking problem. Before that, it was radish cake, Yule logs at Christmastime, beignets, and Hainanese chicken rice. She was constantly trying new things, willing to devote hours, sometimes days, to a single dish, because to her, it was worth it. She enjoyed the process; the little successes that came with capturing that perfect taste, harmony and balance between flavors and textures. It wasn't until I was a little bit older, failing in my own kitchen, that I realized how much artistry went into the way my mom cooks.

I flew to California a few years ago to see my mother. I had plans for the weekend; dishes I wanted her to cook and places I wanted to visit in the Bay Area. She didn't tell me until after I'd arrived that we were going to a death anniversary party for my long-deceased great-grandma.

These gatherings are ostensibly about honoring your ancestors—incense is burned, prayers spoken—but mostly they're an excuse to get the extended clan together to celebrate with an enormous feast. We ate langoustines, plump and sweet, with just a hint of smoke from the charcoal grill. A simple yet complex green papaya salad, shredded into long ribbons on the mandoline and soaked overnight in a sweet brine until the rawness had been tempered. Atop this we laid thin slivers of spicy sweet homemade beef jerky studded with chile flakes, which we then dusted with finely chopped fresh basil from the garden.

My relatives had gone to absurd lengths to procure certain ingredients. There were handmade meatballs for the noodle soup, bought in San Jose from a man who ran a business out of his house, and there was a jar of the finest fried shallots I'd ever eaten, transported all the way from Vietnam. My mom sent me home with a Ziploc bag of fresh lime leaves, cut from the tree out back. When I protested that I could buy lime leaves back in Chicago, she waved me off. "Yes, but these are better."

I was lazy about food for a long time. I was a mindless consumer, ignorant and, worse, vulnerable to self-flattery. I'd often make the mistake of confusing time and effort spent in the kitchen with the quality of the finished dish. With age and experience, my own tastes had evolved, and living with a picky eater really made me examine my food choices closely. I ate more consciously, thinking critically about what I was putting in my mouth, dissecting each element as ruthlessly as my mother would.

When I first moved away from home, I used to dread every time I saw my mom's name on the caller ID, because she only ever called me to tell me when a relative had a terminal illness or had died. We both care deeply about each other, but we never had the kind of relationship where we spent hours talking on the phone. I never asked my mom for advice about school, or clothes, or, God forbid, boys. After I started cooking more seriously, I began calling her to ask about recipes and techniques. She'd call me back a week later to see how the dish turned out. It was a pleasant surprise. After more than two decades of being mother and daughter, we'd finally found something to talk about.

With my mom's tutelage, a steady diet of cookbooks, and a slew of inedible disasters, my cooking improved. I learned from Tom Colicchio's first book that complex-tasting food wasn't necessarily complicated. If you treated them well, you could transform three ingredients into something greater than the sum of their parts. I learned that you didn't need to rely on heavy cream, butter, or copious amounts of cheese to make a good pasta dish. I finally understood why my mother was so particular about minor details, why she'd traveled three thousand miles across the country with a box of free-range chickens. It was because every little thing mattered.

It took many failed meals for me to understand that these rules applied to the kitchen as well as to my work. This is what my mother had been teaching me all those years. It all matters: timing, temperature, and the way the judicious dusting of salt will make a tomato taste more like itself. There is a joy in cutting uniform batons of sweet potato that roast to an even golden hue in the oven, or cooking a glass noodle to the perfect degree of al dente, and there's beauty in an artfully arranged plate of fresh herbs. All these minute details add up, and contribute to or subtract from the success of the final product. I had learned this through my work as a costume designer. The client would never notice if the guts of a costume were shoddily crafted, but I'd know, and I had become the kind of person who could never live with that.

In art school they tell you on the very first day that there is no one path to becoming an artist, and then they make a few halfhearted references to working a day job to support your passion. My early twenties were devoted to figuring out what kind of artist I wanted to be, and how to make a living at the same time. I had to make a lot of mistakes to learn that perhaps those two aspects of my life should be separate. I love that I have a career that satisfies the part of my head that loves order, being creative, and problem solving. But at the end of a long day, I still have room in my brain to make work that is meaningful to me.

Months after I began the arm project, I finally completed it. I painstakingly hand-stitched every single hair, considered the placement of each freckle. It is a strange profession that I've found myself in, but I can't imagine a more natural fit for me. I painted the final highlight on that vagina tattoo, snapped a picture to send to Lucy, and then I thought to myself, *I'm the luckiest girl in the world.*

HANDMADE TOASTED FAZZOLETTI

Once my kitchen successes outnumbered the failures on a more regular basis, I felt comfortable enough to take on more difficult projects. Homemade pasta seemed intimidating at first, but these fazzoletti appealed to me tremendously because they don't require any special equipment beyond a rolling pin. Loosely translated, *fazzoletti* means "handkerchiefs" in Italian. These are rough sheets of dough made with lightly toasted flour, which gives the pasta a wonderfully nutty flavor.

Serves 4 to 6
Prep time: active prep, 30 minutes; resting time, 50 minutes; Cook time: 40 minutes

---

3 cups flour, divided, plus more for dusting (I prefer OO flour, but all-purpose is fine)
1 teaspoon kosher salt
2 large eggs plus 3 egg yolks
½ cup water

Preheat the oven to 350°F.

Spread 1½ cups of the flour in a thin layer on a baking sheet. Bake for about 30 minutes, or until the flour is the same dark blond color as Taylor Swift's hair. Halfway through the toasting process, stir the flour.

Whisk together the remaining 1½ cups of flour, the newly toasted flour, and the salt. Pour this onto a clean cooking surface; create a little crater in the center of the flour and add the eggs, egg yolks, and water. Using a fork, beat the eggs, slowly incorporating in the rest of the flour. Once the liquid has been incorporated, knead the dough for at least 10 minutes, until it is smooth and uniform. Wrap in plastic and let the dough rest for 30 minutes at room temperature. Do not skimp on the kneading or resting steps. Think about how smug you will be when you tell your guests you made this pasta from scratch.

Liberally dust the work area with flour. Divide the dough into 4 balls. Press one of the smaller balls into a flat circle and roll as thin as possible, no thicker than ⅛ inch; dust sparingly with flour if necessary. Ideally, the pasta should be thin enough that you can see the color of your hand through the other side. If you are a fancy person with a pasta machine and the cabinet space to store the pasta machine, just roll the dough on the thinnest setting. On a liberally dusted flat surface, let the pasta dry out for at least 20 minutes, until the texture is slightly leathery. Cut into rough squares no bigger than 4 inches wide.

Bring a large pot of salted water to a boil. Cook the fazzoletti for 2 minutes, or until al dente. Fazzoletti tend to stick together when they sit too long in a colander. It is better to pull them out with tongs when they are done and slip them directly into the pan for the final dish, so time accordingly.

To freeze: Place the pasta on a parchment-lined baking sheet. Take care to not let the pasta pieces touch. Put parchment between the layers of pasta so they do not stick together. Freeze for at least 2 hours before transferring the pasta to a freezer bag. You do not need to defrost before cooking; rather, just add about 30 seconds to the cook time.

TOASTED FAZZOLETTI WITH SPRING VEGETABLES

Serves 4 to 6
Prep time: 20 minutes; Cook time: 10 minutes

2 tablespoons extra-virgin olive oil
1 medium leek, white and pale green parts only, chopped
4 cloves garlic, chopped
8 ounces asparagus, chopped into 4-inch pieces and blanched
4 ounces shelled peas, blanched
½ teaspoon kosher salt, plus more as desired
1 recipe Handmade Toasted Fazzoletti (page 203)
¼ cup cream
½ cup reserved pasta water
Small handful of basil leaves, torn
¼ cup finely grated Parmesan, plus more for garnish
Freshly ground black pepper

Bring a large pot of salted water to boil.

In a large skillet, heat the oil over medium heat. Add the leek and cook until soft and translucent, about 2 minutes. Add the garlic and cook until golden, another 2 minutes. Add the asparagus, peas, and ½ teaspoon of salt.

While the vegetables are cooking, add the fazzoletti to the salted water and cook for 2 minutes, or until al dente. Using tongs, remove the pasta and place directly in the skillet. Add the cream, ½ cup reserved pasta water, and the basil; toss to combine. Garnish with Parmesan and black pepper; serve immediately.

TOASTED FAZZOLETTI WITH WALNUT RAPINI PESTO

Makes about 3 cups of pesto
Prep time: 10 minutes; Cook time: 15 minutes

½ pound rapini, cut into 4-inch lengths
2 ounces basil
1 cup walnuts, lightly toasted
1 cup grated pecorino Romano, plus more for garnish
2 cloves garlic
½ teaspoon kosher salt, plus more as desired
Zest from 1 lemon
½ cup extra-virgin olive oil
1 recipe Handmade Toasted Fazzoletti (page 203)

Bring a large pot of salted water to a boil. Cook the rapini for 8 minutes; drain throughly, squeezing out excess water. In a food processor, pulse together the rapini, basil, walnuts, cheese, garlic, salt, lemon zest, and ¼ cup of the oil until it forms a chunky paste. Drizzle in the remaining ¼ cup of the olive oil and pulse the pesto for another 30 seconds.

Bring a large pot of salted water to a boil. Cook the fazzoletti for 2 minutes, until al dente. Toss the pasta with the pesto, add a bit of the pasta water if necessary, and serve with a generous grating of pecorino Romano. Season to taste with salt.

14

Trail Mix

Lucy

I was speeding down the South Carolina highway in a rented Camry, and I was starving. I had been up since 4 a.m. and I hadn't eaten all day, but food would have to wait. First, I had to find Newt Gingrich.

It was 2012, and I was reporting on the Republican presidential primary. I had been covering the national political scene for a few years now, but this was my first out-of-state trip—and I was terrified. The chief activities I fear in life include speaking on the telephone; talking to strangers; giving people a reason to be mad at me; dealing with people who are mad at me; and asking people to do things they don't want to do. These activities loosely describe the day-to-day activities of being a reporter. Some people get their thrills jumping out of airplanes. I get mine by calling strangers and asking them lightly challenging questions about their lives. This week would put my fortitude to the test.

When I quit my job at the arts magazine it was because I wanted to have opportunities like this one. Sure, it was only for five days, but I was reporting on the trail. If I were to die suddenly, my *New York Times* obituary (fingers crossed!) could officially say I'd been a journalist on the

2012 presidential campaign. On the plane from New York to Charleston that morning I was so jittery with accomplishment that I turned down my complimentary in-flight breakfast. (What a mistake!) Now that I was actually on the ground with a job to do, however, I felt the rising tide of old insecurities. After years of searching for meaningful work, I had found some; now I had to prove that I was actually capable of doing it. *Scary is good,* I told myself as I searched the bottom of my purse with one hand for a possible stale almond to munch on. *Scary means it's worth doing.* No luck with the almonds. I pressed my foot on the gas pedal and sped toward Newt.

In a conversation with Tram before I left, I told her all about my upcoming trip—my excitement, my anxieties, my outfits. Things between us were back to normal, and it was comforting to have her back on speed dial, ready to give me deeply impractical fashion advice at a moment's notice.

"You can't go wrong with a white power suit," she told me, when I mentioned that I was having trouble figuring out what to wear.

I laughed. "I might do something more traditional."

"Like a porkpie hat and a wide tie?" she offered.

In the end I opted for some black pants and sensible ugly blouses. But when I pulled up to the barbecue joint where the Gingriches were speaking, I kind of wished I had taken Tram's advice. Most of the other reporters on the trail had been following the campaign for months. I was just dropping in for a few days, untested and unsure of myself. Perhaps a white pantsuit would have given me an air of authority. Maybe the key to living a life of confidence was as simple as dressing like Diane Keaton at the Oscars.

I sat in the car for a moment. I knew I would have to get out eventually—Jane Mayer did not expose the Bush administration's use of waterboarding tactics from the driver's seat of a rental car—but I wasn't ready quite yet. Was it too late to turn back? I allowed myself exactly one minute to brainstorm escape scenarios. There was still time to turn the car around and watch television in my hotel bathrobe for the next five days. Perhaps Tram would harbor me in Chicago for a few years, until the humiliation of my failure had diminished. A minute passed. I gathered my wits and my backpack full of gear, and I opened the car door.

I had dressed carefully, hoping to look professional but not too corporate mom, but as soon as I walked into the barbecue place I felt like a total nerd. The other reporters were seated casually at a long table; they were wearing jeans and T-shirts and they looked completely at home with one another.

Suddenly I was back in my elementary school cafeteria trying to blend in amid a sea of cruel seven-year-olds. I was a nerdy, shrimpy kid; for years the shortest in my class, not to mention painfully shy and bad at reading social cues. Lunchtime was always stressful. Back in those days my parents refused to buy processed junk food. They sent me to school with sandwiches on thick slices of homemade wheat-germ bread, chocolate chip cookies that my dad had made earlier in the day, and money for milk when obviously what I really wanted was Hi-C or Capri Sun. I thought of Katrina Bockman, queen of the lunchroom, the girl with the whitest bread, the most exciting Lunchables, an ever-changing array of cutting-edge sugary snacks. "Why don't you have a juice box in your lunch?" she asked me once. "Are you poor?"

It occurred to me now that my elementary school lunches sounded delicious. Homemade cookies and cold milk—I would kill for that right now. I set my gear down at the journalists' table and pushed my fears aside.

"Lots of white-haired bearded men," I scribbled in my notebook as I wandered around the room checking out the scene. I chatted with people who had come to support the Gingriches, casually taking the temperature of the crowd. The room, a sea of flannel and scraggly hair, smelled strongly of barbecue sauce. We were at a ribs joint. Did I have time to grab a plate? I looked at my watch. The Gingriches were already running late; I didn't want to be caught with a mouthful of brisket when they walked in.

"Do you know when this is going to start?" I asked the guy next to me. "I kind of want to get some food."

He didn't answer. Huh. Was I not speaking loud enough, or . . . ?

I shrugged and kept my seat.

I definitely could have gotten the ribs. Newt and Callista didn't arrive until what felt like hours later; he with an outsized ego and I'm-loving-this grin, she encased in a golden helmet of hair. Newt gleefully delivered a speech he'd given at least a hundred times before, and I got the whole thing on my tape recorder while assiduously taking notes. Callista gave some similarly well-trod remarks, but with much less gusto. I found myself entranced by her blood-red suit and robotic precision, and my mind started to wander. She did not look like the type of woman who relished life on a bus, with its truck-stop food and shared bathrooms. I was gazing idly at her perfectly coiffed hair when I realized the event had ended. The Gingrich crew was being hustled out the door, and I was already late for the next thing—a rally for Mitt Romney at a middle school auditorium somewhere out in the boonies. I hustled back to my rental car and hotfooted it to the Romney event, woefully eyeing McDonald's signs as I passed them on the highway.

The week was long and sleepless. I drove hundreds of miles and interviewed dozens of South Carolinians. I got lost many times. I also lost track of my rental car not once but twice and spent at least an hour running frantically around downtown Charleston, pressing the unlock feature on my keychain, hoping to hear that telltale beep that would lead me back to my Camry.

There were some small moments of humiliation. In the spin room after a Republican presidential debate, I asked a fellow reporter about the identity of a man who was speaking. She looked me up and down scornfully and then rolled her eyes so far back in her head that I thought perhaps she was in the process of being possessed. Then she mentioned the name of a little-known state representative. I could live with that mistake. Later, in the line to get into a GOP event, I found myself standing by a handful of on-camera reporters from my network. They had no idea who I was.

A couple of minor setbacks didn't faze me. I was too busy—and too hungry. And I mean literal hunger. From the moment I set foot in South Carolina, I struggled to squeeze in meals. I wolfed down crappy room service entrées at 2 a.m. while transcribing hours and hours of tape at a time. I filed articles from the Dunkin' Donuts while inhaling rubbery, overcooked egg sandwiches squished between two cardboard-like pieces of "flatbread." At the GOP debate, I walked up to the flacks handing out the free turkey wraps only to find that they had just run out. All week I felt a gnawing at the pit of my stomach. At the time, I thought it was nerves. Later I realized it was probably malnutrition.

I wasn't eating well, but it didn't matter. I was getting somewhere. I was becoming bolder and less self-conscious. I had stopped caring about my outfits and my low social status among the other journalists. I no longer had to brace myself before entering a building or approaching powerful people for interviews. It turned out I was just as capable of harassing press secretaries as anyone on this earth. I was actually starting to enjoy myself. No one could say I didn't belong.

On the day of the primary election, I worked late into the day doing last-minute interviews and writing the three features I was supposed to file in quick succession after the results were declared. I felt like a comic-strip journalist furiously tearing finished papers out of my typewriter in order to make the deadline. I had finally found my rhythm—and right in time. When the night was over and I had filed my stories, I stretched out on the hotel bed and texted Tram a picture of myself, sprawled out in sweatpants and surrounded by candy wrappers.

"Murphy Brown, at your service."

"Did you get the scoop?" she asked.

"Basically!" I replied.

The next day was my last in South Carolina, and, for once, I had nowhere to be. I got in my rental car and headed straight downtown to the best restaurant I could find. I was going to take myself out to a decent meal.

"Table for one."

I sat down for the lavish southern feast I had been craving all week. And there it was, right on the menu—my dream breakfast: a crab cake eggs Benedict sandwich, complete with fried green tomatoes and grits.

I'm from Maryland and my mom's side of the family is from Missouri, but for some reason all of our familial comfort foods hail from the Deep South. Gummy taught me how to make fried green tomatoes when I was ten. My mother cooked shrimp and grits regularly. For my birthday, we'd have crab cakes—to this day one of my favorite foods. I was hundreds of miles from my apartment, my boyfriend, my family, and Tram. I was as far outside of my comfort zone as I'd ever been in my life, and suddenly, with a big plate of southern food in front of me, I felt completely at home.

I called my mom from the table and told her about my week.

"Gummy is very proud," she said. "Your grandfather would have been, too." I felt a rush of pride. My grandparents had high standards. They had both been journalists—and Gummy, in fact, still was; she was in her late eighties and she wrote for the newspaper at her retirement community. For the first time I felt like I was living up to the expectations I had set for myself way back when I was a kid. My parents and grandparents never pressured me to get especially good grades (although I tried to anyway), but they showed me what it looked like to do work that mattered to you. I had too much pride to be the family slouch, phoning it in and collecting paychecks at a job I didn't love. And now I wasn't. I was a respectable professional and a (mostly) fearless reporter, and I was doing something with my life.

I did not bring down any corrupt political figures that week with my intrepid journalistic wiles. But I did manage to avoid an anxiety-induced trip to the hospital. I worked my butt off and wrote good stories. I asked moderately powerful people intelligent questions. I did the best I could. Next time, I would do even better. I would also bring snacks for the road.

SPICY CAJUN TRAIL MIX

I have always loved snack food. When I was a kid we weren't allowed to have much of it, but my parents did make allowances for long road trips, at which point we would load up on all the salty, crunchy treats we were denied the rest of the year. I liked to go for the industrial-sized trail mix—not the kind with nuts and raisins, but the junky kind, with Fritos and Bugles—because it offered the most variety.

The only problem with store-bought trail mix is that there's always an ingredient in there you don't want. By the end of the bag you're left with a little pouch of disgusting cast-off sunflower seeds, which will mock you for the rest of the twelve-hour ride to New Hampshire while your little sister laughs at you for having bought something that could be perceived as healthy. When making homemade trail mix, you can easily avoid these scenarios by exclusively using your favorite snacky ingredients. The ones here happen to be mine. Feel free to adapt the recipe however you like.

*Serves 1 person who is going to be driving around alone for a while, or 2 people
who are sitting in front of the television*
Prep time: 10 minutes; Cook time: 5 minutes.

¼ cup peanuts
1 cup bite-size pretzels
½ cup sesame sticks
½ cup corn nuts
2 cups plain popped popcorn
1 teaspoon smoked paprika
1 teaspoon cayenne pepper
¼ teaspoon dried thyme
¼ teaspoon garlic powder
½ teaspoon salt
½ teaspoon black pepper
¼ teaspoon white pepper
¼ teaspoon onion powder
2 tablespoons butter, melted

In a large bowl, combine the peanuts, pretzels, sesame sticks, corn nuts,
and popcorn. In a small bowl, combine the spices. Pour the butter over
the snack mix and then add the spice blend. Stir until well incorporated.
Dump the mix in a plastic bag and eat at your leisure.

CRAB CAKE EGGS BENEDICT
WITH FRIED GREEN TOMATOES

When I saw this item on the menu on the last day of my reporting trip, I
knew I had to get it: I love every individual component to it, down to the
English muffin. I was a little worried, though, that all together it might

be decadent to the point of disgusting. I was pleasantly surprised to find that it was, in fact, as delicious as I had hoped. The tartness of the fried green tomatoes cuts through the richness of the crab cakes and eggs, creating a nice balance.

Serves 8
Prep time: 55 minutes; Cook time: 50 minutes.

For the fried green tomatoes:
    1 cup buttermilk
    1 egg
    1 teaspoon salt
    ½ cup all-purpose flour
    ½ cup cornmeal
    ½ teaspoon cayenne pepper
    2 medium green tomatoes, sliced into ¼-inch rounds
    Vegetable oil, for frying

For the crab cakes:
    ¼ cup mayonnaise
    1 egg
    1 tablespoon Dijon mustard
    ¾ teaspoon Tabasco sauce
    1½ teaspoons Old Bay seasoning
    2 teaspoons fresh lemon juice
    Hefty pinch of salt
    1 pound lump crabmeat
    1½ cups panko bread crumbs, plus a little extra
    1 tablespoon chopped chives
    3 tablespoons extra-virgin olive oil

    8 English muffins, toasted and buttered (optional)
    8 eggs, poached

To make the fried green tomatoes: In a small bowl, whisk together the buttermilk, egg, and salt. In a separate bowl, combine the flour, cornmeal, and cayenne pepper. Dip the tomato slices into the buttermilk mixture and then dredge in the flour mixture until thickly coated. In a cast-iron skillet, heat ½ inch of oil over medium-high heat until the temperature has reached about 360°F. In batches, fry the tomatoes for 2 to 3 minutes on each side until golden. Transfer to a wire rack or a plate lined with paper towels to drain excess oil. Cover tomatoes to keep warm until you are ready to assemble the sandwich.

To make the crab cakes: In a medium bowl, mix together the mayonnaise, egg, mustard, Tabasco, Old Bay seasoning, lemon juice, and salt. Fold in the crabmeat, 1½ cups of bread crumbs, and the chives. Divide the crab into 8 parts and form into patties about ½ inch thick. Refrigerate for 15 minutes. While the patties are chilling, pour some panko onto a plate.

In a skillet, heat the olive oil over medium-high heat until hot. Coat the crab cakes with the reserved panko and fry until golden brown, about 5 minutes per side.

To assemble the sandwich, layer a slice of fried green tomato on the bottom of the English muffin. Top that with a crab cake, a poached egg, and the English muffin top. Serve hot.

15

Giving Thanks

Tram

In a lot of Vietnamese families, it is not uncommon to refer to your children by birth rank rather than by name. They begin with the number two so as to not draw too much attention to the firstborn, the most coveted child, lest evil spirits are tempted to steal him away. (It's always a "him"; they'd never bother stealing a baby girl.) My father is one of nine children. The oldest brother, Uncle Two, was called Uncle Crazy, because the whole family thought he was insane. He wasn't insane, he was an artist, but to his conservative brothers those two titles went hand in hand.

Uncle Crazy had decamped to Europe in the early '70s to attend art school. After the fall of Saigon, my paternal grandparents and the youngest children, Aunties Eight, Nine, and Ten, joined him in Brussels. The distance never seemed that far because my relatives were always popping over to the States, their valises brimming with Lacoste shirts and gold-ribboned boxes of pralines. Uncle Crazy came every other year, whenever he was in town to show his work at a DC gallery. He'd sign the poster from the exhibit for me, a parade of grotesque nudes with bloodshot eyes and bulging genitals, which I'd hang up in my pink bedroom next to the honor roll certificates and perfect attendance awards.

My dad's brothers openly teased Uncle Crazy for his strangeness, because he didn't seem to fit into their mold of how a Vietnamese man should look or behave. He wore funny shirts and delicate wire-framed Lennon glasses, and as a ten-year-old I thought that he was the coolest, most bohemian person I'd ever met. He seemed to take the ribbing in stride, until one day I guess he'd had enough. My mom took me aside and told me I was not allowed to call him Uncle Crazy anymore.

When my grandparents left for Brussels, my father, along with his remaining four brothers, said "Non, merci!" to the promise of *moules frites* and socialized medicine, and decided to take their chances in the United States of America. My mother's family had settled in Northern California. After a difficult year of living with my grandpa Harold, who is as kindhearted as he is hardheaded, my mom hopped on a Greyhound bus and traveled three thousand miles across the country to be reunited with my dad in Washington. Despite not knowing each other very well, they married and had me, and five years later they had my brother Jimmy. Growing up, I was always surrounded by Nguyens; Uncles Three, Five, Six, and Seven and their wives and children all lived in the same town. Our already sizable clan seemed to grow every year, with the adoption of friends from the local expat community and the strange new arrivals from the homeland.

Often, on weekends, my mom would fill an enormous stockpot with beef or pork bones; carrots, onions, and jicama for sweetness; and a cheesecloth stuffed with aromatics. It would simmer on the stove for an entire day. The result was a broth complex yet delicate, with a natural silky viscosity that could be achieved only with time and patience. My mom was fluent in an infinite number of noodle soups, many of which included what appeared to be almost reckless combinations of ingredients: blue crab, tofu pillows, tomato, and quail eggs; or poached duck, dried bamboo, and ginger. The one soup that I loved but always found perplexing had crepe-thin layers of omelet sliced into ribbons, wilted lettuce, and poached chicken. She was so particular about these details that if she had forgotten the Vietnamese coriander for the *bun thang*, she would make one last trek to the Asian market, because to serve it without the full plate of accompaniments would be a disgrace.

The doorbell would ring and my uncles would come marching up the stairs, arms laden with cases of Heineken and bottles of Cognac. The wives carried salads, desserts, and the bar snacks that were meant to be nibbled on during the drinking that would follow. I'd eat as quickly as possible and then run off with my boy cousins to watch a kickboxing movie or play a rowdy game of *Predator*. The women cleaned up and gossiped in the kitchen while the men sat around smoking Marlboros and drinking. This wasn't for any special occasion; it was pretty much every Saturday. It was a rotating party, a different family's home and another delicious feast at each week's end. When the Belgians were in town they cooked French onion soup, which we all thought was hilarious. Cheese and bread in a soup! Who ever heard of such a thing?

I loved these feasts as a kid, but as I neared my teens I resented being dragged to the weekly ritual. Although he was handsome and very good at doing the splits, I had a difficult time identifying with Jean-Claude Van Damme's character in *Bloodsport*. I didn't care about *Mortal Kombat*, or the Washington Redskins, or any of the other things most tween boys were interested in. All I wanted was to be left alone, pouting in the corner with a paperback all night.

Tensions at home between my parents didn't help the situation. For years, I could hear them arguing all night, something that happened with increasing frequency, as if there weren't even a wall between our bedrooms. It was just a matter of time before they split up. Uncle Crazy wasn't the only nutty one in the family. My dad's behavior got increasingly erratic and violent. My mom had had a few cancer scares—skin, and then later breast cancer—that required endless tests, and multiple surgeries, and a lot of waiting. She had dodged a few bullets, and she wasn't about to waste the second chance at life she'd been given.

I was relieved when she left my dad and we moved to a house not too far from the home where I grew up. I didn't have to transfer schools, and I'd still be able to see my friends. Nothing would change, my mom assured us. But of course she was wrong. There were many things that my extended family members loved about their adopted country—capitalism and Kentucky Fried Chicken and the sound track to *The Bodyguard*—but progressive gender politics was not one of them. Divorce was practically unheard of in the Vietnamese community at that time, no matter the circumstance. All of those uncles and aunts and cousins on my dad's side of the family seemed to vanish overnight.

Good riddance, I thought. By then, I'd blossomed into a wonderfully sulky teenager, drifting through my new house like a sullen wraith. I adopted Morrissey's rueful melancholia as my own and recognized a kindred spirit in the strangled wail of Ian Curtis. I had my mom and my brother and an extended family that still loved us in California. They were so supportive, in fact, that after the divorce, completely unbidden, my grandpa Harold came forward and generously offered to bankroll plastic surgery for my mom, to give her a leg up in the search for Husband #2. (She declined.)

I was quite content with our small family of three. It was easy to not think about my dad and my former relatives, devoting precious headspace to more important concerns like vintage clothes, boys, and books. The only time I really felt a little lonely was when holiday season rolled around and all of my friends spoke about plans with their own extended clans. It was a lot quieter in my house. Lucy and her family would drive down to her grandparents' place in Virginia to reunite with aunts, uncles, and cousins she hadn't seen in months. After the long weekend, I'd pounce on her, demanding details. Did she play football? What exactly was a Parker House roll? And could I get the recipe for Aunt Marigene's famous pie crust?

I'd been obsessed with Thanksgiving from the moment I learned about it, which was probably in grade school. It seemed magical, a holiday that revolved around a giant golden bird, with fancy little chef hats on its feet and Stove Top Stuffing, which I knew about only from television commercials. My experience with American food was minimal, limited to school lunches and the occasional trip to KFC.

Despite this inauspicious introduction to American cuisine, I still longed for the classic Thanksgiving, with a giant bird centerpiece, an assortment of lattice-crust pies, and family gathered around the table in J.Crew merino wool sweaters. I'd pore over my issues of *Martha Stewart Living*, fantasizing about decorative gourds spray-painted gold and the festive autumnal wreaths that I would never craft. When I was younger, despite the weekly family get-togethers, the American holidays pretty much went unnoticed. Occasionally we'd go out for roast duck or kingdom pork chops at Paul Kee, our favorite Chinese restaurant, on Thanksgiving, but usually my parents treated the holiday like it was just a regular Thursday.

Our first Thanksgivings after the divorce were spent with another Vietnamese family, a single mother my mom had befriended and her three kids. Their father had passed away just a year earlier. We would sit there at the green Formica kitchen table eating dry turkey and boiled Brussels sprouts in near silence. The woman barely touched her food, and, I noticed, neither did my mom. While I sat alone in the living room after dinner reading my book, I overheard the woman say, "I just do it for the kids."

One year, when I was still in high school, I decided we needed to bypass yet another sad Thanksgiving. I announced to my mom and brother that I'd be cooking the dinner. I made the green bean casserole off the back of the French's Crispy Fried Onions can, mashed potatoes, a box of Stove Top Stuffing, and two Cornish game hens—much more practical for my family of three than a giant bird. After many hours spent sweating in the kitchen, I announced that dinner was ready.

We gathered around the dining table to eat what I considered my first American Thanksgiving. My potatoes were lumpy, the casserole was strange, with an odd metallic aftertaste, and the hens were underseasoned and overcooked. For dessert, I attempted to serve a frozen Sara Lee pumpkin pie that I'd neglected to defrost. Dinner was over in about fifteen minutes. We stuck to take-out roast duck every year after that, followed by a family-friendly film that I'd vetted beforehand.

Shortly after I left for art school, my mother bought a restaurant in Berkeley, California, and moved across the country with my little brother. Going home for the holidays didn't hold as much appeal, because I wouldn't get to see high school friends or visit my old haunts, so most years I ended up staying in Chicago. I planned to spend the long weekend eating Chinese takeout and maybe doing something cool, like hosting a personal *Anne of Green Gables* film festival on my laptop. However, my friends were always horrified at the thought of me spending Turkey Day alone. Ignoring my protests, they insisted I put down that raspberry cordial and come home with them. One year, I took the train back with my roommate Amy to the suburbs, where her Taiwanese-Swiss-German family had not just the golden turkey and traditional sides on the table, but also fluffy white *bao* and sliced scallions and hoisin sauce to eat with the bird. Another year, my friend Lamond hosted a massive dinner. He spent two days cooking the meal from scratch, all by himself. There was a glorious thirty-five-pound bird with all the trimmings: mashed potatoes and gravy, wonderfully smoky braised collard greens, a ridiculously rich three-cheese macaroni and cheese casserole, pecan pie, and the pièce de résistance, his grandmother's recipe for sweet potato soufflé. And because Lamond is the consummate host, who worships at the altar of Martha Stewart and Colin Cowie, there were gorgeous autumnal bouquets that he'd arranged himself, in shades of ochre, rust, and crimson, and a wicker cornucopia teeming with decorative miniature gourds.

After we'd been dating for about two months, Romeo took me

home for Thanksgiving. He didn't seem to think this was as big a mile-stone as I did, but he doesn't tend to overanalyze everything the same way I do. After introductions, Romeo's mom, Maria, took me into the guest room. With reverence, she pulled down a framed picture from the dresser. It was a black-and-white photograph of my new boyfriend as a plump, serious-faced baby back in Romania, dressed in a traditional peasant blouse and cowboy boots. She then took my hands in her own and told me with damp eyes, "Tram...I really want grandchildren." I froze, and then thanked her for showing me the picture and said I thought she'd be a wonderful grandmother. Someday.

The dining table was teeming with food: a golden turkey, all the trimmings, plus a few Italian sides, a nod to Romeo's stepdad Rick's her-itage. To my delight, there were many Romanian dishes as well. Maria had spent the days leading up to Thanksgiving cooking; she'd made a massive pot of *sarmale*, cabbage rolls stuffed with rice and pork, enough to keep all of her guests happily sated for the week. In addition to the pumpkin and apple pies, there were platters of delicate, not too sweet, cocoa-and-hazelnut cookies and pastries. The morning that I arrived, to tide us over until suppertime, there was a bowl of yeasted dough for the *placinta*, waiting to be rolled out and filled with tangy sauerkraut or mashed potatoes, then fried in hot oil until they were flaky and golden and eaten while still hot, the steam escaping and burning your fingers as you tore into them.

Romeo laughed when I told him what had happened in the guest room. He said not to read too much into it; it just meant that his mom liked me, and she was just expressing a general desire for grandbabies, not actually commanding me to toss that Ortho Tri-Cyclen in the garbage. I'd been a Thanksgiving nomad for years, accepting the pity invites and often finding myself seated at a table next to strangers, but every year after that, I spent the holidays with Romeo's family and our friends.

Each year, on the two-hour drive to Romeo's parents' house in the country, we talked about the checklist that we'd be subject to: When were we getting married? When would we remodel the kitchen? And, more importantly, when were we going to have a baby? I always felt a little guilty that the answer to these questions was always, "Maybe later?" A few years ago, after the boys had cleaned up and were snoring on leather sectionals in the living room, Maria took my hand, and said, "Tram, I don't care if you have the paper, or a ring on your finger; I want you to know I think of you as a daughter." And this time, it was me who was misty-eyed. For all those years, I had convinced myself that I was perfectly content to be left alone while everyone else was off binge-eating with their loved ones, but I had been missing something. For the first time since I'd left home, I found myself surrounded by people I loved, who not only wanted me around—they also expected me to bring a homemade pie.

These days, I celebrate Thanksgiving with Romeo's parents a week in advance. On the actual holiday, I've introduced Romeo to one of my own family traditions. After a delicious meal at our favorite Szechuan place, our bellies stuffed with three-chile tofu and triple-seafood delight, we spend the rest of the evening at the local movie house, getting tipsy on 2-for-$5 rosé specials. When I get home, I call my mom and my brother, and we compare notes on the different feasts we've eaten, the movies we've watched.

THANKSGIVING TEA-SMOKED DUCK WITH BASIL GINGER SAUCE

There is a reason why most Americans don't eat turkey save for one day out of the year. It kind of sucks. You are much better off devoting your efforts to the anti-turkey: duck. Duck is one of the most luxurious foods imaginable. It comes with its own sumptuous coat of fat, which

is sometimes as thick as a '90s Tommy Hilfiger puffer jacket—nature's own perfectly engineered, built-in basting device.

Serves 2
Prep time: 5 minutes; 2 to 24 hours for the dry brine; Cook time: 25 minutes

For the duck:

- ¾ teaspoon kosher salt
- ½ teaspoon Szechuan peppercorns, ground
- 2 (6- to 8-ounce) duck breasts
- ⅓ cup black tea leaves
- ⅓ cup uncooked rice
- ⅓ cup sugar

For the basil ginger sauce:

- 1 cup tightly packed basil leaves
- 1 (1-inch) piece fresh ginger, peeled
- 1 clove garlic
- ¼ cup extra-virgin olive oil
- 1 tablespoon lemon juice
- 1 tablespoon fish sauce
- ¼ teaspoon sugar

In a small bowl, mix together the salt and Szechuan pepper. Pat the duck breasts as dry as possible. Lightly score the skin, taking care to not cut through the meat, and rub both sides liberally with the salt mixture. Place on a wire rack and refrigerate, uncovered, at least 2 hours or overnight. Take the duck out of the fridge 1 hour before cooking and let come to room temperature.

Line a wok or a stovetop smoker with heavy-duty foil. Spread the tea leaves, rice, and sugar on the foil. Place a wire rack inside the smoker and arrange the breasts, skin side up, on the rack. Partially cover the smoker with a lid and heat on high until you see wisps of smoke. Cover completely, reduce heat to medium, and cook for 15 to 18 minutes, or until the duck is medium rare.

While the duck is smoking, prepare the sauce. Place all of the sauce ingredients in a food processor and pulse until well chopped but not puréed.

Place the duck breasts, skin side down, in a cold skillet. Place the skillet on medium heat and cook until the skin is golden and crispy, about 5 minutes. With the tremendous amount of fat that is rendered, you can almost trick yourself into thinking this is not too unhealthy. Flip the breasts once, turn off the heat, and let them sit in the pan for 1 minute more. Transfer the breasts to a cutting board and let rest for 5 minutes before serving with the sauce.

(ALMOST) MOTHER-IN-LAW CABBAGE ROLLS

I'd never had *sarmale* before I met Romeo's mom, Maria, but they are a regular staple at his family gatherings, and I quickly fell in love with them. *Sarmale* are made from the most humble of ingredients: cabbage, rice, pork, tomatoes, and onion; but after a long braise on the stove, the flavors meld together in the most wonderful way. Bucharest is half a world away from Saigon, but I found the meal strangely comforting, reminiscent of *ca chua nhoi thit*, or tomatoes stuffed with pork, a dish my mother cooked for me growing up. Now I know that if I show up at Christmastime, I will be sent home with enough cabbage rolls to last me until New Year's Day. But what Maria doesn't know is that even though her *sarmale* are superb, I can't resist the urge to doctor them up a bit with soy sauce and sriracha. This dish to me has all the comforts of home, old and new.

This is my version of my almost mother-in-law Maria's cabbage rolls. They are a little Eastern European and a little Vietnamese—not

unlike the hypothetical grandchildren Romeo and I have yet to produce. In lieu of sauerkraut, I top the rolls with chopped kimchi, which lends a nice acidity, heat, and an interesting funk to the broth.

Serves 4
Prep time: 1 hour: Cook time: 2 to 2½ hours

---

1 large head green cabbage (about 2 pounds)
1 tablespoon extra-virgin olive oil
1 medium shallot, chopped
2 cloves garlic, minced
1 (1-inch) piece fresh ginger, peeled and minced
2 teaspoons sugar
4 tablespoons soy sauce, divided, plus more as desired
1 tablespoon toasted sesame oil
1 tablespoon sriracha
1 teaspoon kosher salt
½ teaspoon ground black pepper
1 cup uncooked long-grain rice, preferably jasmine
1¼ pounds ground pork
2 to 3 scallions, green and pale green parts only, chopped
4 cups drained and chopped kimchi
1 (14-ounce) can crushed whole tomatoes

Fill a large stockpot with enough water to submerge the cabbage entirely and place in the pot stem side up. Bring to a boil. As the outer leaves start to cook and turn transparent, about 1 minute, cut the leaves away from the base with a knife and remove with tongs. Repeat this process until you have disassembled the cabbage entirely. Place in a colander and let dry completely. Set aside about 15 of the largest leaves for rolling. With a sharp knife, cut a small *V* at the base of the large cabbage leaves to remove some of the tough center rib. If the leaf still doesn't roll easily, remove a thin layer of the rib, taking care not to slice all the way through the leaf, so you are left with a leaf that is flexible and easily curls.

In a small pan, heat the olive oil over medium-high heat. Add the shallot and sauté for about 2 minutes, or until it is lightly golden. Add the garlic and ginger and cook for about a minute more, until fragrant. Transfer the shallot mixture to a large bowl. Add the sugar, 1 table-spoon of the soy sauce, sesame oil, sriracha, salt, and black pepper. Stir until the sugar has dissolved. Add the rice, pork, and scallions and mix thoroughly until the filling is fairly uniform. You may find it is easier to use your hands.

To assemble the rolls, place about 3 tablespoons of the filling at the base (the stem end) of a cabbage leaf and shape the filling into a log. For smaller leaves, use less filling. Roll tightly, tucking the sides over half-way through rolling, and lay the rolls seam side down.

In a large pot or a Dutch oven, place the cabbage rolls, seam side down, in a circular pattern. Chop up any remaining unused leaves and scatter atop the rolls. Top with chopped kimchi. Spread the crushed tomatoes over the cabbage, sprinkle with the remaining 3 tablespoons of soy sauce, and add enough water to cover the rolls by 1 inch. Cover, bring to a boil on the stove, and then reduce to a simmer. Check occa-sionally, adding more water to keep the rolls submerged. Cook for 2 to 2½ hours, or until the rolls reach an internal temperature of 160°F. Sea-son to taste with soy sauce. Serve warm.

16

Fear of Frying

Lucy

I was lying on the floor, hands outstretched under the couch, while black smoke billowed in the air around me. It was becoming difficult to breathe. Alarms were going off. My neighbors were shouting in the hallway.

"Everyone get out of the building!" someone yelled. "Now!"

The kitchen was on fire.

It all started because of a really good sandwich. During a day trip to the Rockaways the weekend before, I'd had a delicious po'boy—briny oysters that were perfectly crispy, covered in a tangy kimchi slaw and a spicy rémoulade, all tucked into a toasted, buttery roll. A perfect summer sandwich, reminiscent of all those weeks I'd spent at the beach as a kid, reading trashy mystery novels and lazing about in the sun. One sandwich wasn't enough. I wanted more. I was going to re-create it.

The next weekend I stocked up on the necessary ingredients: oysters and the makings for a nice craggy crust; canola oil; lettuce; rolls. A cursory recipe search online suggested I might also want a candy thermometer for gauging the oil temperature, but I didn't bother with that.

I was confident I could just eyeball the oil to make sure the temperature seemed about right.

I had never made po'boys before, and in fact I had never actually deep-fried anything, but I wasn't worried. Deep-frying was just like sautéing, but with a different type of oil, right? I had spent all summer in the kitchen cooking more or less without a recipe. Chilis, salads, crab cakes, and dozens of cold soups—they had come easily. I was a natural home cook, I decided, a late-blooming culinary phenom. I didn't need Ina Garten or any YouTube tutorial to tell me what to do. I briefly considered consulting my mom—my go-to source for southern cooking advice—but decided against it. I didn't anticipate any big problems here. Batter some oysters, dip them into some hot oil, and bam. The most delicious sandwich of all time!

Rob was out of town, so I invited my friend Amanda to join me for lunch. She arrived and we gossiped idly about her latest summer escapades as I battered the oysters and shredded the lettuce. At some point, I dumped a tub of oil in a pot to heat it up. When I checked it a few minutes later, however, nothing seemed to be happening in there. The oil was supposed to reach a rolling boil, right? I put the top on the pot to speed up the process.

After a while, I figured it was time to get down to business.

"So, I just drop a few oysters in the pot and let them get crispy?" I asked Amanda, who at this point was lying supine on the couch, in the optimal gossip position, definitely not paying attention. How much time had passed since I'd turned on the stove? It could have been five minutes or it could have been fifteen. Amanda is a very good conversationalist.

I casually lifted the top off the pot.

"These are going to be delicious," I bragged.

A few seconds later, the oil exploded into flames.

I screamed. I turned off the stove and jumped back. I screamed again.

Amanda, who is great in a crisis situation, sprang into action. She found the fire extinguisher Rob had bought when he and I moved in together the year before, and she opened it onto the flames. The fire died down, and for a moment we felt optimistic. Then it returned; huge, bursting flames leapt from the pan, nearly hitting the ceiling and filling the room with a thick cloud of smoke.

"This is the part where we call 911," she said.

She picked up the phone and dialed while I stood there staring at the fire, frozen in panic. I couldn't quite figure out what was happening. Wouldn't someone turn off those horrible alarms?

"I don't want to call the fire department," I said. "My neighbors are going to hate me!"

"Lucy, it's time to get out." Amanda ran into the hallway and started knocking on the neighbors' doors, telling them to get the hell out of the building. Soon everyone was running down the stairs. I could hear sirens in the distance.

Amanda popped her head back in. "Lucy, let's go!"

"You go ahead. I have to get the cat!" I screamed over the wail of the smoke alarm.

"Oh my God, we do not have time for that!"

"Go! I'll be right there!"

I adopted Dizzy when she was just six months old, a tiny wildcat traumatized by early abuse and abandonment. She is not one of those sweet, docile cats you see in the Fancy Feast commercials. She's a streetfighter. She once gave me a black eye. But I love her, and she did not escape life in the back alleys of Brooklyn just to die at the hands of some amateur with a po'boy experiment. I was going in.

I covered my mouth with my shirt and got down on my hands and knees to look for her. Animals are supposed to have such good instincts; you'd think they'd run from smoke and fire. But Dizzy was hiding. When I found her under the couch, she darted away. I chased her around the apartment as the air around us grew thick and black. Was this how

it would all end for us? *Rob will kill me if I die for this cat*, I thought, growing increasingly panicked. Time started moving in slow motion, and I
wondered if I was experiencing some interesting side effects of asphyxi-
ation. I imagined Rob and my family, devastated by my needless death.
What would they say at my funeral? I wondered. And, speaking of which,
who would show up? As the smoke started to fill my lungs, I realized I
was getting carried away. There was still some time. I was going to save
my cat.

I found her under the bed. We locked eyes; she growled. "I'm not
dying in here with you, little monster!" I screamed as I grabbed her paw
firmly and yanked her to my chest. She writhed, bit, and scratched,
bloodying my arms and my stomach with deep gashes. Then she let
out a piercing, ghoulish cry, the sound you might hear from a hyena
being burned at the stake. I clutched her to my T-shirt and sprinted out
of the apartment and down the stairs. As I put the cat in the doorman's
bathroom, firemen began storming through the building—dozens of
them, it seemed. Outside, my shirt torn wide open, soot on my face,
and bloody cat scratches running down my exposed stomach, I met
my neighbors for the first time. As I cried sooty, maniacal tears, I heard
someone call my name. I looked up. It was a girl from college who had
called me a slut not once but twice. She didn't even live in New York.

"Oh my God, Lucy, what happened to your shirt?"

It didn't take long for the firemen to put out the flame—thankfully, it
had never left the pot—and then, after they had roundly mocked my
cooking skills, they sent me upstairs to recover, or at least to hide out in
shame. The kitchen was coated in a thick layer of soot and ash; so were
the twenty beautiful oysters, all wasted. I took a picture and texted it to
Tram: "Oops??"

Over the next few days, I attempted to make the apartment look
halfway presentable again. I wiped away the ash that had taken resi-
dence on every surface. I scrubbed the walls ineffectually until they

became a splotchy gray. Eventually, I overcame my humiliation enough to start venturing out of the house. My doorman, Randolph, offered some kind words and told me not to get discouraged about my cooking. I shook my head. I would not be touching a pan anytime soon.

I had spent a good portion of my childhood in the kitchen. As an adult, cooking had more or less formed the basis of my relationship with my mother; after years of driving each other crazy, she and I had found common ground over food. I would call her for advice about bake times and pizza dough techniques, and she'd learn a little about my life in the process.

Oh well! I thought now as I curled up on my bed in the fetal position, hugging Dizzy against her will. Cooking wasn't for me anymore. I'd just have to start a new family history.

In the past, I had been fearless in the kitchen. I wasn't the most skilled chef, but I was always up for a challenge. It had never occurred to me that cooking could be dangerous. Now, the menacing possibilities were all I could see.

For weeks, I stayed away. I ordered delivery for dinner and grabbed ham-and-cheese sandwiches from the deli for lunch. Even when I was forced to make my own food again—my budget did not support the take-out lifestyle—I ventured back into the kitchen for only the most basic tasks. I was terrified to do more than fry an egg or boil some water. When I toasted bread in the oven and my oversensitive smoke detector went off, I almost fainted with fear. Dizzy hid under the bed for three hours. "I think the cat and I are traumatized," I told Tram over the phone. I was kidding, but she agreed with me.

"You make those po'boys yet?" Randolph would ask as I left the house in the morning.

"I'll never fry again!!" I told him. He laughed, because he thought I was joking.

A few weeks later, talking to Gummy on the phone, I told her about the fire. I hadn't wanted to. After all, this was a woman who had been deep-frying food for about seventy-five years; as her progeny, I felt it was my birthright to know my way around a vat of hot oil. But when she asked me what I'd been cooking lately, I couldn't bring myself to lie.

"I'm afraid to cook right now," I said. "I almost burned my apartment down in a grease fire and it's freaking me out."

"Oh, a little grease fire is no big deal," Gummy said casually. "Next time, just throw some baking soda or salt onto the flame. Or cover the pot with the lid."

"There won't be a next time!" I said. "I'm never touching oil again."

"You can't let it get to you, Lulu," she said. "It's life! You just need to know what to do."

Frying is not a big deal to my grandmother. Growing up in Kansas City, Missouri, her mom, Bobo, was famous in the neighborhood for her southern fried chicken. Additional house favorites included homemade French fries and "fraaaaad paaaas," otherwise known as fried pies, which are what they sound like. In fact, when we spoke on the phone Gummy told me that she'd recently made Bobo's fried chicken for a friend who lives in her retirement community. "It wasn't quite as good as Bobo's," she said, "but it was close."

My eighty-eight-year-old grandmother was making fried chicken in the retirement home, while one little grease fire had put me off cooking for life.

"Uncle Jim knew how to fry, too," Gummy told me, twisting the knife into my wounded pride. "He used to make oyster stew for our Sunday night suppers at Balclutha, and we'd eat it with fried shad roe on toast."

Uncle Jim—nicknamed Bow-Wow—had been married to my great-great-aunt Weesie (née Genevieve), and the two of them made a very glamorous couple. Everyone in the family idolized them. Weesie, my grandfather's aunt, had been a young suffragette, a teenage newspaper columnist, the daughter of a politician. She was gorgeous, smart, and beloved by my family. Bow-Wow, meanwhile, was a handsome newspaperman. Eventually they settled down in Berryville, Virginia, at a big old country house they called Balclutha. It was there that my grand-mother, mom, and aunt lived for eight months when my grandfather was diagnosed with tuberculosis.

My mom was born a few days before my grandpa was shuttled off to the sanatorium, and the legend is that she slept in a laundry basket at Balclutha for the first several months of her life. It was terrifying for my grandmother, but looking back on it everyone remembers the experience as a kind of wild adventure. Gummy and her two young daughters—a one-year old and a newborn—carted off to a southern estate to live with glamorous older relatives, and doted on hand and foot by the cook. Weesie and Bow-Wow were not exactly dripping in diamonds, but they were from the South; they knew their way around a debutante ball. ("What happened to all that money?" I asked my mom once I was old enough to understand that my family had apparently once had some. "Don't ask me!" she said. "But my understanding is that it ran out with relatives like Bow-Wow and my great-aunt Dimple.")

Throughout their adult lives, Weesie and Bow-Wow employed a number of cooks. My mother especially remembers a woman named Margie, a beloved figure from her childhood who spoiled her and her siblings rotten. She kept green glass bottles of coke in the cooler on the back porch, and every afternoon she let the kids use them to make ice cream floats when they were supposed to be resting. She baked minia-ture loaves of bread, which she'd then wrap in used Wonder Bread paper and distribute to the kids as little gifts. Everyone lived in eager anticipa-tion of her popovers and her bombe, which was layered with dark choco-late and pistachio ice cream, plus cocoa powder and crumbled nuts.

Margie and the other cooks at Balclutha took care of all food-related matters. And yet, despite having no obligations whatsoever in the kitchen, Bow-Wow apparently still knew how to fry a damn shad roe.

This would not do. I could not be the only home cook in my family history to fear the fryer.

I decided to fix the situation. And so, I called Tram.

*   *   *

Tram and I had been cooking together since we were teenagers, and I trusted her with everything in the kitchen. I always consulted her when I was figuring out a dinner party menu. When I was stuck on a recipe, or when I couldn't get a dish quite right, I called her to pick her brain. Like my mother, Tram always seemed to know the answer to any cooking-related question. I sometimes questioned my own culinary skills, but I never doubted hers.

I had been planning a trip to Chicago, and fried chicken was the perfect project to take on during the visit. Deep-frying seems far less scary when you do it with another person—especially if that friend is a trusted confidante who, as she herself would tell you, has tyrannical tendencies when it comes to cooking. See, I had a secret plan. Usually when Tram and I make dinner together, my role is somewhat decorative. This is because, at least in her own kitchen, Tram likes to run the show. She'll sometimes give me an obviously fake task to make me feel included, but for the most part she does all the work. I personally love this routine. I enjoy cooking, but I am equally content to sit at the counter with a glass of wine, peeling potatoes and gossiping.

I figured it'd shake out like that this time, too: I would watch Tram fry the chicken, I would see that it was not scary, and then, one day, when I was good and ready, I would attempt to make it on my own. Thus I would "confront my fears" without having to do anything especially difficult. We planned a dinner party for the Saturday night of my visit and invited a bunch of friends.

After we settled on the plan, I took a picture of Bobo's recipe from the family history and texted it to Tram. Then I actually looked at it. It was very simple, almost suspiciously so, but one thing terrified me: you had to fry the chicken with the lid on the pan. Wasn't that what had gotten me into trouble the first time? I e-mailed my mother for clarification.

"Bobo's recipe sounds DANGEROUS," I wrote. "Close the lid?

Doesn't she know that's how I started my grease fire? I am going to have to make some tweaks."

My mother, who made Bobo's fried chicken on special occasions throughout my childhood, responded in no uncertain terms: "YOU CANNOT TWEAK BOBO'S RECIPE!!!!!"

We would see about that.

Newly acquired candy thermometer in my suitcase, I touched down at O'Hare on a brisk fall morning. But as soon as I arrived at Tram's doorstep, I could tell something was wrong. She was moving very slowly, and if I walked out of her peripheral vision, she'd turn her whole body— not just her neck—to see me.

"What's the matter?" I asked.

Lately she had been having some trouble with her neck and back, she explained, and the night before it had escalated badly. She was in excruciating pain. She couldn't rotate her head; in fact, she could barely move her upper body at all.

"We have to cancel the party," I said. "You should be in bed, resting!"

"Don't be ridiculous," Tram said. "You came all this way to fry some chicken. And we have guests on the way."

I wasn't sure what to do. Tram was not in any shape to throw a dinner party. But we had planned my whole trip around this activity. I didn't want to give up.

"I'll get started on the pie," I said. Tram nodded and loaded up a stretching app on her phone. Before I knew it the mellifluous sounds of a male yogi were trilling through the apartment. As I sifted flour for the pie crust, Tram lay on the floor and stretched. Every few minutes I would glance over and see her move her head about 10 degrees. It looked very relaxing. It must have been, because before I knew it, she had fallen asleep in Child's Pose.

When she woke up a few minutes later, Tram had the yoga mat imprinted on her face. Her neck was still sore, so we formulated a backup plan: she would load herself up with painkillers and watch six straight episodes of *Gilmore Girls* while I cooked the entire dinner. "You can advise from the sidelines. This is my project, anyway."

I shouldn't have even had to say it. Ostensibly that had been the plan all along. Tram didn't know that I had been counting on the possibility that she would do the tricky part of this project for me. Now that I knew I had to do it by myself, the whole scenario was much less appealing. But there was no turning back. To do so would mean telling Tram about my intent to take advantage of her culinary expertise—with good intentions, but still!—and I was too proud for that.

To make the process as straightforward as possible, Tram and I decided on a relatively simple menu: in addition to the blueberry galette, I would make the chicken and mashed potatoes, and if Tram could move by the time the guests arrived, she would throw together an arugula salad with her trademark shallot vinaigrette.

"No problem," I said, attempting to appear casual after Tram and I had solidified the plan. Then I started to sweat. I did not feel casual. I was freaking out.

It's one thing to start a small fire in your own home, and it is another much worse thing to start a fire in someone else's home. But to start a fire in Tram and Romeo's home would be a crime. They both have impeccable taste, and, what's more, they had recently remodeled their kitchen. It had always been nice, but now it was state-of-the-art. State-of-the-art, and white. Gleaming white. I could literally see my reflection in their pristine cabinet walls. *Oh my God*, I thought. *Whose dumb-ass idea was it to make fried chicken here?*

I had waited until our friends showed up to start frying the chicken, because I knew it would be at its best hot out of the pan—plus, I was seriously procrastinating. The whole day had been building up to this moment in a foreboding way, and I was dreading it. I had visions of Tram's kitchen charred and melting—all that remodel money down the drain—while I was carted to jail in a paddy wagon full of failed fry cooks. I knew Tram would never speak to me again after I burned down her house.

When the guests arrived, I immediately started ranting about my ineptitude, despite the fact that I had just met them that night. "I have no idea what I'm doing!" I wailed. "I'm afraid of burning the house down! This is a disaster!"

Tram's friend Dawni stepped in with a calming assurance.

"It's simple. I've watched my dad do it a million times," she said. "You've got nothing to worry about."

I calmed down. Dawni was right. This was not rocket science. Since the fire, I had studied my mistakes. I had gotten advice from my mom and my grandmother, and I had read everything I could about how to do this right. Before, I had been careless; I had let the oil overheat. That would not happen this time. This time I was prepared.

Over the next hour, Tram and Dawni stood by, watching as I battered, seasoned, flipped, poked, prodded, and ultimately fried a bunch of chicken. It was not exactly Bobo's recipe, but it was delicious. Crispy but tender, salty and with a little warm spice from a dash of smoked paprika—a victory. The house was safe. At the end of the night, so stuffed we couldn't even touch the galette, the group of us sat around the table, happy, full, and a little bit tipsy.

"That was great, but thank God it's over," I said. "I thought I was going to throw up the whole time."

The next day, in a taxi on the way back to the airport, I started scheming about my next fried chicken party. This one would take place next summer, and I'd serve it with Champagne and Margie's famous bombe. I would use Bobo's fried chicken recipe. It no longer seemed terrifying at all.

BEGINNER-FRIENDLY FRIED CHICKEN

When I was a kid, my mom used to make this fried chicken in the summer on special occasions; I have vivid memories of her in a flour-dusted button-down shirt, shaking a big paper bag filled with chicken and flour. There was nothing better than hearing the shake-shake-shake of chicken in that recycled paper grocery bag. It meant delicious food on the table that night.

When I decided to try my hand again at frying after the grease fire disaster, I wanted it to be as simple as possible. That translated into using boneless chicken thighs, because I knew the meat would cook more quickly and more uniformly. This recipe, therefore, is about as quick and easy as fried chicken gets—even for the rookie who has no clue what she's doing. (Just don't skimp on the candy thermometer.)

Serves 2
Active prep time: 20 minutes; 1 to 12 hours to marinate; Cook time: 20 minutes

---

1 quart full-fat buttermilk
1 teaspoon Tabasco sauce
1 tablespoon plus 1 teaspoon salt, plus more as desired
1½ pounds boneless chicken thighs
1 cup whole milk
2 eggs
2 cups flour
1 teaspoon paprika
1 teaspoon ground black pepper, plus more as desired
1 to 2 cups Crisco shortening

In a large sealable container, combine the buttermilk, Tabasco sauce, and 1 tablespoon salt. Whisk together and add the chicken. The buttermilk should cover the chicken entirely. Seal the container and refrigerate for 1 to 12 hours.

In a medium-sized bowl, whisk together the milk and eggs. In a large bag (a paper grocery bag or large ziplock bag would be ideal), combine the flour, 1 teaspoon salt, paprika, and pepper.

Remove the chicken from the buttermilk marinade and pat dry. In batches of 3 or 4 pieces, dip each thigh into the milk-and-egg mixture, then immediately drop it into the flour bag. Once you have a few pieces in there, shake the bag to coat each piece of chicken generously with batter. Don't be afraid to use your hands to make sure the flour mix gets into every crevice of the chicken. Your hand will turn into a gross, gummy mess, but it's worth it. Once each piece of chicken is battered, set it aside on a plate.

In a large, flat, heavy-bottomed skillet, melt the Crisco over medium-high heat. Melted, the shortening should come about halfway up the side of your skillet, no higher. With the help of a candy thermometer, heat the Crisco to 350°F. When the fat has reached the appropriate temperature, gently place a few pieces of chicken in the skillet. Don't crowd the pan; you'll probably have to cook the chicken in batches. Fry each side 6 to 8 minutes, until dark golden brown and crispy on the outside, then flip. The length of time you need to fry the chicken will vary greatly depending on the size and thickness of the chicken piece, so monitor closely. To test the doneness of the chicken, measure the temperature with a meat thermometer. The meatiest part should reach 160°F. Once cooked through, remove the pieces from the pan, lay them on a cooling rack, and season with salt and pepper.

Serve and eat immediately.

BOBO'S SOUTHERN FRIED CHICKEN

This recipe is taken directly from the pages of my family history, an assiduously researched 350-page tome my grandfather wrote when I was growing up. Part of its charm is how wonderfully old-fashioned it is: Bobo leaves it to you to figure out the details. There is no mention of quantities, measurements, or a candy thermometer—and yet, to my knowledge, this recipe has never caused anyone to burn down her kitchen.

Cut broiler-fryer chicken into small pieces, trying to leave wishbone in if possible. (You might have to get a whole one and learn to do it yourself.)

Rinse well; put pieces in paper bag with flour and shake to coat well. Fill skillet up to one-half full with Crisco or similar fat and get hot so it sizzles when bread cube is dropped in; put chicken in skillet and turn gently to brown a little.

Reduce heat to medium and cover with the lid for 15 minutes.

Remove lid and cook another 10 to 15 minutes on medium heat, turning occasionally—you can turn up heat the last few minutes if chicken doesn't seem brown enough. Add salt and pepper during cooking to taste. Drain on paper towels and savor. (It will be good, but probably not as good as Bobo's, for some reason we can't explain.)

MARGIE'S BOMBE

I used to beg my mom to make this dessert, not only because it tastes so good but also because of how beautiful it is. Bombes are not popular these days, which is why I love making them. It's a simple process, but the resulting dish has an ornate look and an old-fashioned charm. If you

don't like pistachios, swap in a different nut, or something else entirely. The nice thing about a bombe is that you can pretty much add whatever you want between the ice cream layers.

Serves 6
Prep time: 2 hours; Cook time: none

¼ cup unsweetened cocoa powder
3 tablespoons sugar
1 pint dark chocolate ice cream, softened
½ cup pistachio nuts, pulverized in the food processor
1 pint pistachio ice cream, softened

You will need an old-fashioned bombe mold or a 1-quart bowl with an 8-inch diameter. Whatever you use should be made of metal, not plastic.

In a small bowl, whisk together the cocoa and sugar.

Fill the bottom half of the bombe mold with a 2-inch layer of chocolate ice cream. Sprinkle a generous 2 tablespoons of the cocoa mixture in a thin layer to cover the ice cream, followed by about 2 tablespoons of pistachio nuts. Put in the freezer to harden, about 30 minutes. Add a 2-inch layer of pistachio ice cream. Cover with a thin layer of the cocoa mixture (about 2 tablespoons) and pistachio nuts (about 2 tablespoons). Let harden in the freezer, about 30 minutes.

Repeat this process, alternating ice cream flavors, until the mold is filled.

When you are ready to serve, run the mold under warm water and unmold the ice cream onto a platter. Quickly dust the unmolded ice cream with the remaining cocoa mixture and chopped nuts. Serve immediately.

17
The Trip Back

Tram

While she was on vacation in Mexico, in between sipping frozen daiquiris poolside, Lucy sent me an e-mail. She boasted—as she usually does whenever she is near a beach—that her skin was so tan she was "brown as a nut" (highly unlikely considering the *Mayflower* stock from which she descends). She spent a bit of time reiterating her '90s figure-skating loyalties ("Tonya forever"), and then she breezily slipped this in at the very end: "Oh, and by the way, Rob and I are planning a wedding." That was pretty much Lucy's entire engagement announcement. I had watched countless friends get married in recent years; my summer weekends were booked solid with nuptial ceremonies. I'd shed a thousand tears and drank Moscow mules from dozens of mason jars, but seeing one of my oldest friends on the cusp of this major life event was a shock to my system. We were adults now. After we exchanged a few manic texts and the excitement had died down, my thoughts naturally turned to how this was going to affect *me*. And then I realized, *Oh crap, I'm going to have to give a speech.*

*   *   *

A few months later, Romeo and I drove the thousand miles from Chicago to DC. More accurately, Romeo drove the entire way, because I'd let my driver's license expire seven years prior. I hadn't been back to Maryland for almost a decade, because up until that point, I hadn't had a reason. My mom had sold the house and left for Berkeley years earlier, and all of the friends I still kept in touch with had moved on to bigger cities. But I needed to deliver costumes for one of my clients, a beer company with an office in Silver Spring, and it seemed as good a reason as any to make the trip. It would be a triumphant homecoming. I was an adult now, with an actual career, marketable skills, a boyfriend, and an SUV packed to the brim with giant beer bottles.

In the back of my mind I secretly hoped this trip would result in some kind of self-revelation. Perhaps if I went back to the place where our friendship first began, I'd learn something about myself and instinctively know exactly what to say on the day of Lucy's wedding.

Lucy had asked me, apologizing the entire time, if I would be willing to give a toast at the reception, alongside our closest friend Naomi. As much as the thought of talking in front of more than a hundred people made me want to die, I would have been more offended if she hadn't asked me to do it, so I agreed. What exactly Naomi and I would say, I wasn't sure. How do you even begin to sum up an almost two-decade-long friendship without resorting to Hallmark clichés? Naomi suggested improvising the whole speech, which would have worked out fine if she were giving the toast solo. She is a natural born storyteller, and probably one of the most charismatic people I know. If we went up there without a plan, she would share a hilarious, touching anecdote, and when it was my turn to speak, I'd sob into the microphone until someone took it away from me. Winging it was off the table, but I wasn't too worried. The wedding was still a long way off, and I was sure I'd find some inspiration at home.

I could have shipped them, but I didn't trust FedEx to safely transport the costumes I'd toiled over for months. And because the bottles were the size of an average NBA power forward, flying with them in my carry-on luggage wasn't an option. It was much more practical to hand-deliver the costumes myself. After much coaxing, I convinced my patient, overindulgent boyfriend that we should drive the entire fourteen hours. It was going to be great! We'd learn life lessons! We'd follow in the footsteps of famous spiritual nomads like Bob Dylan, Bruce Springsteen, and Britney Spears in *Crossroads*. On the open highway, you could gaze out that window and witness the passage of time, minute by excruciating minute. I queued up *Darkness on the Edge of Town* and told Romeo that we were time traveling. I had every intention of savoring this journey, treating each fleeting moment as if it were precious, and finding some kind of existential truth in that endless stretch of concrete and sky. Afterward I'd know exactly what to say in my toast, something deep and profound about the meaning of friendship and all the ways Lucy and I have changed. But as Indiana turned into Ohio, and Ohio into Pennsylvania, I was lulled by the monotonous blur of dotted yellow lines on pavement, red lights disappearing beyond the horizon, and I fell asleep.

I did not wake up again until we arrived at our destination. As we merged off the highway, I looked at the street signs, and the names were familiar, but I no longer recognized the place. I was shocked at how foreign Silver Spring appeared, the lush greenery and lurching hills a dramatic contrast to the wide, flat planes of the Midwest to which my eyes had grown accustomed. The formerly sleepy downtown area where Lucy and I had spent countless lazy afternoons was gone. The area had flourished in the past decade, with high-end condos, fast-casual chain restaurants, and pedestrians strolling the newly poured concrete walkways. We drove by my mom's house, and I knew it was irrational, but I almost expected her to emerge from the garden holding a trowel, wearing a big straw sun hat. Perhaps there would be a guy digging a koi pond in the backyard. But of course, my mom was in California, and there were strangers living in my house now. I'd turned my back on this place, but I didn't expect it to have kept going on without me.

After Romeo and I safely delivered the costumes to the client, we stopped for lunch at the hole-in-the-wall Thai restaurant that my family loved growing up. The last time Lucy and I had eaten there, the entire place was just one room that could seat maybe twenty patrons, max. The restaurant had been located in a shabby strip mall, nestled in between a dry cleaner and a currency exchange. But when we arrived, I was dismayed to find that other people had discovered my secret. The restaurant had expanded, taking over the space next door, and the dining room was filled with a decidedly non-Asian clientele.

For the last ten years I had rhapsodized about the food that I'd grown up with, complaining loudly to anyone who was unfortunate enough to ask me for restaurant recommendations that there was no good Asian food in Chicago. But in the suburbs of DC, you couldn't coast by with mediocre food. There were simply too many good options.

When I was younger, weekend mornings were devoted to shopping for the week, followed by lunch out. Sometimes, my mom and I would stop in to eat at the secret restaurant hidden in the back of a grocery store. Seven dollars bought you a huge plate of noodles, enough for two to share; slick with sesame oil, complex and smoky, with just the perfect amount of char from the wok. If we felt like braving the brunch crowds, we'd go to Good Fortune for dim sum. An army of surly older Asian ladies with bowl cuts would push metal carts around the bustling dining room, calling out their wares: "Har gow! Shu mai! Char siu bao!"

Some Saturday nights, my family would roll into our favorite Chinese place as the clock neared midnight. The restaurant would be packed and raucous with other families, even at that late hour. I'd peer through the open service window, watching as old men in grease-stained chef's whites moved about in a kitchen the size of a railcar, wielding butcher knives and heavy woks, their movements equal parts brutal and exacting. In a matter of minutes, the lazy Susan in the center would fill up with steaming bowls of Hong Kong–style shrimp dumplings in broth; salty sweet stir-fried beef and pickled mustard greens; shrimp and scallops and squid, battered and deep-fried until crisp and flash-fried with salt, pepper, and jalapeño; and whole ducks, roasted until the skin was lacquered a deep mahogany.

After all those years, my secret Thai restaurant was completely unrecognizable to me save for the name. I suddenly felt unsure of my previous claims. What if my memories proved false? Back then I was an ignorant child, with an almost indiscriminate appetite. I was an adult now, with presumably grown-up, sophisticated tastes. What if the dishes we'd eaten were never that good to begin with? I ordered a few old favorites and waited with unease as they appeared on our table. Romeo's eyes widened as he took that first bite. Instead of the gloppy, syrupy, Americanized facsimiles that we'd been settling for in Chicago this food was explosive, bright, balanced, and complex. It held nothing back in its delicate interplay of bitter notes tempered by creamy fats and a judicious use of palm sugar, its bracingly hot chiles and cooling fresh herbs. It was the real thing, and it was better than I could have dreamed.

After my eyes had adjusted to the surface changes, my hometown still felt oddly the same. I wasn't a miserable teenager anymore, but I found that I hadn't changed all that much either. Completely shedding my past, my family, and my identity would have meant losing the best parts of myself as well. I still loved the same things I had always loved. My palate was now more adult and refined, but the food was as good as it had been in memory. I had traveled back in time to trace how far I'd come, only to my surprise, future me looked very much like the past me, albeit slightly less insecure and with better eyebrows.

My soul-searching road trip was a delicious failure. I'd had the expected epiphany, but what I'd learned about myself was somewhat disappointing. I couldn't base a whole speech around the fact that after all these

years, we were still the same people we had always been. The date of
Lucy's wedding loomed ever closer. Naomi and I workshopped a few
more ideas, but nothing felt quite right. I knew rationally that my
friend's wedding reception was not a competition, but that wouldn't
stop me from treating it as such. It wasn't going to be an easy win. We'd
be up against Lucy's brilliant brother and sister, and Rob's friends who
were professional comedians. On top of this, we'd be speaking to a
crowd of writers and performers. Despite the formidable competition,
Naomi and I were out for blood. We were determined to crush the other
toasters and stomp all over their self-esteems. And of course, say something heartfelt and meaningful about Lucy.

Naomi pointed out that everything we'd already written felt like
a graduation speech—too sappy and not funny enough. Going in the
opposite direction, I suggested we do the entire routine from Eddie
Murphy's *Raw*. A slightly unrealistic plan, because it would be pretty
tough to track down matching red leather outfits. Finally, Naomi and I
decided that if we couldn't think of anything spectacular, we'd go with
the nuclear option: a short, sappy speech, followed by a PowerPoint presentation of embarrassing pictures. She would either break up with us
or murder us after that little stunt, but at least it would be memorable.

I would have been happy to spend the winter chained to my sewing
machine, whipping up leather pantsuits for Lucy's wedding, but suddenly it wasn't clear what condition I'd be in by the time the big day
rolled around. The first time I saw the alarmingly steady stream of
blood coming from my left breast, I thought I was hallucinating. I was
thirty years old—the exact same age my mom was when she'd had her
cancer scares. This was too scary, too real. I needed to talk to Lucy. I
turned to her when I had news, good or bad. I needed her voice in my
head telling me it was going to be fine. And if it wasn't fine, that at least I
wasn't alone. I snapped a picture of my breast and texted it to Lucy.

"Kind of freaking out? WebMD says it might be cancer..."

Alarmed, she immediately called me and begged me to go to the emergency room. The next day I went to see a real doctor, a brusque Russian lady, whom I liked because she reminded me of my own no-nonsense mom. I asked her if she wanted to see my boob pic. She ignored me and instead referred me to a breast cancer specialist.

There were months of tests with still no diagnosis. Instead of sleeping, I hung out on cancer message boards and did self-exams compulsively. To my friends, I cracked jokes and was blasé about the whole thing, but internally I was freaking out. The earliest they could schedule me in for testing just happened to land on Tet, the Lunar New Year. My mom wouldn't have been happy if she knew I was getting an MRI on that day, so I didn't tell her. In fact, I didn't tell her about any of my health concerns because I didn't want her to worry. Old habits are hard to break. In Vietnamese culture, we believe that how you live on New Year's Day will set the tone for the rest of the year, so you actively avoid negativity and try not to get into any fights. My mother also told me that if you ate duck on that day, you would be doomed to walk like a duck all year long. I never quite understood if I was supposed to take that literally, but I avoid eating Peking duck just in case.

There are a few things that no one ever tells you about the process of getting an MRI. They *will* open your hospital gown all the way and if you accidentally wear sexy lace underwear, it makes the imaging technician super uncomfortable. Also, MRIs are boring. As I lay in that little plastic tube and listened to the machine drone, I passed the time by divvying up my prized possessions. I would bequeath two pairs of my beloved high-heeled Timberlands to Lucy and Naomi. Perhaps they could get together once a year to lace up their inherited boots, listen to Bruce Springsteen, and think of me. After I had given away all of my worldly goods, I still had a good thirty-five minutes left in the machine, so I did Kegels.

My Russian lady doctor, who is remarkably efficient when she is trying to shoo me out the door or upsell me a blood test I don't need, was surprisingly laconic when it came to giving results. A few days after I was to hear back, sick of waiting, I called the office. The tests came back negative. No cancer, no cysts, no surgery. I was going to be fine. Romeo was sitting with me when I got the good news. After I'd composed myself, and drank a little glass of wine to celebrate and calm my nerves, the first person I called was Lucy.

I didn't have a serious illness, but for the months when I was waiting for results, I *could have*. I did a lot of self-reflection that winter. When your house is on fire, what do you take with you? (Your cat, obviously. But I didn't have a cat.) The only things that ever really mattered to me were my relationships. I've always had a wildly independent streak. When I was younger it was partly out of necessity, but as I grew older, it was a point of pride for me to be self-reliant. So much so that I often forgot I needed other people at all. That was never true. It took me a long time to realize that the lone-wolf narrative I'd been infatuated with for so long was wrong.

Even when there were thousands of miles between us, even when there was emotional distance, Lucy and I never completely lost touch. Passed notes in Mr. Grossman's tenth-grade geometry class turned into daily e-mails about music and books, shared recipes, and teenage crushes. I survived friendlessness and self-pity during my stint in France by writing her every single day I was there. She e-mailed me from Internet cafés in Quito and Cuenca, recounting her adventures on the weeks-long solo trip she took across Latin America. As grown-ups with real jobs, we probably spent several hours every day Gchatting with each other when we should have been working. She was my lifeline when I needed it, and she was with me to experience all the ups and downs of my early years. The world feels more real, the colors richer, the emotions in sharper relief when you experience it with someone you love. It's almost as if I hadn't lived through something until I'd shared the memory with my friend.

When I first sat down to compose the speech, I thought it would be a list of all the ways we'd transformed ourselves and how far we'd come. We've seen each other through ill-advised, early-oughts haircuts, bad outfits, adult acne, and the new lines where previously there were none. We have grown older, we have matured—but who we are has remained essentially unchanged. She was always that brilliant, fearless adventurer; I was just there to remind her of her own strengths when she needed it. And she has done the same for me. In my lowest moments, her voice and her words reminded me that I was someone worthy of her friendship. In Lucy's eyes, I was already the woman I hoped to become one day: smart, funny, creative, and kind—even if I didn't yet believe it myself.

I knew what I was going to write for my speech. I wasn't going to write anything. I didn't need to; I had the whole of our friendship, documented in thousands of letters and messages between us over the past two decades. To the crowd Naomi and I would read a (highly edited) selection of Lucy's personal, private e-mails. They covered her early years in New York when her greatest desire was to have a bedroom with a door, crazy crash diets, and falling in love—first with her cat, and then with Rob.

At Lucy's wedding, I downed three Manhattans and Naomi's glass of white wine to steel my nerves, but I was so high on adrenaline they had little effect. My heart was pounding in my chest as I made my way to the mic. I looked out on that sea of strangers, and when I found Lucy's beautiful face smiling back at me, my fears vanished.

CREAMY ASPARAGUS AND BLUE CRAB SOUP

Where I grew up in Maryland, the blue crab trucks that appeared on the side of the road in June marked the official start of summer. We'd buy them by the bushel and invite the entire extended clan over. Then we'd lay down newspaper on our patio table, and my parents would dump out huge steamer pots of crabs, their shells now a vivid orange from the heat. I'd spend hours happily cracking the claws with my little wooden mallet and feasting on the sweet, buttery meat.

They are delicious simply steamed, but my mom liked to slip a bit of blue crab into everything during the season—soups, salads, and dumplings. One of my favorite soups growing up was *sup mang cua*, a mainstay of large family gatherings like weddings and first birthday parties. I've leaned a bit more heavily toward the French influence of the original soup, substituting a potato and cream for the cornstarch that is usually used as a thickener.

Serves 3 to 4
Prep time: 15 minutes; Cook time: 40 minutes

---

2 tablespoons extra-virgin olive oil
1 tablespoon butter
1 medium leek, white and light green parts only, chopped
1 pound asparagus, cut into 2-inch lengths
1 medium potato, peeled and cut into ½-inch cubes
4 cups low-sodium chicken stock, preferably homemade
½ teaspoon sugar
½ teaspoon kosher salt, plus more as desired
8 ounces cooked lump crabmeat
½ cup heavy cream
1 teaspoon fish sauce
¼ cup chopped scallions
¼ cup chopped cilantro
Lemon wedges for serving
Freshly ground black pepper

In a large stockpot, heat the olive oil and butter over medium-low heat. Add the leek pieces to sweat for 3 to 4 minutes, until they are soft. Add the asparagus, potato, chicken stock, sugar, and salt. Partially cover, bring to a boil, and then reduce the heat to medium low and simmer

for about 20 minutes, until the asparagus is very tender. Turn off the heat and let the mixture cool for about 10 minutes. Using an immersion blender, or carefully transferring in batches to a traditional blender, purée the soup until smooth and return to the pot. With the heat on medium low, stir in the crab, heavy cream, and fish sauce, cooking for 5 minutes more. To serve, garnish the soup with scallions, cilantro, a squeeze of lemon, and salt and pepper to taste.

CRISPY SOFT-SHELL CRAB SALAD WITH CARAMELIZED SHALLOT VINAIGRETTE

The only thing better than Maryland blue crabs are *soft-shell* Maryland blue crabs. These are lightly dusted with cornstarch and fried until the outsides are crisp and the insides are ultracreamy. I balance out that richness by serving them with a simple salad made with the shallot dressing that weirded out my first Chicago roommates so much.

Makes 2 appetizer-size portions
Prep time: 10 minutes; Cook time: 20 minutes

---

3 tablespoons extra-virgin olive oil
2 small shallots, sliced about ⅛ inch thick
3 tablespoons lemon juice (about 1 large lemon)
1 teaspoon sugar
½ teaspoon kosher salt, plus more as desired
½ teaspoon fish sauce
2 soft-shell crabs (about 4 inches wide), rinsed, cleaned, and patted dry
1 cup cornstarch
Peanut oil, for frying
1 small head butter lettuce, torn

Heat the olive oil in a small saucepan over medium-low heat. Add the shallots and cook for 10 to 15 minutes, until golden, stirring occasionally to prevent burning. Turn off the heat and leave the shallots in the pan to cool. They will continue to cook, turning a little darker in color.

To prepare the dressing, in a small bowl, mix the lemon juice, sugar, ½ teaspoon salt, and the fish sauce. Stir to dissolve.

In a medium bowl, sprinkle the crabs with the cornstarch, tossing to coat evenly. Fill a medium-sized pot with 1 inch of peanut oil and heat over medium-high heat until the oil reaches 360°F. Working in batches to avoid crowding the pot, carefully slip the crabs into the oil and fry for about 2 minutes per side. Monitor the oil temperature and adjust the burners accordingly to maintain an even 360°F. Cook until golden, and then transfer to a wire rack or a few layers of paper towels to drain. While the crabs are still glistening with oil, season generously with salt.

As soon as the crabs are cooked, toss the lettuce with the dressing. Garnish with fried shallots and drizzle with the remaining shallot-infused oil. Arrange the salad on a plate, place the fried crabs atop the salad, and serve immediately.

18
Cake Love

Lucy

It was 3 a.m. the day before my wedding, and I was standing in the kitchen, covered in confectioners' sugar, sculpting tiny 3-D marzipan cats.

"Ohh, that's a nice kitty," I whispered to myself. "But how do I make it dance?"

I heard Rob stir in the other room. "What's going on out there?"

I froze.

Rob and I had gotten engaged in Mexico City the year before, and I had not experienced a single moment of doubt about our decision to get married. Rob was the most loving, funny, supportive person; locking it down was a no-brainer. But as I started to actually plan the wedding, I discovered I did have some qualms about being a bride. The word alone left a bad aftertaste in my mouth. I had spent my twenties trying to get people to take me seriously. Even to be able to take myself seriously had been an all-consuming process. My sense of self was a delicate construction I had assembled, piece by piece, over fifteen excruciating years—but I had confidence in it now. I knew who I was and I liked that person.

But suddenly, seemingly out of nowhere, it felt like the world expected me to be someone else. Someone who would wear a frilly white dress that I had picked out with my mother; who did a first dance to some sappy love song; who was "given away" by my father to my husband. It made me feel uncomfortable, not to mention vaguely insulted. It wasn't enough to just be myself? I started imagining all of the embarrassing ways in which I might be perceived in this new "bridal" role. Lucy the Bridezilla. Lucy the trying-too-hard-to-be-a-nonconformist. Lucy who is spending too much (but also not enough!) money on her dumb wedding.

"I'm just going to do my own thing," I told Tram on the phone. "No bridesmaids, no shower, no tulle. And none of this stereotypical descent into madness behavior, either. I'm going to be a chill bride."

"Lucy, in what universe have we ever been chill?" she asked, laughing.

"I mean it!" I insisted. "All I have to do is find a way to do exactly what I want while also doing exactly what everyone else wants me to do."

There was a pause on the other end of the line.

"Well, try not to make yourself too crazy about it all," Tram said. "It's going to be great no matter what."

"I told you, I'm chill!"

I was not chill. I had thought I would be able to skim over some of the wedding conventions, no problem, but I kept running into objections. If I didn't have my dad walk me down the aisle, friends said, everyone would think we hated each other. If I told my mom no on the bridal shower, her feelings would be brutally hurt. When I mentioned to my brother that I planned on buying my dress online instead of at a boutique with my mother, he went on a lengthy Gchat tirade that ended with, "Mark my words: this is a terrible idea."

I didn't want to make anyone feel bad, but I resented the fact that people seemed so comfortable telling me how to behave. No one was trying to push Rob around. It felt like there was a law in the universe that gave special dispensation for the entire collective population to tell me what to do now that I was getting married.

"I don't get it," I told Tram. "I'm an adult. My mom and I haven't been shopping together since I was twelve, and it was miserable even then. Not because we hate each other. Because we hate *shopping*. We always have! Why would we start loving it now?"

My mother and I were never great at the conventional mother-daughter bonding activities. When I was little she would take me to the mall twice a year to buy school clothes, and I'd cry the whole time because she wouldn't let me invest in a wardrobe that consisted exclusively of neon green bike shorts and skorts. When I was a preteen our shopping expeditions typically ended with me sitting sulkily on the floor of some filthy department store dressing room, refusing to speak to her because she wouldn't allow me to go off to the Limited Too on my own.

I always wanted to do things by myself. I still remember the first time I was allowed to ride my bike solo to the candy store a mile away from our house—such a sweet victory, to be able to buy that Snickers bar without parental supervision. I got my driver's license the day I turned sixteen so that I would no longer have to ask my parents for rides to orchestra practice or cross-country meets. I loved my parents, but I also liked my privacy, to have the time and space to clear my head without being scrutinized. The first time a boy came to pick me up for a date, I refused to let him inside the house—until he told me he had to use the bathroom.

"Fine, but don't talk to anyone," I told him. He ignored me, and not long after that I dumped him.

I had dreamed of moving to New York because I wanted to be independent. Maybe I didn't know exactly who I was back then, or what I was going to do with my life, but I wasn't going to let anyone else—and certainly not my parents—try to dictate the answers. When my mom tried to convince me to apply for full-time jobs my first summer in the city, I not only refused to listen to her, I stopped replying to her e-mails altogether. As I got older, I became increasingly confident in what I wanted—and the less I wanted to hear from the peanut gallery. Even when I asked Tram for advice, I was usually just looking for confirmation of a plan I had already decided on. As for my family, I liked to keep my distance, lest anyone think they could get away with telling me what to do.

I took a similar tack with the wedding. I knew my mom wanted to be involved, but I felt very protective of it. This thing was between Rob and me. I didn't want to surrender it to all the various family members who might want to have a say. I was more than familiar with the momzilla trope—I'd seen it play out in real life a startling number of times—but I didn't think that had to be the standard operating procedure. *Just say no*, I thought, every time one of my friends complained that her mother was insisting on a certain type of gown, this venue, that ceremony. I couldn't see my mom turning into a control freak, but I *could* see her getting uncomfortably up in my business. So I simply froze her out, as I always had.

But after talking to Tram, I realized I was being preemptively harsh. My mom just wanted to be included. She wasn't asking me to have a Latin-language Catholic ceremony or to wear a Princess Di dress. And when I shut down the idea of a shower, she didn't complain. She was bending over backward not to alienate me, but I was punishing her anyway, out of habit. So I decided to compromise. I would involve her in a way that felt meaningful to us both. I would ask her to bake my wedding cake.

Once upon a time, before I became a sullen teenager, baking had been our thing. Mom always made cakes for special occasions growing up, and I would often help—even if it was just to hand her a cup of flour she'd already measured, or stir melting chocolate in a double boiler on the stove. I loved sitting on a kitchen stool after school, waiting to snatch a piping-hot cookie off the cooling rack, or lick batter off the beater after she'd popped cupcakes in the oven. She and I always had the best conversations when we were in the kitchen, focused on the food, not trying too hard.

Plus, baking is in our blood. My grandfather baked wedding cakes for both my aunt and my uncle. My mom made her own, plus a million other cakes over the course of her lifetime. For one of my brother's book parties, she prepared literally five hundred mini cupcakes. Baking-induced mania was a celebratory tradition! And it was a way to let her in without ceding to conventions that made my skin crawl.

She signed on with no hesitation. We went over the details of the recipe on the phone, as we had so many times when I called her to ask for cooking advice. Her cake, we decided, would be a classic, tiered affair. Simple and elegant, just a smattering of flowers. We were going over the plan when something occurred to her.

"But Lulu," she said, "my cake won't feed 150 people. We might need some backup desserts."

Caught up in the moment, I had a brilliant idea.

"I'll make one, too!"

"Aren't you going to be busy leading up to the wedding?" she asked. "Maybe you should think about it."

I promised I would, and I did. By the end of the week, my thoughts had led me to a new plan—an even better one. I would not make just one cake. I would make *many* cakes. Big cakes, small cakes, layer cakes, bundt cakes—there would be a table filled with them. The whole wedding would be a festival of baked goods. My mom's cake would be the centerpiece.

Once again, I called Tram and told her the plan.

"Girl, have you lost your mind?" she asked.

"I know it sounds like a lot of work. That's why I'm going to make them in advance and *freeze* them," I said.

"What does Rob think of this idea?"

"Well, he says it's crazy and that I'm not allowed to do it," I responded. "So I'm not going to tell him. I'll bake while he's at work and then hide the cakes in the freezer."

"Won't he notice a freezer full of cakes?"

"I might need to find something off-site," I conceded. "I'm looking into some rental spaces."

"Lucy, I love you, but this sounds insane," Tram said. "What if you pared it down a bit?"

At first I ignored Tram. How dare she try to stomp out my vision for a thousand secret wedding cakes? But after a few days, I started to take her words to heart. It was possible I was taking the whole "you don't know my life" rebellion act too far, especially considering that I was thirty-one. One cake might suffice. One from me, and one from my sister.

I called Devon and laid out the plan: She and I would keep it simple. Just a layer cake, no big deal. Devon could make whatever she wanted, and I'd develop a recipe for my own with weeks to spare. I'd test it multiple times before freezing the layers, and then I'd defrost and assemble them the day before.

Of course, it was more complicated than that. For months, I agonized over possible recipes. I tested a chocolate hazelnut (too sweet), a devil's food (too dry), a vanilla hazelnut buttercream icing with chopped nuts (tasted good, but took on an unfortunate poop-like patina after sitting for too long). None of them were up to my standards. At night I would lie awake, cursing myself for this dumb idea, which naturally I was unwilling to abandon. I would randomly bolt out of bed at 4 a.m. to make panicked lists of various cakes and icings I should test out: a chocolate tart from Mimi Thorisson's cookbook; a hazelnut, ginger, and olive oil cake from Dorie Greenspan; a German chocolate layer cake from *Cook's Illustrated*. Rob would wake up in the morning and I'd be sitting there on the couch, pounding espresso, watching YouTube videos of frosting techniques, no closer to having figured out a recipe.

After months of agonizing, I was as far as ever from a solution—and I was losing patience with desserts. They were fickle, they took hours to make, and they required endless precision and pounds and pounds of expensive butter. And yet, at the end of the day, they were all so . . . *sweet*. I turned to the only person I knew who would truly understand.

"I still have no recipe," I told Tram on the phone. "At this point I honestly don't even know if I like cake."

"I agree," she said. "Cake is disgusting."

Tram enjoys a good pastry—a flaky pie crust, a delicate cream puff—but she has no time for cakes and cookies. When we were teenagers baking at my house, Tram refused to actually eat any of the cakes we made together—to the point that it was almost insulting. But now that I was eating a slice basically every night, I finally understood where she was coming from.

"Do you think I can make wedding fries instead?" I asked her.

"No," she said. "What other flavors do you like?"

I told her I wanted to make something that was rich and chocolaty but not crazily sweet, something with a little spice maybe.

"What if you throw some cayenne pepper in the cake to cut through the sweetness a bit? Kind of like Mexican hot chocolate."

My mother had a similar idea.

"What about adding chipotle peppers?" she suggested, in one of hundreds of e-mails we exchanged on the subject. "Is that too crazy?"

Nothing was too crazy for me. It was two weeks before the wedding. I would try anything.

*   *   *

I resumed the recipe-testing process in marathon, middle-of-the-night baking sessions, late nights fueled by caffeine and obscure figure-skating competitions that I watched via live stream on my laptop, which I perched atop an upside-down mixing bowl. Finally, a week, twelve tests, and thirty or forty sticks of butter later, I figured it out: I would bake a sour cream chocolate cinnamon cake with a bit of espresso and a dash of cayenne pepper. It would be rich but not cloyingly sweet. I felt good about it. I had tested cake after cake after cake. I was confident. This one would be delicious.

But how would it look? I had become so maniacal about coming up with a recipe that I'd forgotten to figure out how to make it pretty.

Awhile back, in the early planning stages, I had taken a cake decorating class. I was a mediocre student when it came to buttercream roses, but I absolutely excelled at marzipan fruit. My miniature carrot was authentically ridged and just the right amount of knobby—I might have plucked it from a garden in the wild. My tiny peach, with its cherubic dimples and soft blush, belonged in a museum. If I was such a marzipan genius—and I believed that I was—I figured I could sculpt a cat or two, easy, and then paint them some opulent color, like gold. How cute would it be to top the cake with a couple of small golden cats, spooning? Or better yet, slow-dancing? Now, in the middle of the night, a day before the wedding, was my chance to discover my inner sculptress.

I texted Tram a picture of the cats in progress.

It was 3 a.m., but she was still up; she was busy writing the toast I had asked her and Naomi to give at the wedding.

"Omg," she said. "Amazing."

Rob found me the next morning, passed out on the couch still wearing my apron, the kitchen counter caked in sticky marzipan.

"Wow."

"Just a few more tries and I think I'll really have it," I said, bleary-eyed, sleep-deprived, and clearly delusional.

Rob looked at me, mystified and genuinely a little scared. Thankfully, at that moment my sister and mom arrived and he quickly fled to the bedroom. It was cake decorating day. We filled the space with our offset spatulas, spinning plates, and my mom's enormous tool kit of supplies. We got to work in a rhythm that felt cozily familiar—the whirring of the standing mixer; the dull thwack of rubber spatulas scraping against bowls; the plop of icing on cake; all those sounds that reminded me of growing up. We took turns using the KitchenAid, chatting and strategizing as we worked. My sister's cake was objectively the simplest to prep, so she went last, whipping up a simple cream cheese icing. As I tinkered with my little marzipan creatures from the night before—not looking so hot in the light of day—I heard a whimper.

"Something is not right," Devon said, her voice wavering. "Look at it! It's flat and soggy. It's a mess!"

My mom and I peered down at Devon's cake, assessing its possibilities. It was true; something was off. The layers were barely thicker than pancakes, and they had an unsettling damp quality to them. One had broken apart as Devon attempted to handle it.

The cake wasn't perfect, but then again, it probably wouldn't kill anyone. And we didn't have a lot of time. The rehearsal started in two hours.

"It's probably okay," I said. "Just use a lot of icing. No one will notice."

Devon started to cry. "It's disgusting! I can't serve this thing!"

I had known a moment like this was coming, but I thought it would be me, not my sister, having the eleventh-hour episode. After all, Devon is the responsible sister, the steady sister, the sister who teaches elementary school children for a living. I, on the other hand, had spent the last several weeks—if not the greater part of my life—on the brink of an epic meltdown. I turned to my mother, the resident expert in both cake and hysterical children.

"What should we do?"

She was calm and reasonable, as she always is when one of her children is on the verge of a fiasco.

"We'll just bake it again. It doesn't take long, and Lucy has most of the ingredients here," she said. "Devon, you and I can do it tomorrow morning before the ceremony."

Then she turned to me, on a roll.

"And Lucy, ditch the marzipan cats."

The next day, Devon and my mom arrived at the apartment bright and early, ready to bake. I was at the hotel hanging with Tram when I got a text from Rob: "Devon now realizing she used baking powder instead of baking soda."

Tram helped me get ready at the hotel, and for the first time in weeks I felt totally calm. Everything was going to be fine. I had my best friend. I had Rob. I had my mom and my sister, my dad and my brother, a huge extended family of people who cared about me.

"Wow," said my wedding photographer as we snacked on room service in the hotel room, "you are a seriously chill bride."

Tram and I laughed.

Naomi and my good friend Sarah joined the party and we cracked some Champagne. Then, two hours before the ceremony, Devon came busting in, hair done up fancy and ready to get a face full of makeup. She showed me a picture of the cake, which she had delivered downstairs only moments before. It was gorgeous.

"What the hell?" I said. "It's prettier than mine!"

Devon grinned. "You know what is not in good shape? Your kitchen. There's cream cheese icing *everywhere*. Sorry!"

Finally, it was time. As I walked down the aisle—wearing a white dress I had picked out online—Matt, Rakesh, and our friend Marcus played a New Order song, one Tram and I had loved fifteen years before. Rob and I exchanged our vows, and Rob's had the crowd laughing and weeping in equal parts, as I knew they would, which was why I insisted on going first.

Then came the speeches. There were several of them, and they were all great—how did we even know so many kind, hilarious people?—but Tram and Naomi's had people crying tears of laughter into their arugula-and-goat-cheese salads.

Tram has always had a way of seeing my life in its most flattering light—even when I'm in the middle of trying to convince her of how crappy it is. That night as she read from letters and e-mails I had sent her over the last ten years, she turned the mirror on me again. In her telling, I wasn't just some broke and depressed layabout with no walls; I was a gutsy heroine who was willing to take risks in order to find the life I wanted. That was the message she had been hammering into my brain for years. She had faith in me. She thought I was already as good as I was so desperately trying to be. I probably would have seen that myself one day, but thanks to Tram, I got there a lot faster.

It had been sixteen years since we met; I was different but the same. I was stronger, more sure of myself, and I had finally realized that it was okay if I didn't know exactly what the rest of my life would look like. Some uncertainty about the future was fine, because now I knew who I was. I had traveled and had adventures; I had dated some horrible men and one really, really good one; I had taken up—and then quit—smoking; I had even resigned myself to the fact that I would never genuinely love malbec. Things were pretty good. They might even improve. Why not? When I quit my job at the fashion magazine all those years before, my boss had left me with some wise words.

"Lucy, I'll be honest with you. Being in your twenties is really hard," she said. "Your thirties are much better."

At the end of the night I was standing by my seat, momentarily taking a reprieve from all the action, when Tram walked up to me, a slice of chocolate cake in hand.

"Lucy," she said. "This has been absolutely amazing."

A NOT-SO-SWEET, SLIGHTLY SPICY CHOCOLATE WEDDING CAKE

(Recipe adapted from Rose Levy Beranbaum's Chocolate Domingo Cake)

After months of experimenting, I finally landed on a cake recipe that I knew I would not get sick of. I love the depth the sour cream adds, and the cinnamon and cayenne add just a hint of spice to the rich chocolate flavor. For my wedding I made a three-layer cake, but two will also suffice.

Makes one 10-inch 2-layer cake
Prep time: 15 minutes; Cook time: 30 minutes

Nonstick cooking spray
1⅓ cups full-fat sour cream
4 large eggs, at room temperature
¾ cups plus 2 tablespoons Dutch-processed cocoa powder
1 tablespoon vanilla
3 cups plus 2 tablespoons sifted cake flour
2 cups sugar
1½ teaspoons baking powder
½ teaspoon baking soda
1 teaspoon salt
½ teaspoon nutmeg
½ teaspoon cayenne pepper
4 tablespoons espresso powder
2 teaspoons cinnamon
1¾ cup unsalted butter, softened

Preheat the oven to 350°F. Grease the cake pan with nonstick cooking spray, insert a cake round, and grease again.

In a medium bowl, mix the sour cream, eggs, cocoa, and vanilla until smooth.

In the bowl of a standing mixer, combine flour, sugar, baking powder, baking soda, salt, nutmeg, cayenne pepper, espresso powder, and cinnamon for 30 seconds on low speed. Add butter and half the cocoa mixture to the dry ingredients and mix until the dry ingredients are just moist. Increase the speed to medium and beat for 2½ minutes. Gradually add the remaining cocoa mixture and mix for an additional 1½ minutes, scraping the sides down if necessary. Pour batter into the cake pans and smooth out the top. Bake for about 30 minutes, or until you can stick a toothpick in the center and bring it out clean. Let cool in the pan for 10 minutes, then remove the cakes and place on a rack until cool.

CHOCOLATE GANACHE ICING

If, like me, you find buttercream icing a bit on the sweet side, chocolate ganache is a great alternative. It's rich and chocolaty but it layers on thinly, so it does not overwhelm the flavor of the cake as icings sometimes do. It has the added bonus of being incredibly elegant, which makes decorating unnecessary. Unless, of course, you happen to be very skilled in the art of marzipan cat-making.

Makes enough icing for a 2-layer cake
Cook time: 12 minutes

3 cups bittersweet chocolate
3 cups heavy cream

Put the chocolate in a heatproof bowl. In a saucepan on medium-low, heat the cream to just under a boil. Remove from heat and pour over the chocolate. Let the mixture sit for a few minutes, until the chocolate is partially melted. Stir until smooth. While the icing is still warm, pour it over the cake and level it out with an offset spatula.

Acknowledgments

Thanks to our agent, Brettne Bloom, for plucking us from the Internet and giving us the opportunity to write this book, and for being eternally supportive and helpful throughout the process.

Thanks to Sara Weiss, Karen Murgolo, and our publisher, Grand Central Life & Style, for taking a chance on us.

To our editor, Brittany McInerney, and our designer, Lisa Honerkamp, we'd like to express gratitude for all of your hard work.

To Naomi Levine, a Cher among mortals. We love you.

Nancy, Jimmy, Gloria, Emma, and Olivia, you are the best family Tram could have hoped for.

Romeo, you already know.

To Jane and Chris, for being loving and infinitely patient, and for teaching Lucy how to cook. To Gummy, for being a constant inspiration. To Bennett and Devon for giving Lucy so much material.

Rob: See dedication.

A big thank-you to our friends and family members too numerous to name, who listened to our constant hand-wringing, who ate our failed experiments in the kitchen, and who talked us down from the ledge time after time.